# PAGANISM

## ABOUT THE AUTHORS

Joyce and River have taught Paganism classes throughout the past decade. They have planned and organized local and national Pagan gatherings, written articles for Pagan publications, appeared on radio and television broadcasts, spoken at Christian and Unitarian churches, and attended interfaith councils. They also helped found the Council for Alternative Spiritual Traditions, which hosts public Pagan and alternative events in the Midwest.

## TO WRITE TO THE AUTHORS

If you wish to contact the authors or would like more information about this book, please write to the authors in care of Llewellyn Worldwide and we will forward your request. Both the authors and publisher appreciate hearing from you and learning of your enjoyment of this book and how it has helped you. Llewellyn Worldwide cannot guarantee that every letter written to the authors can be answered, but all will be forwarded. Please write to:

Joyce and River Higginbotham
℅ Llewellyn Worldwide
2143 Wooddale Drive
Woodbury, MN 55125-2989

Please enclose a self-addressed stamped envelope for reply,
or $1.00 to cover costs. If outside U.S.A., enclose
international postal reply coupon.

Many of Llewellyn's authors have websites with additional information and resources. For more information, please visit our website at:

http://www.llewellyn.com

# PAGANISM

## AN INTRODUCTION TO EARTH-CENTERED RELIGIONS

Joyce & River Higginbotham

Llewellyn Publications
Woodbury, Minnesota

First Edition
Twenty-third Printing, 2024

Book design and editing by Joanna Willis
Cover image © 2002 by Corel Professional Photos
Cover design and interior illustrations by Gavin Dayton Duffy, Llewellyn art department
Excerpts from the *God of Jane* by Jane Roberts © 2000 by Robert F. Butts. Reprinted by
    permission of Moment Point Press, Inc.
Permission to quote from *A Book of Troth* granted by Runa-Raven Press

**Library of Congress Cataloging-in-Publication Data**
Higginbotham, Joyce
    Paganism: an introduction to earth-centered religions / Joyce & River Higginbotham.—
1st ed.
        p.          cm.
    Includes bibliographical references and index.
    ISBN 13: 978-0-7387-0222-3
    ISBN 10: 0-7387-0222-6
    1. Neopaganism.  I. Higginbotham, River, 1959–  II. Title.

BF1571 .H54 2002
299—dc21
                                                                          2002022239

Llewellyn Publications
A Division of Llewellyn Worldwide Ltd.
2143 Wooddale Drive
Woodbury, MN 55125-2989
www.llewellyn.com
Llewellyn is a registered trademark of Llewellyn Worldwide Ltd.
♻ Printed in the United States of America on recycled paper

*This book is dedicated to teachers everywhere,*
*but especially to Moriah MacCleod and Jane Roberts,*
*our first teachers.*

*This book is also dedicated to the memory of Vito John Ponticello,*
*who brought so many seekers together—*
*including the two of us.*

# CONTENTS

# EXERCISES

# ACKNOWLEDGMENTS

We wish to thank Lowell McFarland for helping us track down obscure demographic information; Scott Russell for sending us his dissertation and discussing the results of his national survey; Selena Fox and Dennis Carpenter for sharing their many years of survey information gathered at Circle Sanctuary, a Pagan land sanctuary in Wisconsin; the physicist who reviewed chapter 5 and gave us invaluable feedback; and Joyce's dad, the television engineer who inspired the Cosmic TV. A warm thank-you goes to those on the local Pagan chat list who shared scriptural research and debate, and to members of the Legion of Loki for insights into the Satanic movements.

We also send a thank-you to Jodi, Naomi, Dave, and Jenny at the Meadville/ Lombard Theological School in Chicago for their helpful research and discussion regarding the origins of panentheism, and to Tom Chapin for his insights into Taoism and Confucianism.

We also thank our friends and family for being supportive of our spiritual searching over the years; or if they couldn't be supportive, then for at least being catalysts of growth and change. We also wish to thank Regina Clarke for reviewing the manuscript and raising issues that never occurred to us; Dana Eilers and Blaine Drayer for their encouragement; Frank Medina for being a connector into the creative current; Morgan T. Forrest for being a companion on the journey and taking Joyce to Mystic Valley for the first time; fellow authors Dorothy Morrison, Trish Telesco, M. R. Sellars, and Silver RavenWolf for their encouragement; and our many students over the years who asked us so many questions.

# INTRODUCTION

If you are curious about Paganism, you have come to the right place. Perhaps you are curious because one of your friends or family members is a Pagan and you want to understand him or her better. Perhaps you are taking a world religions class or are studying the Pagan movement through your church or Sunday school. Perhaps you are interested in Paganism for yourself and want to discover if this is the spiritual path for you. Whatever your reasons for being here, you have found a good starting point. We hope to make Paganism approachable and easy for you to understand.

As we wrote this book, we wanted to be sure it accomplished two goals. The first is to provide facts and information about Paganism in order to help you better understand the Pagan movement. The second is to provide you with tools to help you move forward in your personal and spiritual development. To help you meet both of these goals, we've included a number of activities that can be used by any number of people in a variety of settings, including classrooms, Sunday schools, study groups, or private study. You can certainly use this book on your own, but if you know of others interested in Paganism, you may find it enjoyable and enriching to study it with them.

We also highly recommend that you acquire a journal or notebook before getting started, especially if you are using this book as an aid to spiritual development. A journal is an ideal place to take notes, write down your thoughts, answer the discussion questions, and do the journaling exercises. Each chapter contains one or more sets of journaling exercises designed to help you identify who you are right now and why, and where you might like to go next. Your journaling captures a snapshot of who you are at this moment. Seeing parts of yourself on paper can help you gain insight on many levels. If you are working through this book with a group, sharing parts of your journaling with others can be meaningful for everyone. Some of our best memories in class come from students sharing their journaling with us—describing their struggles and successes, uncovering an old belief, writing a poem, or seeing something in a new way. Years from now your journal will make an interesting record of your spiritual journey.

As you will already have noticed, this book is jointly written. Because River and I developed our understanding of Paganism together, we decided to write this book together. Generally, we refer to ourselves as "we," and occasionally as "River and I" or "Joyce and I." In those rare instances when "we" or "us" is used to mean people in general, we will clearly say so. When one of us is reminiscing or telling a story, we identify which of us is speaking as we tell the story in the first person. Writing as a team and deciding which voice to use has presented some unique challenges, but we think you'll find that we keep shifts in voice to a minimum and those we do make are easy to follow.

This book is organized in chapters whose concepts build on each other as they progress. Chapter 1 begins with an overview of Paganism, defines traditions that fall under the Pagan umbrella, explains the Pagan sacred liturgical year, explores Pagan worship (called *ritual*), identifies the typical elements of ritual, and, finally, sets out seven principles of Paganism. If you have time to read only one chapter of this book, then this is the chapter to read. Chapter 2 explores Pagan approaches to the issue of belief and belief systems, and investigates the idea of religion as a type of belief system. In this chapter you will be encouraged to examine your own beliefs, where they come from, and where they are likely to take you. Chapter 3 explores beliefs as they relate to images of God or Deity. We examine the range of beliefs about Deity that people have frequently adopted over the centuries, and look at the sorts of beliefs Pagans often hold. Chapter 4 fearlessly addresses the issue of Satan and the historical developments that led to Paganism's occasional and inappropriate association with Satan. We also encourage you to examine your own issues involving "cosmic boogeymen" and explore what you fear spiritually. Chapter 5 lays the groundwork for Paganism's belief in a living, conscious, cooperative universe, the existence of which forms the basis for much of Paganism's magickal practice. Chapter 6 then applies the view of the living universe to the practice of magick, and explains what magick is, the types of magick, its applications and limitations, and how it is often performed by Pagans. You will have an opportunity in this chapter to begin to enhance your own magickal connections with the universe in a series of visualizations and exercises. Chapter 7 concludes the book with a discussion of ethics and human nature from a Pagan perspective. It sets out two ethical systems followed by many Pagans, and provides a year-long system for developing virtue and values within yourself. At the back of the book you will find a recommended reading list by chapter so that you can pursue those subject areas of most interest to you.

As was mentioned earlier, one of our goals in writing this book is to help you in your journey of personal and spiritual growth. To support this goal we've included numerous exercises, journaling and discussion questions, and personal rituals and visualizations for you to experience. Through these hands-on activities we hope to give you a taste of the kind of self-inquiry Pagans encounter in their studies of Paganism. Whether or not you decide to be a Pagan once you finish is not as important as having provided you with tools to help you identify your values and goals. Why do you believe what you believe? Who are you and what is your spiritual nature? Who is God to you, how do you relate to the Divine, and what do you want from your relationship with the Divine? What is your place in the universe and how do you interact with it? What is evil to you and what do you fear spiritually? What are your values and how did you arrive at them?

Unlike some religions, "becoming" a Pagan is not about accumulating facts or knowledge, becoming theologically adept, memorizing holy text, or adopting a predetermined belief system. Instead, becoming Pagan often involves learning how to let go of attachment to dogma, to approach belief systems as objectively as possible, to accept responsibility for the beliefs and ethics you choose to adopt, and to take responsibility for the consequences of your beliefs as exhibited in your behavior. Spiritual development in some religions is measured by the degree to which you know the belief system and adhere to it in your daily life. Spiritual development in Paganism can be measured by the maturity of your actions and the degree to which you participate in the interconnectedness of the universe.

We certainly hope that when you finish this book you will have a deeper understanding of Paganism's beliefs, values, and practices. We also hope that you will have a deeper understanding of your own beliefs and values. Our efforts will have been successful if in some small way we help each of you move forward in your spiritual journey, wherever it may take you.

Blessed be.

# 1

# WHAT IS PAGANISM?

Paganism, also called neo-Paganism, is a new religious movement whose adherents are found throughout the world. Paganism is an umbrella term that describes a variety of denominations—known to Pagans as *traditions*—which for the most part organize themselves and operate without a centralized religious body or a standardized dogma. While variety of belief and practice is a source of pride for Pagans, it can sometimes be a source of confusion for others. In the pages that follow we present what we believe to be the fundamentals of Paganism. We explore such questions as why Paganism is called an earth-centered religion, how many Pagans there might be in the United States, what Pagans are like, how the Pagan sacred year is arranged, what Pagans do in ritual, what magick is, and what Pagans believe about God, worship, human nature, and ethics.

Over the years we have met thousands of Pagans throughout the United States. We have watched the Pagan movement grow from a fairly small, insular movement to one that may now number more than a million in the United States. We have spoken to numerous Pagans individually, participated in discussions and debates about the nature and future of the Pagan movement, and helped organize local and national Pagan events. For more than a decade we have explained and taught Paganism to many people in a variety of likely and unlikely places. We've taught Sunday school at Christian churches, given the main address at Unitarian churches, attended interfaith councils, taught world religions classes, demonstrated Pagan ritual for Mensa, given retreats, spoken at festivals and conventions, and provided newspaper, radio, and TV interviews on the subject. For most of these years we've also offered private class instruction in Paganism at beginning and intermediate levels. It is from this source of accumulated personal experience that we have collected and developed the concepts we present in this book. While elements of the topics covered here can be found in other books on Paganism, the beliefs we identify as fundamental to Paganism and how we interpret them are uniquely our own.

We have on occasion been asked to name the most important belief or concept of Paganism. This is difficult given the many traditions within the movement. However, if we could reduce Paganism down to its essentials, we believe its two most central concepts are *interconnectedness* and *blessedness*.

The belief that every part of the universe is profoundly interconnected shapes how Pagans view the nature of the Divine, the sorts of relationships possible with the Divine and the universe, and forms the Pagan approach to prayer and magick. Most Pagans believe that all parts of the universe, whether "animate" or "inanimate," are connected at very deep levels that extend beyond the boundaries of space-time as we know them. Because of this interconnection, many Pagans believe they are able to interact with the universe and the Divine as co-creators. This concept is further explored in chapters 5 and 6.

The belief that every part of the universe is blessed in its nature, and that there is nothing wrong with the universe or with you, means that the purpose of Pagan spiritual practice differs from that of religions focused on issues of purification and salvation. Paganism takes the position that human beings are unflawed in their natures, are not spiritually doomed or damned, are born with all the tools and skills necessary to live ethically and spiritually, and are naturally oriented toward their own greatest growth and development. No part of Pagan belief, practice, ritual, or sacrament is designed to "save" Pagans from a flawed or corrupt nature, or to avert supernatural punishment arising from such supposed flaws. Elements of this concept are developed throughout the book, particularly in chapter 7.

By contrast, most world religions today teach the opposite of one or both of Paganism's central themes. They teach that the elements of the universe are separate from each other and that there is something fundamentally wrong with all of us. They may teach separateness by asserting that the universe contains distinct bits of matter not connected at deeper levels, that each of us is irretrievably separated from others and the Divine by nature, or that the universe is split between what is spiritual (and therefore good) and what is physical (and therefore bad).

Most world religions also teach that human nature is flawed, and that there is something fundamentally wrong with all human beings that must be corrected in order to reach that religion's idea of salvation or enlightenment. This wrongness may be called original sin or ego or desire or free will or any other of a number of names, but the existence and overcoming of this inherent wrongness is the basis of the spiritual practices, sacraments, and ethics practiced by their members. In such religions, the wrongness frequently doesn't end with human beings but extends into the entire physical world so that we are seen to be surrounded by wrongness, to be spiritually unsafe, and are encouraged to feel that life is a very dangerous undertaking. The concepts of separateness and wrongness are so ingrained in each one us and in our culture that most of us are often not even aware they color our perceptions, life experience, and spiritual growth.

Paganism soundly rejects both of these concepts, and unequivocally affirms the interconnectedness of all parts of the universe and the inherent rightness or blessedness of the universe and human nature. Certainly Pagans believe that humanity can improve itself, but Pagans do not equate the human *ability* to make bad choices with a flawed nature.

Joyce and I believe that the concepts of interconnectedness and blessedness are what link together most of the divergent paths and traditions within Paganism. Yet they are not the only common threads Pagans share, as you shall see throughout this book. However, if you come away from here with no other knowledge of Paganism than the concepts of interconnectedness and blessedness and what Pagans mean by them, then you will have gained something of value.

## GENERAL CHARACTERISTICS OF PAGANISM

In addition to the two central themes of interconnectedness and blessedness, what other characteristics common to Paganism as a whole can we identify?

**Paganism is a religion.** As in other religions, Pagans seek answers to ultimate questions such as what is the meaning of life, what happens after death, is there a God, what is our basic nature, and how do we interact with the greater universe. Pagans seek these answers in the context of a religious and social community. Pagans gather in churches, homes, or outdoors, and meet in groups that may be called, among other things, circles, covens, churches, or groves. Unlike members of some religions, however, Pagans generally do not actively proselytize. They do not send out missionaries, hold revivals, or try to gain converts. Almost none of the Pagans we know "converted" to Paganism in the traditional sense. They became Pagan by deciding that Paganism reflected what they already believed and then adopted the word "Pagan" to describe themselves.

Like other religions, Pagans have clergy who perform religious functions such as marriages and funerals. Pagans also observe a sacred year and have religious holidays and other celebrations. Most modern Pagan traditions are described as "earth-centered." Pagan holidays often fall on dates that mark the change of seasons or are otherwise seasonally important. We take a look at the Pagan sacred year and how it is celebrated later in this chapter.

**Paganism is a modern religion.** Paganism is a new religion, even though it may borrow concepts and practices from any spirituality, including those now fading or extinct. Paganism is classified as a new religion by social scientists who report that Paganism exhibits all six features of new religious movements. These are (1) a pronounced religious individualism, (2) an emphasis on experience instead of belief and doctrine, (3) a practical perspective on matters of authority and practice, (4) an acceptance and tolerance of other religions and worldviews in general, (5) a holistic worldview, and (6) an open, flexible organizational framework.[1]

Pagan traditions also meet the test of a religion as applied by the U.S. courts. Characteristics that courts look for include historic longevity, number of devotees, the existence of clergy, religious literature, ceremonies, and holidays. The federal courts correctly recognized Wicca, the largest of the Pagan traditions, as a religion in the case of *Dettmer v. Landon* (1986).[2] In this case, the court found that Wicca exhibits the characteristics of a religion as outlined above.

**Paganism has no central hierarchy or dogma.** Paganism is a religion that as a whole has no central hierarchy or dogma, though individual traditions may adopt an internal governing structure and specific beliefs. Some Pagan paths have a specific ethnic focus, such as the Asatru, African, and Celtic Traditionalists. Others pull together many Pagan and non-Pagan religious beliefs and practices and blend them into a unique religious expression, such as the Eclectic and Blended paths. (We look at a variety of these traditions later in the chapter.) Most Pagans enjoy spiritual diversity and would not think it appropriate for all Pagans to believe the same things, practice in the same ways, or be organized under the same structure.

**Paganism stresses personal responsibility.** Most Pagan traditions stress personal responsibility and put the burden of developing spiritual practices, beliefs, and ethics on to the individual. Even those traditions that offer established beliefs and methods encourage their members to test ideas so that members build the mental muscles necessary to judge the soundness of beliefs for themselves. Those traditions that offer established moral guidelines also tend to encourage their members to explore ethical ideas so that members can find their own ethical sense and form their consciences accordingly. With this freedom comes a corresponding responsibility; a responsibility for one's beliefs, behavior, and degree of spiritual development. As friend and fellow author Dana Eilers once humorously observed to us, "Some religions are a restaurant. You sit down and they bring you what they're serving for dinner. Paganism is a buffet. If you want to eat, you have to get up off your butt and serve yourself."

On the whole, Paganism's approach to the issue of personal responsibility is very empowering for the individual. It is also empowering for the greater society as the number of mature and self-directed individuals in it increases.

**Paganism offers a different worldview.** Paganism is one of the first religions that deliberately incorporates new perspectives from science, metaphysics, and mysticism into its spirituality and consciously breaks from the traditional Newtonian view of the world. (These concepts are explored further in chapter 5.) Pagans tend to see all parts of the universe—from the smallest atom to the largest planetary system—as sacred and having some form of consciousness or spark of intelligence. Most Pagans believe that this living universe is able to communicate to all parts of itself on one or more levels, and that these parts can choose to cooperate together for specific ends. Pagans call this cooperation *magick*.

**Paganism is a spirituality.** Paganism is a way of living, praying, and connecting to the flow of the universe. Pagan spirituality addresses the existence and nature of Deity, the relationship of ourselves and the universe with the Divine, the nature and scope of human existence, what happens to us after death, the nature of the physical and nonphysical universe, and our relationship to that universe. Spiritual practices among Pagans are quite varied and include everything from formal ritual to meditation, quiet walks, singing, dancing, healing, divination, ecstatic sex, working with herbs, gardening, and massage. Just about any activity can be incorporated by a Pagan into his or her spirituality.

**Paganism is protected by law.** The freedom to hold and practice the religion of one's choice is a hallmark of liberty in the United States as well as several other countries. It is a right enjoyed by American citizens regardless of their affiliation as a liberal, conservative, Democrat, or Republican. President George W. Bush, a Republican conservative, stated in a speech given to a joint session of Congress on September 20, 2001, following terrorist attacks against the United States that, "No one should be singled out for unfair treatment or unkind words because of their ethnic background or religious faith." He also pointed out that if the citizens of the United States intend to defend their principles, then their "first responsibility is to live by them." Paganism is protected in the United States under the First Amendment and various civil rights acts. One of the largest of the Pagan traditions, Wicca, is formally recognized as a religion in the case of *Dettmer v. Landon,* as mentioned earlier. Pagans in the military are allowed to practice their religion on military bases, as are Christians, Buddhists, Jews, Muslims, and Hindus.

## WHAT DOES "PAGAN" MEAN?

The word *Pagan* comes from the Latin word *paganus,* which means "country dweller." It may have been a derogatory term created by city dwellers to describe "those hicks out there," much like the word "redneck." Because "pagan" tended to have a negative meaning, it was later adopted as an insult.[3] During the Crusades, the Christians called the Muslims "pagans," and later, Protestants and

Catholics flung the word at each other.[4] Eventually, "being pagan" meant someone without religion.[5]

Since the word "Pagan" has been adopted by the Pagan movement, some of its perceived stigma has lessened. At the very least, the word helps us to think about the labels history applies to those who differ from conventional Western thought. Some Pagans don't like the word and use other terms to describe their path, such as African Traditional Religion, Native Spirituality, Celtic Spirituality, Heathenry, Earth-Centered Spirituality, European Traditional Spirituality, the Elder Faith, and the Old Religion.

Joyce and I occasionally run into Pagans having a debate over whether the term "Pagan" or "neo-Pagan" should be used. The term "Pagan," after all, refers to ancient, tribal, and usually pre-Christian cultures that are mostly extinct. To avoid confusion between historical Paganism and the modern movement, many social scientists and Pagans alike have decided they prefer the word "neo-Pagan."

The noted author and Druid Isaac Bonewits goes further. He uses the word "paleopaganism" to describe "the original tribal faiths of Europe, Africa, Asia, the Americas, Oceania and Australia." A few of these tribal faiths, such as Hinduism, Taoism, and Shintoism, whose adherents number in the millions, have survived to the present. Next, Bonewits describes "mesopaganism" as re-creations of paleopagan systems, usually with influences from Judeo-Christian thought. Some of his examples are Freemasonry, Rosicrucianism, Theosophy, Voudon, Santeria, and Sikhism. His third category is "neopaganism," which he defines as religions created from the 1960s onward, and that "have attempted to blend what their founders perceived as the best aspects of different types of paleopaganism with modern 'Aquarian Age' ideals."[6]

We leave it to you to decide how to refer to your spiritual path. In this book, however, we use the word "Pagan."

## WHO IS A PAGAN?

The word "Pagan" is a label that identifies you as a person who agrees with one or more parts of Pagan philosophy, and who may participate in observances or practices common to Pagans. In the broadest sense, Paganism is an umbrella term that describes a multitude of religious and spiritual traditions. This is not unique to

Paganism. Most of us are already familiar with Christianity as an umbrella term that describes a myriad of denominations and groups. These include Methodists, Catholics, Baptists, Mormons, Episcopalians, Presbyterians, and Jehovah's Witnesses, to name a few. If we try to define Christianity in a sentence we will find it difficult. Moreover, we will not be able to capture in that sentence the differences between Catholics and Mormons, for example. Pagans are in the same boat, and yet are frequently asked by friends, family, and journalists to describe all of Paganism in a sentence or a sound bite.

Let's take a look at the Pagan umbrella (Figure 1.1). Under Paganism's umbrella are found such diverse traditions as Wicca, Shamanism, Asatru, Eclectic, Family Traditions, Celtic Traditionalism, Druidism, Strega, Santeria, Voudon, Ceremonial Magick, Mystery Traditions, solitaries, as well as a wide variety of Blended paths such as Judeopaganism, Christopaganism, Buddhistpaganism (or Easternpaganism), and so on. These traditions, while spanning many centuries and cultures, share at least one of several characteristics: they are indigenous, earth-centered, contain magickal elements, recognize both male and female deities, were suppressed or eradicated by another religion, or stress a connection to and respect for the natural world.

In other words, Paganism is a broad term that acts as an umbrella under which many different traditions find a home. Joyce and I have been asked, "So are you Wiccan or are you Pagan?" This like asking, "So are you Baptist or are you Christian?" Wiccans are Pagans, but not all Pagans follow a Wiccan path, in the same way that Baptists are Christians, but not all Christians are Baptists. To answer the question of what Joyce and I are, we would reply that we are "Eclectics." What does that mean exactly? Below we take a brief look at each of the Pagan traditions. Unfortunately, it is beyond the scope of this chapter to explain the various traditions in detail. The study of even one tradition can, and does, fill many books. So many books, in fact, have been written on most of these paths and traditions that you should have no trouble finding further reading. Just check with your bookseller by subject.

**Wicca.** Wicca is the single largest tradition within Paganism; nearly half of all Pagans are Wiccan.[7] Wiccans follow an earth-centered calendar of eight festivals a year, and believe that Deity manifests in both male and female forms often called "the God" and "the Goddess." The Wiccan ethic is set out in the Wiccan Rede, which states, "If it harm none, do what you will."

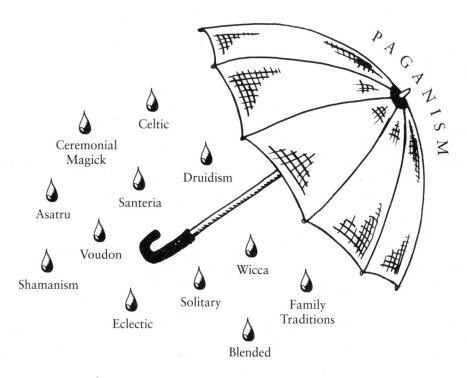

**FIGURE 1.1**
The Pagan umbrella.

**Gardnerian Wicca.** This is the name given to the branch of Wicca begun by Gerald Gardner in 1939.

**Alexandrian Wicca.** This is an adaptation of the Gardnerian tradition. It was begun by two of Gardner's students—Alex and Maxine Sanders—during the 1960s. Both Gardnerian and Alexandrian traditions tend to use set ritual forms and more hierarchical degrees of training than other forms of Wicca.

**Dianic Wicca.** This is a Wiccan path that focuses on the strong female Deity Diana. Dianic groups often allow only women members and may concentrate only on Goddess energy. Specifically, they work with the images of Goddess as maiden, mother, and crone, known as the Triple Goddess. The term "Dianic" was first used by Margaret Murray, author of *The Witch-Cult in Western Europe* in 1921.[8]

**Faery Wicca.** Those who practice Faery Wicca work specifically with nature spirits.

**Strega.** This is an Italian tradition of Wicca that emphasizes herbal knowledge and tends to be strongly matriarchal.

**Shamanism.** Shamanism is a Pagan tradition that involves going into a trance state in order to perform a variety of works, which may include healing and divination. Shamanism is considered by some to be the oldest Pagan tradition.[9] It is also found in cultures and religions not necessarily considered Pagan. The shamanic Pagans we know may follow a particular shamanic tradition or combine practices from several; they do not necessarily use Wiccan techniques such as casting a circle, calling the directions, and inviting Deities, although they might if they consider themselves Shamanic Wiccans.

**Asatru.** Those who practice Asatru devote themselves to the Nordic, Germanic, and Icelandic Deities, and may do so to the exclusion of all other Deities by a voluntary covenant.

**Eclectic.** Those who practice Eclectic Paganism combine what they believe to be the best elements from a variety of Pagan, and possibly non-Pagan, traditions.

**Family Traditions.** This Pagan tradition involves beliefs and practices that are passed down through a family over the generations. The practice of the tradition may be informal and involve no ritual, but its origins are frequently Pagan. The connection to Paganism may be downplayed, denied, or combined with Christian elements. A well-known surviving example is the Germanic Pow-wow tradition, which has its origins in German witchcraft and has been modified into faith healing.[10]

**Celtic Traditionalism.** This describes groups, or clannads, whose goal is to re-create pre-Christian Gaelic religion and society.

**Druidism.** Druidism is a revival tradition that attempts to re-create the Druidic system and may or may not be combined with Celtic Traditionalism. Since the Druids left few written records of their practices and rituals, modern Druidism tries to infer what was done.

**Santeria and Voudon.** These are traditions that developed among Africans, especially followers of the Yoruban religion, which later spread into Central and South America. Voudon is based in Haiti, and Santeria in Central America,

South America, Puerto Rico, and some portions of North America. As was mentioned earlier, Isaac Bonewits describes Santeria and Voudon as "mesopagan" traditions. Many, though not all, of the Pagans we know who combine aspects of Santeria, Voudon, or Yoruba into their spirituality are ethnically connected to these cultures and have frequently told us that their study of these "mesopagan" faiths brings them closer to their cultural origins.

**Ceremonial Magick.** This describes traditions that usually involve precise rituals, words, and tools, and draw heavily on the writings of Aleister Crowley and the Order of the Golden Dawn. The Golden Dawn was a prominent occult society founded in Britain in 1887 by a small group of Rosicrucians. Its complex set of rituals are set out in the book *The Golden Dawn* by Israel Regardie. Ritual magicians who focus on Crowley's works and ritual forms are known as Thelemics.

**Mystery Traditions.** This Pagan tradition includes those who study the ancient Greek, Roman, or Egyptian Mystery Traditions, particularly those practiced between three and five thousand years ago.

**Solitary.** This term describes a person who practices alone, regardless of tradition. This does not mean that solitaries never enjoy being with a group or community of Pagans. We know many solitaries who attend public Pagan functions in our city. They do not, however, have an interest in joining a circle or coven on a permanent basis.

**Blended Traditions.** This term describes traditions that deliberately blend together two paths. Examples include Judeopaganism, which is often strongly matriarchal and blends certain ancient Jewish customs with an earth-centered practice. We have a friend who calls herself a "Jewitch," for example. Christopaganism blends some Christian beliefs and practices with Paganism. Christopagans may pray the rosary and work magickally with angels, archangels, and other spirits. In our experience, most Christopagans revere Jesus and believe that his teachings are loving and beneficial to the world and are in no way in opposition to the principles of Paganism. We have also met Pagans who blend some aspects of Buddhism and other Eastern traditions into their spiritualities. In addition to Pagan observances, their spiritual practices may include periods of meditation, yoga, t'ai chi, or the martial arts.

# HOW MANY PAGANS ARE THERE?

Since there are no membership lists, getting a head count of Pagans is a challenge. Modern efforts to document Pagans began in Britain in the 1950s during a revival of interest in Paganism. The revival was encouraged by the repeal of the antiwitchcraft laws in England in 1951 and the publication of Gerald Gardner's book *Witchcraft Today*.[11] At that time, the number of Pagans in the United States was probably low, but no records were kept. The British revival grew and by the 1960s Paganism had become fairly popular in the United States. However, the emergence of a sizable Pagan presence in the U.S. did not occur until the 1970s, and was aided by the publication of two books, Margot Adler's *Drawing Down the Moon* and Starhawk's *Spiral Dance,* both of which are still popular today.

One of the earliest scholarly studies of Paganism was conducted by Marcello Truzzi in 1972. At that time he estimated Wiccans to number 3,000 in the United States, but gave no data on the number of Pagans as a whole.[12] Based on data collected in the mid-1980s, religious academics in the early 1990s estimated the number of Pagans in the United States to be approximately 300,000, a rather remarkable rate of growth in one decade.[13] The mid-1980s population numbers were generated by the analysis of book sales, attendance at Pagan festivals, and studies of group membership patterns.

How many Pagans are there now? Unfortunately, there has been no population data collected by religious academics since the mid-1980s. Informal data can be found in polls and surveys, however, and these offer some food for thought. The website Survey.net conducts an ongoing religious survey for Internet users. Their survey includes categories such as Wicca, Druid, Faery, Old Gods, New Age, Ceremonial Magick, and Goddess Traditions. Near the beginning of 2002, 6.5 percent of Internet users who responded to the survey identified themselves as belonging to one of these categories.[14] In September 2001, the United States government conducted a study in which it determined that Internet users in the U.S. numbered 143 million people.[15] If we extrapolate the Internet survey percentage to U.S. Internet users as a whole, then as many as 9.3 million Internet users may be Pagan, or follow paths closely related to Paganism.

Another interesting figure comes from the Hart and Teeter Research Companies. The organization conducted a poll in October 1997 in which 4 percent of respondents answered they are involved in an "alternative religion."[16] Although

Pagans often refer to their spirituality as an "alternative religion," the term would obviously include many religions other than Paganism. Even so, it is interesting that such a large percentage of the population, or approximately 10.8 million people if we extrapolate the survey percentage to the U.S. population as a whole, identify their spirituality as "alternative."

Along these same lines, a survey conducted in 1995 by Yankelovich Partners reveals that 8 percent of those polled had participated in "New Age" rituals and practices such as contacting the dead, spirit channeling, investigating past lives, mental telepathy, healing through mind power or crystals, consulting a fortuneteller or astrologer, or making plans based on their horoscope.[17] This survey includes practices that are not exclusively Pagan. However, if we apply the survey percentage of 8 percent to the U.S. population as a whole, then it does indicate that 21.6 million people were apparently open enough to New Age, Pagan, and other alternative practices to participate in them.

We discussed the issue of Pagan population figures with a religious academic who has published studies on Paganism, and he believes that at the beginning of the twenty-first-century Pagans in the U.S. numbered about 1.25 million people. This is just his opinion, however. We will have to wait for another academic study to be released before we will know if he was correct.

How do the number of Pagans compare to other religions in the United States? According to *2002 World Almanac* figures for "northern America," which excludes Latin America and South America, Buddhists number just under 800,000, Hindus 1.3 million, Jews number 6 million, and Muslims number about 4.5 million. Even using the mid-1980s Pagan population figure of 300,000, Pagans constitute a significant minority. If future academic studies support the estimate of one million or more Pagans, then Pagans would indeed constitute a significant religious minority in the United States as of the turn of the twenty-first century.

## WHERE PAGANS COME FROM AND WHAT THEY'RE LIKE

Pagans are one of the most diverse groups of people you are ever likely to meet. They come from a wide variety of religious and educational backgrounds, and work in a wide range of professions. We know Pagans who are doctors, lawyers, clerks, computer programmers, teachers, mechanics, accountants, waitresses, and small-business owners. Most Pagans we have met are bright, intelligent, and well-read. To get an accurate idea of what Pagans are like, we look to the most recent national survey of Pagans, conducted by Scott Russell in 1996 at nine different Pagan festivals across the U.S. Russell's survey states that Pagan women only slightly outnumber men, and that the majority of Pagans are between the ages of twenty-six and forty-one. The largest income brackets for Pagans puts them solidly in the middle class, and almost half of all Pagans have bachelor's degrees or higher.[18]

Also according to Russell's survey, if Pagans belonged to another faith before becoming Pagan, they were most likely Protestant. Those who were Catholic and those who described themselves as "other" are almost equally divided. Nearly half of all Pagans have identified themselves as Pagan for less than five years, and slightly more than half have been Pagan for five years or longer. The numbers of Pagans who practice by themselves and those who practice in groups is about equally split.[19]

It is also interesting to note that a large majority (69 percent) of Pagans state they have never been persecuted for their religion.[20] We find this significant and believe it may indicate that Paganism is becoming more accepted in the United States. Pagans are well educated when it comes to their legal and civil rights, and, in our experience, are aggressive in asserting and protecting them. In the early years when numbers were much smaller, many Pagans were fearful of speaking out for themselves. Now, however, Pagans can be quite vocal and quick to write letters, speak to state representatives, give testimony in court and legislative actions, join interfaith ministerial groups, and demand equal time from the media. There are several civil rights organizations who devote themselves to help protect the civil liberties of Pagans. They are easy to locate by searching the Internet.

If you ever feel that you have been discriminated against because you are Pagan, you can best help yourself and other Pagans by exploring your legal rights and remedies. Contact an attorney, the Equal Employment Opportunity Commission (EEOC), the American Civil Liberties Union (ACLU), or a Pagan civil rights organization for a referral to an attorney. If you are Pagan, you belong to what may be one of the fastest growing religious minority groups in the United States, many of whose adherents are highly educated, well-read, employed in good positions, and pay their share of taxes. Pagans have every right to be proud of who they are, and to insist that the precious gift of religious freedom be applied to *every* religion in this country, large or small.

## WHAT PAGANS DO AND WHEN THEY DO IT

As with other religions, Pagans meet to celebrate, worship, pray, learn, discuss, and have fun. Pagans gather in big groups and small groups, in churches, homes, and in nature. Pagans gather for seasonal celebrations and to mark life passages. Pagans gather for special occasions and events like conventions, picnics, and festivals. Pagans who prefer to practice alone are called "solitaries," but even solitaries join in group ritual and festivities from time to time.

Pagans on the whole have no prescribed religious ritual form to follow, so spiritual experiences are quite diverse. A religious gathering may involve singing, dancing, quiet meditation, prayer, healing, ritual movement, chanting, or magick and energy workings.

What occurs at any given gathering will depend to a large extent on the goals of those who plan it. The organizers may choose to stay within the structure of their tradition, blend several traditions together, or ask a guest group to share theirs. The location of the ritual, size of the group, and purpose for the gathering are also considered. Some traditions have prescribed ritual forms that are always followed. Some groups have no prescribed forms. Some groups work only with certain energies or Deities, or excel in certain kinds of magick, which is described further in chapter 6. Pagans enjoy learning about many traditions and, if they choose, participating in different kinds of religious experiences. A typical gathering for ritual where we live, called "Open Full Moons," may be attended by eighty or more people who may represent ten, twenty, or even more different traditions. Planning a ritual that is meaningful to such a diverse group can be quite a challenge! However, it is our opinion that this sharing of traditions and openness to a variety of religious experiences is a real strength of Paganism.

As in other religions, many Pagans observe a sacred, or liturgical, year. The Christian liturgical year, for example, begins with Advent and the birth of Christ, continues through his death and resurrection, ends after Pentecost, and then begins again. Many other religions in addition to Christianity build their liturgical years around the lives and deeds of their founders, their ethnic history, or their Deities. Most Pagan traditions, on the other hand, build their sacred year around the cycles and seasons of the earth. Because of this, Paganism is often referred to as an "earth-centered" religion.

# AN EARTH-CENTERED RELIGION

Many Pagan religious observances are built around the flow of the seasons, which mark not only the passage of time, but also moments of spiritual significance.

Pagans call their earth-centered cycle the Wheel of the Year. The Wheel begins with Yule at the Winter Solstice and ends with Samhain, or Halloween, passing through a total of eight celebrations. In some Pagan traditions these celebrations are known as Sabbats, a word drawn from the Hebrew *Shabath,* which means "a day set aside for rest and worship." Together they comprise the eight religious holy days, or holidays, observed by most Pagans, and are spaced such that a Pagan holiday occurs about every six or seven weeks. Many Pagans also observe the Esbats, which are the thirteen full moons of the year.

As fun as the welcoming of the seasons is in and of itself, the observance of the seasons is also about honoring aspects of life and spirituality. Let's take winter as an example. The Pagan celebration of the arrival of winter is not only about winter, but those times in our lives when we are stripped bare and proceed in faith through darkness. It's about the hard times, the times we endure the loss of loved ones, illness, injury, a lost job, a period of depression. It's about watching our parents and friends age; it's about our own aging and death. Winter is also about quiet, rest, recovery, simplicity, and openness to change. We can say, then, that faith, loss, change, and rest are some of the spiritual lessons of winter.

Pagans celebrate their personal seasons as well. Pagans call these personal seasons "life passages" or "rites of passage." The passages of life most often celebrated are pregnancy and birth, baby welcomings, handfasting and marriage, handparting, coming of age, croning for women, saging for men, death, dedication to a path or course of study, and ordination. We look at each of these later in the chapter. Life passages can either be observed as they happen or tied to other seasonal celebrations of the year.

# THE WHEEL OF THE YEAR
## The Quarter Points

Let's begin our exploration of the Wheel of the Year with the four solar holidays that mark the astronomical beginnings of the seasons (Figure 1.2). These solar holidays are also referred to as Quarter Points of the year. In the Northern Hemisphere

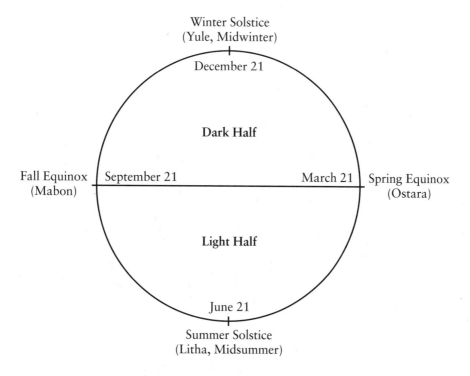

**FIGURE 1.2**
The Quarter Points of the Wheel of the Year.

they are the Winter Solstice on December 21, the Spring Equinox on March 21, the Summer Solstice on June 21, and the Fall Equinox on September 21. These dates occasionally vary by a day or so from year to year, so check your calendar.

### Winter Solstice

The Winter Solstice, also called Yule or Midwinter, occurs on December 21 and is the first Pagan holiday celebrated after the ending of the old year at Samhain. It is located in the north on the Wheel of the Year, which represents the land of dark nights and the cold grip of winter. When Winter Solstice arrives, we know we are halfway through the dark part of the year.

The darkness that has been growing since the Fall Equinox reaches its peak at the Winter Solstice, making this the shortest day of the year. Starting the day after Winter Solstice, the length of sunlight begins to increase day by day until it reaches its peak at the Summer Solstice. Many view Winter Solstice as the day on which the "sun is reborn," as indeed it is. The Pagan Solstice celebration is just one of many festivals of light that occur this time of year, including Christmas, Kwanzaa, Hanukkah, St. Lucia's Day, and La Posadas.

Yule traditions include the burning of the Yule log, which represents the increasing light of the season. It is a common practice to keep a piece of it to light the next year's Yule log, and to scatter some of its ashes over the fields. Kissing under the mistletoe, whose white berries symbolized semen to the ancient Druids, may be the remnants of an ancient fertility practice. Better watch out who you kiss! Holly and evergreen are both symbols of the promise of the return of life and springtime, since their leaves do not turn brown and die like other trees.

### Spring Equinox

Daylight has continued to grow since the Winter Solstice. At the Spring Equinox, daylight has grown to the point where there is as much daylight as darkness in a day. Light and darkness are in perfect balance on this day, March 21, and will not be again until the Fall Equinox on September 21. The Spring Equinox, then, marks the beginning of the light half of the year. It is a time to celebrate balance and the arrival of spring. The trees are budding, and the earliest flowers are blooming. Its position on the Wheel of the Year is in the East, which represents the land of dawn, the freshness of a new day, and new beginnings.

Most of the Spring Equinox traditions that we observe today relate to fertility and renewal of the life force. The most familiar is the coloring of eggs. The egg was the symbol of the German goddess Ostara, known to the Anglo-Saxons as Eostre, and which may also be derived from the Phoenician Astarte and Babylonian Ishtar, all of which are spring fertility goddesses and from whose names come the words *East* and *Easter.*

### Summer Solstice

The Summer Solstice occurs on June 21 and is known as Midsummer or Litha. It marks the time when the sun is at its maximum power and is the longest day of the year. The Summer Solstice marks the midpoint in the light half of the year. The themes of this season are growth, fruitfulness, abundance, and strength. Its position on the Wheel of the Year is in the South, the realm of heat, fire, and creativity.

The celebration that occurs before Solstice day is known as Midsummer's Eve, and is considered a night of potent magick. Many herbs, including mistletoe, were considered to be at their peak strength at the Solstice. It was believed that fairies roamed the land on Midsummer's Eve, a belief that was incorporated into Shakespeare's *A Midsummer Night's Dream*. It is common for Pagans to light bonfires at the Solstice to celebrate the warmth and light of the sun.

### Fall Equinox

As with the Spring Equinox, this is the point at which light and darkness are in equal balance. The Fall Equinox, also called Mabon, occurs on September 21 and marks the change from the light half of the year to the dark. From the Equinox forward until the spring, there will be more darkness than daylight every day. The Fall Equinox is a time of harvest, appreciation, reflection, and preparation for winter. Its position on the Wheel of the Year is in the West, the land of sunset and approaching darkness. This is a time of transition as we watch gardens fade and leaves turn color and drop. The balance experienced here is different from that of the spring, which is poised and ready to leap into action! Here we experience the calm of rest after labor.

The Fall Equinox is celebrated as a harvest festival; it is usually the second harvest festival, with Lammas being the first (see below). In ancient times, the harvest was crucial. Was enough grown and gathered to support everyone through the winter? Were enough seeds saved for good planting next spring? Pagans celebrate the end of the harvest with feasting and visiting with friends. Since the fall is also associated with the harvesting of grapes and the making of wine, a tasting of the year's vintage may be in order. Decorations made of corn, squash, vines, and pumpkins is a harvest custom practiced not only by Pagans but much of the culture.

## The Cross-quarter Points

The Wheel of the Year is divided into four additional points known as Cross-quarters, which fall more or less directly between the Quarter Points. In some Pagan traditions the Cross-quarter Points are celebrated as the "high" festivals and the Quarter Points as "low" festivals, while other traditions make no distinction. In general, the Quarter Points are considered solar holidays since they relate to the strength and position of the sun throughout the seasons. The Cross-quarter Points are considered agricultural holidays, as they tend to mark key moments in the planting, growing, and harvesting of crops.

The Cross-quarter Points are Imbolg on February 2, Beltane on May 1, Lammas on August 1, and Samhain on October 31 (Figure 1.3).

### Imbolg

Imbolg (pronounced *IHM-bowlg* or *IHM-bowlk*), also called Candlemas, occurs on February 2nd, midway between the Winter Solstice and the Spring Equinox. Imbolg reminds us that daylight is growing and that winter will soon be gone. As a symbol of the growing light, Pagans bless and light many candles on this holiday, as do those Christians who still observe Candlemas. Candlemas is also known as St. Brigid's Day. Brigid is a Celtic goddess of fire (an appropriate figure for this holiday), who was later canonized by the Catholic Church. Imbolg also corresponds with Groundhog Day, a modern version of testing for the return of spring!

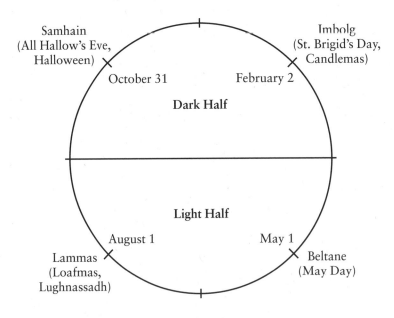

FIGURE 1.3
The Cross-quarter Points of the Wheel of the Year.

Imbolg can be celebrated with candlelit processions, the ceremonial lighting of fires and solar wheels that are lit and rolled down hills, and by sending blessings to the fields and farm animals. A principal theme of Imbolg is purification and cleansing, a time to clean out mental, spiritual, and emotional cobwebs as we leave winter behind and make room for spring.

### Beltane

Beltane (pronounced *BELL-tain* or *bay-ALL-tin*), also known as May Day, occurs on May 1, halfway between the Spring Equinox and the Summer Solstice. This is an exuberant holiday that celebrates sexuality, fertility, and the unfolding of spring. It is a time when the divine male and female energies come together in a union whose fruits are ourselves, the crops, and livestock. The month of May was set aside to honor this "divine marriage." Human marriages were discouraged until June, which is why June is a traditional month for weddings.

A well-known Beltane celebration is the Maypole dance. A pole, traditionally cut from a fir tree by young men, is topped with red and white streamers and a crown of flowers and placed into the ground. The pole, of course, is a phallic symbol, which represents the male aspects of divinity, and the streamers represent male fertility. The streamers are taken by two circles of dancers, one circle of which dances clockwise (or deosil) to represent the forces of life. The other circle dances counterclockwise (or widdershins) to represent the forces of death. Typically, one circle consists of young men and the other of young women. As the dancers weave the streamers in and out, they weave together the forces of life and death.

Other celebrations of Beltane include wearing wreaths or crowns of flowers, the crowning of a May Queen, and the lighting of bonfires.

Joyce and I participated in a powerful Beltane ritual a few years ago at a Pagan festival. It was the night before Beltane, and a large bonfire was lit. The men left the circle area and began drumming and chanting. The women stayed at the circle area and divided into two lines, facing each other closely enough that they could touch the shoulders of the woman across from them. This line formed a symbolic "birth canal," as all life is birthed through the female. The men then moved toward the women and entered this birth canal single file. The women remained standing close enough together that the men had to struggle to push their way through. As they went, both the men and the women expressed themselves in whatever way they felt moved, whether by chanting, singing, or crying out.

After the men had passed through the canal, the line of women then "birthed" itself into the circle, which now surrounded the bonfire. The men and women stayed apart for most of the ritual and chanted across the fire at each other, raising male and female energy until at last they came together in an explosion of song and dance that continued most of the night.

### Lammas

Lammas, also called Loafmas, or Lughnassadh (pronounced *LOO-nah-sahd*) by the Celts, is the first of the harvest festivals and marks the beginning of the harvest cycle. It falls between the Summer Solstice and the Fall Equinox and occurs on August 1. Lammas literally means "loaf mass," and celebrates the first grains harvested for the baking of bread. Lughnassadh refers to the Celtic god Lugh, a fire, sun, and grain deity who by legend fights and defeats an older god and then demands the secrets of planting, growing, and harvesting from him. His legend sometimes also combines him with a Corn King deity who sacrifices himself and is scattered over the land as corn.

Lammas is celebrated with feasting, games, and contests. Loaves of bread are baked and blessed and shared by all. For those enacting the legend of the Corn King, a loaf of bread may be broken and scattered over the ground in remembrance of the god who sacrificed himself so that life may go on.

### Samhain

Samhain (pronounced *SOW-un*, where "sow" rhymes with "cow"), popularly known as Halloween, is celebrated on October 31. Samhain falls between the Fall Equinox and the Winter Solstice, and marks the end of the Pagan sacred year. It is the first festival to occur in the dark half of the year. Samhain is a Celtic word that means "summer's end," and indeed by the time Samhain arrives, we are clearly on our way to winter. This is the time of year when agricultural societies decided how many animals to slaughter based on available grass and feed, the number of breeding livestock needed for the following year, and the amount of meat required to survive the winter. Serious mistakes in these calculations could mean death and starvation. For the ancient Pagans then, Samhain was a time of death in a very real way.

As observed by Pagans today, Samhain is a festival that celebrates several things: the end of the harvest, a change from the activities of summer to the quietness of winter, the beginning of the new Pagan year, and the honoring of ancestors and the dead. It is also a time when we acknowledge and honor the sacrifice of animals we kill in order to live. It is a time when we come to terms with death and are openly encouraged to process our fear of it. It is a time when we acknowledge the hard moments of life that we usually do not think or talk about. If there are things we need to let go of, Samhain is a good time to release them.

On this night, the veil between the worlds is considered at its thinnest and the dead are thought to return and visit. Pagans may encourage this visit by setting a place at the table for ancestors who care to join them. They may honor their ancestors by speaking their names and recalling fond memories. Pagans enjoy Halloween customs as much as anyone else, and are right in there with costume parties, trick-or-treating, bobbing for apples, and making jack-o'-lanterns.

The tone of Samhain religious services is usually more solemn than other festivals of the year. Not long ago Joyce and I attended a Samhain ritual near the Vietnam War Memorial in Washington, D.C. In this very powerful and moving place, a number of Pagans created a sacred space and invited our dead to come and be remembered. We invited those who died in war, from illness, accident, and violence. We invited our departed children, who were taken from us too soon. We invited our relatives, ancestors, and friends. We each lit a candle, named a deceased friend or relative, and put our candle into a large pot filled with sand on the center altar. Visitors to the war memorial—people we didn't know—came and joined our circle, asking if they could add their candles. Together, Pagans and non-Pagans alike, we stood in that powerful place and mourned our dead. It was a solemn and moving experience neither of us will soon forget.

exercise                                   **WALKING MEDITATION**

Take a half hour to go outside and enjoy the feeling of the season. If the temperatures are extremely hot or cold, wait until a day when you can go outside safely, and be sure to dress for the weather.

There is a rhythm and a flow to the seasons. Each one has its own taste, smell, and mood. As you go for your walk outside, get in touch with the message of the season for you. Feel your sense of connection to the earth, trees, grass, animals, and people around you. Let your walking and your breathing fall into a rhythm that helps you feel connected.

Make a mental note of which Pagan holiday you are nearest and think about its meaning for you. How does this holiday speak to the events happening in your life right now? How does the Earth reflect these messages to you? What is it saying?

Before you come in, pick up an object that reminds you of the season. Put it somewhere where you can see it and let it remind you of the connections you made on your walk.

## questions to discuss                          PAGAN HOLIDAYS

1. Which season of the year is your favorite? What do you remember from your childhood about this season that has special meaning for you? How do you celebrate this season now?

2. Have you ever been to a Pagan holiday ritual? If so, what did you think? Describe what occurred in the ritual and what you liked about it.

3. What do you think about Paganism including celebrations of fertility into its sacred year? Do you think that the Pagan celebration of fertility offers something positive to the culture? If so, what, and if not, why not?

4. What do you think about Paganism including the processing of death into its sacred year? Do you think that the Pagan celebration of aging and dying offers something positive to the culture? If so, what, and if not, why not?

# RITES OF PASSAGE

The celebration of the personal seasons of life is important to most people, Pagans included. The passages of life most often celebrated by Pagans are pregnancy and birth, baby welcomings, coming of age, handfasting and marriage, handparting, croning for women, saging for men, death, dedication to a path or course of study, and ordination. Some traditions have specific rituals for observing life passages and others do not. Many celebrations are created at the time, specifically for those involved, and may be highly personalized. Although Pagans do not have sacraments as such, rites of passage resemble sacramental rites, and generally serve the same purpose.

## Pregnancy and Birth

Celebrations focused on pregnancy and birth are designed to give support and encouragement to parents expecting a new baby. It is a time to bless the mother, the father, and the baby, to wish them good health during and after delivery, and to give gifts and advice.

Joyce and I attended a celebration for friends of ours expecting a baby several years ago. The ritual began with the lighting of candles and incense and the playing of soft music. The expectant mother sat in a comfortable position, leaning back in her husband's arms. The rest of us came forward, two or three at a time, and rubbed the mother's feet and hands with massage oil. As we did so, we offered both the father and mother our support and energy for the coming delivery. The massaging enabled a very direct energy exchange to take place between us and the mother. Occasionally someone would share advice or a funny story, bringing a round of laughter to the group. The ritual was very relaxed and unstructured, and continued until everyone present felt that they had offered all the blessings they wished, and exchanged the degree of energy with the mother that they desired. After the ritual was over, we gave baby presents and had a feast!

On the Wheel of the Year, pregnancy and birth fall between the north and the east, or between winter and spring. The new life is not here, but its promise is definitely felt and eagerly awaited.

## Baby Welcomings

After a baby is born, its parents may wish to "present" the child to the Pagan community for a formal welcoming and ask for the help and support of their friends as the child grows. Pagans do not baptize either adults or infants, so this is not a christening or baptismal service. Pagans do not pledge an infant to membership in a faith, so this is not a service where a baby "becomes" Pagan. This celebration welcomes the arrival of new life and gives the community an opportunity to gather around the parents, show their support, and offer blessings for the future.

Joyce remembers a baby welcoming she attended at a Pagan convention in the late 1980s. The ritual began, a circle was cast (see "What Happens in a Ritual?" below), and the parents brought forward their child, now several months old. The woman acting as priestess held the child, and together she and the parents approached each person in the circle. The priestess presented the baby to each person, one at a time, and asked what special gift or blessing they wanted the child to enjoy in his or her life. A lot of responses were given, from love to romance to music to a happy heart. A preschooler was there, and he added his blessing of lots and lots of toys!

On the Wheel of the Year, birth sits squarely in the east, or springtime, the dawn of the day and of life. It is the very point of beginning in all its wonder, newness, and freshness.

## Coming of Age

Pagans celebrate the coming of age and the reaching of puberty as a spiritual event as well as a physical one. It is a time when young people cross the threshold into adulthood and full participation in the community. It is a time when they begin to experience themselves as sexual beings and struggle with the difficulties of getting dates, fitting in, understanding themselves, and communicating their feelings. Adults are very important at this time as a source of advice and support. Most of the coming-of-age ceremonies we have been to are same-sex rituals; that is, the men hold a ceremony for the boys, and the women for the girls. This seems to be more comfortable, and allows adults and youths to share their experiences about growing up, puberty, dating, and sex more openly.

Pagans are generally not inhibited about discussing sex when it is appropriate, and they want their young people to have solid and accurate information. Pagans want to cultivate an atmosphere where youth feel comfortable approaching the adults in the community—especially their parents—with questions and problems. The coming-of-age ceremony can be one step in this process of trust and communication, and is an important way in which the community demonstrates to young people that they have permission to discuss these issues.

In many aboriginal and ancient cultures, the coming-of-age rite involved passing through some kind of test or ordeal. This is not usually done in Paganism, though in some cases a young person may make a vision quest, or go through a symbolic trial, such as the answering of questions or demonstration of certain skills.

On the Wheel of the Year, coming of age falls between east and south, or between spring and summer. It is not quite yet the time of full maturity and productivity, but the energy is building.

## Handfasting and Marriage

Pagans can choose to be either handfasted or married, and both are recognized as valid partnerships within the Pagan community. A marriage is the legal union of a heterosexual couple, although a few states allow same-sex marriages. A marriage must be performed by a Pagan minister having the authority to do so in that state, and usually requires witnesses and a license. A legal marriage is a condition created and defined by state law and can only be dissolved by the state. It establishes certain parental and property rights, which are regulated and enforced by the state.

A handfasting is recognized as a marriage within the Pagan community, and is usually performed by Pagan clergy, but it has no legal status. This may be because the parties involved are not interested in obtaining legal status, or because the laws of the state do not include their arrangement in its definition of legal marriage. Examples of the latter are marriages between homosexuals or the union of three or more people who decide to form an extended family. A handfasting may be entered into for a limited period of time such as a year, at which point the union automatically dissolves, or it may be for an indefinite period. We have friends who handfast for one-year intervals. Each year at that date they are free to leave the relationship, but if they decide to stay together, they renew their vows privately.

On the Wheel of the Year, handfasting and marriage are found in the south, the summer, the land of flowering adulthood, fertility, and productive unions. It is a realm of great energy, life, and abundance.

## Handparting

This is the Pagan equivalent to separation, divorce, or dissolution. If the parties involved are legally joined, they must also go through whatever legal process is required by their state in order to end the relationship. If the parties are hand-fasted, no legal action is likely required, and either a formal or informal hand-parting is usually sufficient.

The purpose of a handparting ritual is to mark the end of a relationship or other involvement, and to help those involved say goodbye and let go. It provides ritual space in which to heal, forgive, and to grieve. In the general culture, the ending of a relationship is often seen as cause for shame and failure, which the parties usually endure alone. A handparting is not a stigma for Pagans. As we saw in our review of the Wheel of the Year, there is always a season when things must end, when change and transition occur. It is a natural, even though painful, process. A handparting openly acknowledges the personal season of letting go, and can occur with all involved parties present, or with only some. It may be done publicly, or as a private goodbye with a few close friends.

On the Wheel of the Year, we find handpartings in the west, the land of letting go as well as the realm for reflection, processing, and evaluating what we have accomplished and experienced.

## Croning and Saging

The croning of women and the saging of men is a supportive rite of passage for those Pagans who have passed through their middle years and are now esteemed as elders in the community. The croning of women often occurs near menopause. The saging of men occurs whenever appropriate, though it is frequently associ-ated with retirement. It is a passage that reaffirms for those approaching elderhood that they are a valued part of the Pagan community. It marks for them a transition to a stage of life where they can enjoy the fruits of their labors and maybe even relax a little bit!

On the Wheel of the Year, croning and saging is found in the west, the land of autumn and sunset. This life passage brings out the energies of quiet, rest, reflection, and wisdom. It is a time for letting go and being open to transition as children leave home, jobs are left behind, and women leave their childbearing years.

## Death

Death can be the most difficult of the life passages. It can also be the most inspiring and uplifting. Pagans see death as a natural and expected part of the wheel of life, necessary for the renewal of the body and the spirit and the processing of life experience.

For those who are dying, a rite of passage celebrated at this time can be a great comfort. They may want friends and family near. They want to know they are leaving a legacy that will be remembered. They may need help in their own transition and letting go, and finding the courage to step out into the realms of death. It is important that they have the support of their family and community, and that they know it is all right for them to do what they need to do, whether that is to heal and recover, or to pass over.

After death, these rites help those of us who remain to grieve, support each other, and remember our loved ones. Pagans may decide to have funerals, memorial services, graveside services, or private services. They may choose to be buried or cremated. Pagans have no rules concerning the method of interment or the type of service that must be held, though some Pagan paths may observe certain traditions.

On the Wheel of the Year, death and dying is found in the north, the land of darkness and the cold of winter. It is here that life sleeps and awaits its next cycle.

## Dedication to a Path or Course of Study, and Ordination

Dedication rites can occur at any time during life, and may occur more than once. They include all forms of initiation and self-dedications. They may be performed alone or in the presence of a group or community that a Pagan wishes to join. The dedication may be renewed from time to time.

Ordination takes this dedication one step further. In this instance, a Pagan church will grant clergy status to one of its members. As with other clergy, Pagan ministers can perform weddings. Pagan clergy are not required to remain celibate, and usually hold jobs and raise a family. Pagan clergy is essentially a volunteer force, though there is no obstacle to paid, professional Pagan clergy either. Any Pagan can choose to study to become clergy and apply for that status through a Pagan church.

## WHAT IS A RITUAL?

Throughout our discussion of the Wheel of the Year and rites of passage we have frequently mentioned "rituals" we have attended. So what is a ritual? A "ritual" is what Pagans call their church services. The fourth edition of the *American Heritage Dictionary* calls ritual "The prescribed order of a religious ceremony," and that pretty well sums it up.

## WHAT HAPPENS IN A RITUAL?

What happens in a ritual is up to those who plan it. They consider the time of year, the purpose of the gathering, how many people there will be (which can range from one to several hundred), whether they are indoors or out, and what they want from the ritual. Some traditions have regular forms that are followed. These might be quite precise or only provide a framework that the group fills in for itself.

You will hopefully have the opportunity to attend many rituals. Below are the typical elements of ritual you are likely to come upon no matter where you go or what tradition you encounter.

The typical ritual consists of six parts. These are (1) the preparation of the space, (2) the preparation of the people, (3) the creation of sacred space, (4) the calling of quarters, deities, or other energies, (5) the magickal or energetic working, and (6) the dismissals.

### Preparation of the Space

Since Pagans don't necessarily meet in churches, they don't have a pre-existing sacred space. They typically have to create sacred space every time they meet. The Preparation of the Space involves the choosing of a location and getting it set up for ritual. It may need to be straightened and cleaned up both physically and energetically. Some Pagans like to cleanse a space energetically by sprinkling salt, sweeping the area with a broom, or by using the Native American practice of smudging, which is the burning of sage and sweet grass.

## Preparation of the People

The people who will be in the ritual—both those planning it and those participating—are coming with all their stresses and concerns attached. They may have sat in traffic for an hour, had their dinner boil over, and endured the kids fighting over the TV. So when people show up for ritual, they need to relax, calm down, and let go of the day. There are many ways to do this, including guided meditation, massage, silent preparation, and listening to music. The group may go through the process together, or the participants may do it on their own, but either way, it is important that it be done. Generally, the participants will feel better and get more out of the ritual if they take time to prepare.

A common way to get prepared is called Grounding and Centering. In a nutshell, Grounding is the plugging in of your energy centers so that you connect smoothly to all parts of yourself, the Earth, and those around you. It's like hooking yourself up to a psychic lightning rod that allows you to pull energy in from the universe when you need it, and then to feed it back out when you want to get rid of it. In the event you get a larger jolt of energy during ritual than you care to keep, Grounding the excess will usually take care of the problem.

Centering is the process by which you open up energy centers in your body, and then place your focus there. It is similar to the focusing done by those in the martial arts, who place their power or focus in their solar plexus. Many Pagan rituals focus the energy into the heart center, although this will vary based on purpose, time of year, and the nature of the work.

Grounding and Centering are discussed further in chapter 6. If you are fortunate enough to be taking classes or have a teacher, ask to learn several methods.

In addition to Grounding and Centering, the persons attending a ritual may prepare by being smudged, passing through the smoke of incense, being cleansed with the sprinkling of water or salt or anointing with oil, or discussing the work of the ritual beforehand.

## Creation of Sacred Space

Remember the sacred space Pagans create every time they hold a ceremony? Well, casting a circle is one of the most common ways to do it. Casting a circle is like drawing the walls, floors, and ceiling of an imaginary church within which to do spiritual work. It's a portable church, really. Pagans cast it when they want it and take it down when they're done. It is an energetic filter that keeps the static out and holds in the energy that they want to build. It exists only on an energetic level, but is very palpable when done well.

There are many ways to cast a circle. There is no right or wrong way, but only what works, although some traditions specify a particular method. Circles can be cast by walking the perimeter of the circle one or more times, standing in the center and using a finger, sword, or athame (a knife used for magick and ritual) to draw the circle in the air outside the ring of people, dancing, or a wall of sound created through singing or chanting. A circle may be put up and taken down by an entire group or only by those conducting the ritual. A circle may be marked by stones, candles, or the sprinkling of tobacco, salt, or cornmeal, or by nothing at all.

Why cast in a circle? Most rituals occur in the round mainly because the participants can all see each other that way. Pagan rituals are very participatory and theater seating would just not be very practical or fun.

## Calling of Quarters and Deities and Other Energies

What occurs in this part of the ritual will depend entirely on the participants' tradition and point of view. Some traditions call before the circle is cast and some after. The Quarters are the four directions: north, south, east, and west. They are called in their energetic roles as representatives of the Wheel of Life and the sacred year. Just as the Christian cross points to the four directions and may represent, in addition to the crucifixion, the spreading of divine energy to the four corners of the Earth, so, too, do the four Quarters sum up the totality of divine energy for Pagans.

Those Pagans who work with Deities will then call them into the circle to lend their energies to the work ahead. Which Deities are called will depend on those running the ritual and their particular tradition. Wiccans typically call "the God" and "the Goddess," who they may or may not envision as actual personages, but who certainly represent universal forces of polarity. Whether the Pagans involved see Deities as actual beings or not, they are almost always called for the particular archetypal energies they represent. See chapter 3 for a further discussion on Pagan views of Deity.

## Magickal and Energetic Working

This is where the real work of the ritual is done. Whatever the purpose of the ritual is, it will occur at this point. Those who design and plan the ritual decide what magickal and energetic working will be done, and usually make it known to the participants beforehand. They may decide on a working that is based on a theme or is related to the season of the year. Common purposes of rituals are healing, prayer, empowerment, manifesting a desire or goal, experiencing spiritual connection, and specific projects. Specific projects may include magickal work designed to affect weather, lower crime, or send help to someone in need. See chapter 6 for a more thorough discussion of magick.

## Dismissals

This section marks the ending of the ritual. Going in reverse order from how the ritual began, any energy raised in the magickal working is first thoroughly grounded, then the Deities and four directions are thanked and their energies released. Finally, the circle is taken down and the ritual is over. After the ritual it is typical for there to be drumming, dancing, and singing, and sometimes feasting and partying.

Not all rituals contain the six parts outlined above, but most do. Those who work in some Eastern traditions, in Tantra, Asatru, or Shamanism may not cast a circle or call directions or Deities. Ritual is fluid. Attend a variety of them and see for yourself. Try out several traditions, work with their methods and energies for awhile, and see what clicks for you.

# RITUAL TOOLS AND SYMBOLS

Probably the most common Pagan symbol is the *pentacle,* or five-pointed star (Figure 1.4). The five points represent the essences of physical existence as we

FIGURE 1.4
The pentacle.

know it: earth, air, fire, water, and spirit. Together these five essences make up earthly life. Many pentacles are also surrounded by a circle, which represents spirit, the unbroken wholeness of the universe, and the profound interconnectedness of all things. To many Pagans the pentacle is an extremely meaningful statement of their faith and personal philosophy, and they wear it proudly as a sign of their religious beliefs.

The first four points of the pentacle—earth, air, fire, and water—are known as the *four elements* and they represent all the forms matter takes in this physical universe as we currently understand it. The *earth element* represents matter in its solid form, and is also associated with the physical body and the concerns of the physical body, such as food, clothing, shelter, and the money to purchase these things. The *air element* represents matter in its gaseous form, and is also associated with the mind, thought, genius, and inspiration. The *fire element* represents matter in its plasmic form, and is also associated with spirituality, willpower, passion, and creativity. The *water element* represents matter in its liquid form, and is also associated with the emotions, the subconscious, wisdom, and intuitive work.

As we've already seen in our discussion of the Wheel of the Year, each of these elements are associated with a *direction:* earth with the north, air with east, fire with south, and water with the west. Each of the directions is further associated with a *stage of life:* east/air with the sunrise and the spirit of youthfulness; south/fire with the productive, abundant, creative time of adulthood; west/water with the reflection and wisdom during the sunset of life; and north/earth with elderhood and stepping over into death.

Each of the elements is further associated with certain tools, colors, sounds, perfumes, animals, minerals, gemstones, herbs, trees, or flowers, which are too numerous to cover thoroughly here. When Pagans prepare for a ritual they frequently include these associations, known as *correspondences*. A table in the north, for example, may be covered with a dark-colored cloth and decorated with black, green, or brown candles, some crystals, stones, ears of corn, a container of salt or cornmeal, and even a buffalo skin. The ritual tool associated with the north is the *staff,* a symbol of age, experience, wisdom, and the solidity of the physical realm.

In the east you may see a table covered with a green, yellow, or white cloth and decorated with candles of the same colors, incense, feathers, bells, or a fan. The ritual tool associated with the east is the *sword,* which represents the power of the mind and the ability of thought to cut through all distractions.

In the south you may see a table covered with a red or orange cloth and decorated with red candles, incense, desert sand, representations of snakes, salamanders, or the coyote. The ritual tool associated with the south in some traditions is the *athame* (pronounced *ah-THAW-may* or *ATH-ah-may*), which is a knife, and in other traditions it is the *wand*. Both the athame and wand are phallic symbols, and represent action, intention, and energy as they are projected by the practitioner into the outer world. The athame and wand are used as extensions of the hand while the person directs energy through them. Circles, for example, are frequently cast by a person using an athame to draw the circumference of the circle. The wand is used in much the same way, and is frequently tipped with a crystal.

In the west you may see a table covered in a blue cloth and decorated with blue and aqua candles, seashells, a fountain, cups and chalices, or even a bear skin or claw. The magickal tool associated with the west is the *chalice* or the *cauldron*. Sometimes the cauldron is used as a symbol of the north, but in either case both the chalice and the cauldron are feminine symbols representing the womb of life, quiet inner reflectiveness, and the fluidness of intuition and the subconscious.

Correspondences vary from tradition to tradition, however, and sometimes those variations are significant. Although the elemental associations and directions given above are the most common, you will encounter variations if you attend enough rituals. The correspondences and associations adopted by a tradition are

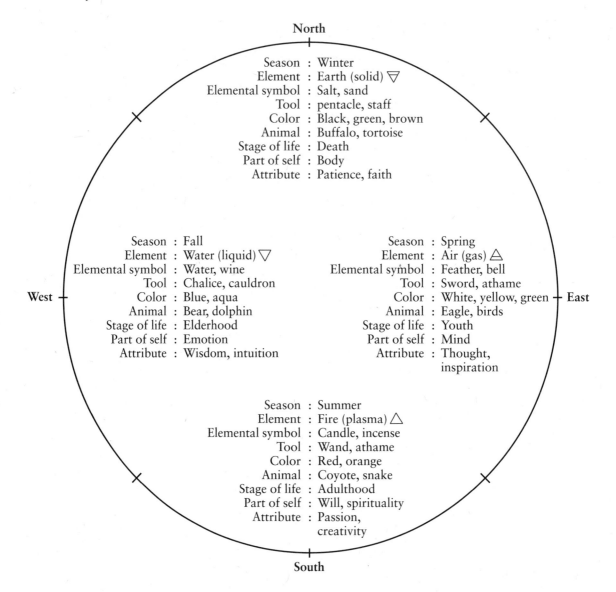

North

Season : Winter
Element : Earth (solid) ▽
Elemental symbol : Salt, sand
Tool : pentacle, staff
Color : Black, green, brown
Animal : Buffalo, tortoise
Stage of life : Death
Part of self : Body
Attribute : Patience, faith

West

Season : Fall
Element : Water (liquid) ▽
Elemental symbol : Water, wine
Tool : Chalice, cauldron
Color : Blue, aqua
Animal : Bear, dolphin
Stage of life : Elderhood
Part of self : Emotion
Attribute : Wisdom, intuition

East

Season : Spring
Element : Air (gas) △
Elemental symbol : Feather, bell
Tool : Sword, athame
Color : White, yellow, green
Animal : Eagle, birds
Stage of life : Youth
Part of self : Mind
Attribute : Thought,
inspiration

Season : Summer
Element : Fire (plasma) △
Elemental symbol : Candle, incense
Tool : Wand, athame
Color : Red, orange
Animal : Coyote, snake
Stage of life : Adulthood
Part of self : Will, spirituality
Attribute : Passion,
creativity

South

**FIGURE 1.5**
Wheel of the Year correspondences.

not an end in themselves, but rather a means to help us mentally order the universe
to interact with it meaningfully. Therefore, Pagans do not view one tradition's correspondences as right and another's as wrong. Pagans respectfully accept and adapt

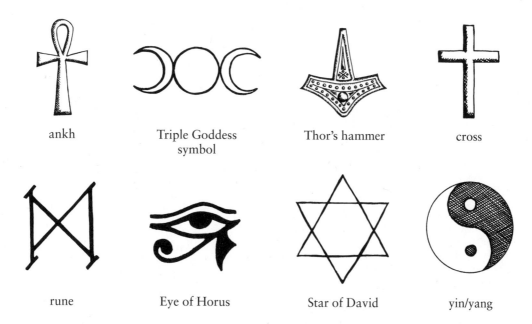

ankh          Triple Goddess          Thor's hammer          cross
                  symbol

rune          Eye of Horus          Star of David          yin/yang

**FIGURE 1.6**
Other Pagan symbols.

themselves to the associations of whatever tradition is leading the ritual. Some of the more common correspondences Joyce and I have encountered are listed in Figure 1.5.

The tables that were mentioned in the examples for each of the four directions are known as *altars*. An altar, for a Pagan, is any surface used for the placing of ritual and magickal tools, candles, decorations, and other items needed for a given working.

None of the tools discussed are a necessity for the doing of good and effective ritual or magick. Although many Pagans are more comfortable using their tools and may feel they have formed a bond with them, the tool itself is not the magick. Ritual and magick can be done without any tools whatsoever. See chapter 6 for an in-depth look at what magick is and how it works.

Many other symbols in addition to the pentacle are meaningful to Pagans, and these vary according to individual taste or the tradition followed. Some of these symbols include the Egyptian ankh and Eye of Horus, Thor's hammer, rune signs, the yin/yang, and even the Star of David and the cross (Figure 1.6).

# IS RITUAL ALL PAGANS DO?

Formal ritual—privately or with a group—is only part of what Pagans do to nurture themselves spiritually and celebrate the sacred year. There are a multitude of other spiritual practices that are popular with Pagans. These include meditation, prayer, t'ai chi, martial arts, tantra, working with herbs and essential oils, aromatherapy, camping, massage, healing, belly dancing, vision quests, tarot readings, other forms of divination, retreats, gardening, reading and studying, ecstatic sex, nature walks, learning an ancient language, magickal cooking, weaving, sewing, and on and on. Pagans are open to so many cultures and ways of connecting spiritually that there are few activities that cannot be made a part of their spiritual practice.

# WHAT DO PAGANS BELIEVE?

When describing Pagan beliefs, the question "Which Pagans?" arises. Shall we talk about what Wiccans believe, or Asatru, or Santerians? These groups are so diverse that we cannot define all of Paganism by looking at only one tradition.

Critics tend to seize on this diversity as a sign that Pagans don't believe anything, but a quick illustration will show that Christians are in much the same situation. Let us say that we are asked to define what Christians believe about baptism. First, perhaps, we can say that all Christians must be baptized. There are, however, several denominations where baptism is rarely practiced and is not a requirement for membership, while in other groups baptism is an absolute requirement. So, we cannot say baptism is or is not required, but only that the practice varies.

Let's keep going. Perhaps we can say how and when Christians are baptized, such as, baptisms are performed on infants by the sprinkling of water. Once again, there are denominations that not only do not practice infant baptism, but condemn it strongly. A hot debate rages in some circles as to whether sprinkling even qualifies as baptism, and accept no baptism that hasn't been accomplished by complete immersion. Looks like we can't say anything definite about the age or method of baptism either, but only that the practice varies.

Let's try one last time. Surely we can say something common about baptism that is true for all Christians everywhere, like, at least the baptized person is alive! That seems pretty obvious, don't you think? Not so fast. At least one denomination routinely baptizes for dead people and does so by the millions.

Shall we conclude, then, that Christians have no definitive beliefs about baptism? Of course not. It's no more difficult to accept diversity in Pagan beliefs and practices than in Christianity. Even so, it is possible to distinguish Pagans from the rest of the religious universe through certain principles that are held, for the most part, by many Pagans regardless of tradition.

# PRINCIPLES OF PAGANISM

The principles of Paganism presented below are not drawn from any one Pagan tradition, but are our synthesis of principles encountered in a variety of Pagan traditions. Most Pagans we know agree with most or all of these principles. These principles are not a list of beliefs a person must adopt in order to be Pagan; rather, they are statements that embody Paganism's worldview that point to the development of one type of relationship with the universe and the Divine rather than another, and that outline the direction in which spiritual and personal growth might proceed for a Pagan. The actual beliefs adopted by Pagans on these issues are not as important as the underlying process of spiritual growth and personal development these principles represent. It is our opinion that spiritual maturity tends to express itself in similar ways at common stages of development regardless of a person's culture or religion. We hope to present a study of this pattern of spiritual growth and its particular application to Pagans and Paganism in future books. In the meantime, we offer these principles both as concepts most Pagans agree with, and as a direction in which spiritual growth may likely proceed for persons who choose to pursue a Pagan path of development.

1. **You are responsible for the beliefs you choose to adopt.** You are in control of what you choose to believe, especially when it comes to ideas about spirituality, ethics, values, the nature of the Divine, the nature and purpose of the physical world, and your place in it. The power to choose your beliefs resides in you—not in an institution, church, or government. It is important that you take responsibility for the beliefs you adopt because beliefs act as templates around which you build your reality. You will tend to interpret experience and information to fit what your beliefs tell you to expect, while filtering out information that does not fit. To a great extent, then, your beliefs shape both

the interior and exterior world you create for yourself. Regardless of the beliefs impressed on you in the past, you are in control of what you choose to adopt as your beliefs now. Pagans accept their responsibility to become more self-aware, identify the beliefs they are allowing to operate in their lives, and then to examine the merits of those beliefs periodically.

2. **You are responsible for your own actions and your spiritual and personal development.** The development of a conscience, or personal ethic, and then the application of that ethic to everyday life is the responsibility of every person. Any resource, teacher, practice, or holy writing that helps you move toward your goal of spiritual maturity can and should be used. Resources, teachers, and holy books cannot be substituted for the effort each person must give to his or her own growth, however since growth is a muscle you must exercise yourself. Spiritual muscles don't get strong by letting other people do your work for you. Pagans strive to become spiritually mature and to take responsibility for their beliefs, actions, and spiritual growth.

3. **You are responsible for deciding who or what Deity is for you, and forming a relationship with that Deity.** Someone who joins a particular faith has gone through the process of deciding what Deity is for them and that the faith they are joining is a good match. Pagans openly acknowledge this process and are open to a variety of ideas about Deity. Pagans have many images of Deity, including multiple images, male, female, animal, energy or spirit images, or no images at all. This topic is covered in chapter 3.

4. **Everything contains the spark of intelligence.**[21] From the smallest atom to the largest planetary system, each part of the world contains a form of consciousness or spark of intelligence. In the physical realm, consciousness exhibits as awareness, personality, energetic vibrations, or other characteristics that are in keeping with the particular physical form. Science and mysticism both suggest that consciousness is multidimensional, that it folds and unfolds into physical reality from unseen realms, and its expression in the physical world is only a part of its greater reality. This concept is explored further in chapter 5.

5. **Everything is sacred.** Sacredness means different things to different Pagans. To some it means that all parts of the universe are precious, and worthy of respect

and careful handling. To others it implies a feeling of kinship, of connection, a kind of cosmic brother- or sisterhood. To others sacredness means that something is holy, having been created, blessed, or approved by a Deity. Some ways that Pagans view and relate to the universe are discussed in chapter 5.

For some Pagans, this principle also relates to how Deity is involved with the physical and nonphysical universes, and whether by its nature the universe is good or evil. Many Pagans see Deity as penetrating the universe in one way or another. We discuss this and other views about Deity in chapter 3. The result of this particular view, however, is that if Deity permeates everything, then everything is sacred. Nothing is cut off or isolated from the Divine Ground. The dualism that says that the physical is bad and the spiritual is good has no meaning to a Pagan. The dualism that says that what is physical is at war with what is spiritual has no meaning to a Pagan. This brings us naturally to the second point, then, since if nothing is cut off from the Divine Ground, then neither are you. Your human nature is not inherently flawed. Do not confuse this issue with one of behavior. People can choose to act in ways that are destructive, but Pagans tend to treat behavior as a separate issue from the question of whether or not human nature is corrupt. See chapter 7 for more on this point.

6. **Each part of the universe can communicate with each other part, and these parts often cooperate for specific ends.** Here is the crux of magick. Magick is a completely natural process, which, in its simplest form, is the communication and cooperation of many consciousnesses. Other religions call this same process prayer, meditation, inspiration, synchronicity, or miracles. The basic principles of magick are explored in chapter 6.

7. **Consciousness survives death.** Consciousness, as was earlier suggested, exists on multiple levels simultaneously, and physical reality is only one expression of it. Physical existence can be seen as the intrusion of consciousness into the world of matter, and death as the withdrawing, or enfolding, of it back into other dimensions. Pagans hold a variety of views of what happens after death, and most, though not all, believe in an afterlife. This topic is explored further in chapter 7.

**questions to discuss**                    **IMPRESSIONS OF PAGANISM**

1. In what ways is Paganism influencing movies, music, commercials, consumer products, businesses, and other religions? What was the first Pagan reference or idea you encountered in the general culture?

2. What was your impression of Paganism before you began studying it? What do your friends and family think of your new interest?

3. Why are you studying Paganism at this time, and what do you most want to gain from this book?

4. Who was the first Pagan you ever met? How did you go about finding Pagans? How did you hear about Pagan events? How do you think Pagans can improve their accessibility to those who are looking for them?

5. Have you ever attended a Pagan festival or convention? What was it like? How was it different from what you expected, and in what ways did it meet your expectations? What would you say to someone going to their first Pagan festival or convention? Their first ritual?

6. What experience have you had with Paganism so far that has been the most fun, the most rewarding, or made the deepest impression on you?

**my journal**                              **DISCOVERING PAGANISM**

- I came to know about Paganism because . . .
- Three things about Paganism I don't understand or that concern me are . . .
- Three things about Paganism I would be interested to study further are . . .

If I am a Pagan or think I may be:

- My religion before I was Pagan was . . .
- Five things I appreciate about my previous religion are . . .
- Three things I wish I could have changed about my previous religion are . . .
- I am attracted to Paganism because . . .
- The Pagan tradition I am most interested in right now is . . .
- The reasons why I am interested in this tradition are . . .
- The reaction of my friends and family to my interest in Paganism is . . .

**keys to success**

**HOW TO FIND PAGANS**

If you are looking for Pagans, Pagan events such as festivals and conventions, or want to find a teacher or a group, then here are some suggestions in the order we would try them:

**Go to your local metaphysical bookstore.** Once you're there, talk to people, ask about classes, groups, and gatherings. Tell them what you're interested in and ask them to help you make connections. Pick up whatever flyers and calendars you can find and check out what's happening locally. Buy a few periodicals that have calendars and contact information in them.

**Get on the Internet and search for groups and activities in your area.** Check out what festivals and gatherings are planned for your region. Sign on to some chat lists. Spend a few afternoons surfing and see the variety of traditions that are available.

**Go to rituals and other gatherings.** Once you have discovered what is going on and where, get out and go! Try to attend local public rituals and also make plans to attend one or more festivals and conventions. While rituals are usually free, festivals and conventions generally have registration fees and require a larger investment of your time. Most festivals and conventions last for a weekend, and a few last an entire week. You may have to plan ahead for a festival or convention, but try to go to at least one. You will meet a variety of interesting people, and possibly connect with a teacher or group.

**Take classes.** Try to find classes or a teacher in your area. Some groups offer training for new Pagans. Books are fine to start with, but there is no substitute for hands-on experience.

**Join an organization.** Some towns, cities, and regions have councils and planning groups that plan and put on Pagan events and lectures, hold open circles, or work to build up a Pagan community in their area. Searching the Web will help you find these groups. Ask around at rituals and festivals. If there is a Pagan organization near you, you'll find out about it. Then sign up! Become a member, and if possible, volunteer to help plan and put on events. You'll get to know a lot of Pagans this way, and have fun while you're doing it.

# YOU ARE WHAT YOU BELIEVE

Ideas are powerful. What you believe about yourself and your world determines to a large extent the kinds of experiences you will have and how you will interpret them.

The ideas you accept as true are your beliefs. Beliefs act like a filter through which information passes before it reaches you. The belief filter acts so strongly that it usually allows in only information you already believe to be true. Contradictory information is either ignored, explained away, or rejected.

What you decide to accept or reject as your beliefs will literally create your world. If you believe you cannot be a certain kind of person, then you won't. If you believe you must have only certain types of relationships, then you will never experience others. If you think you can't go to college or learn a skill, then you never will. If you believe that God is one way, then you will never experience God any other way. If you think that certain topics and questions are forbidden, then you will never explore them. One of our favorite sayings about beliefs comes from Henry Ford, who said, "Whether you think you can, or whether you think you can't, you're right!"

Power such as this is awesome. It mobilizes nations, creates religions, begins and ends wars, and defines new civilizations. On a more mundane level, it can even influence the kind of toothpaste you buy! Advertisers understand the power of getting you to believe what they want you to believe. So do politicians, governments, and religious leaders. Beliefs set a vision around which people take action.

What is your vision? What kind of life do you want to live? What kind of world do you want to create? What beliefs are best going to get you there? These questions are not annoyances to rush through so you can start "being a Pagan." These questions are the heart of the matter. They are so central, in fact, that the first principle of Paganism addresses the issue of beliefs. This principle states, "You are responsible for the beliefs you choose to adopt." Because beliefs set a vision around which people act, the second principle flows directly from the first and states that, "You are responsible for your actions and your spiritual and personal development."

These two principles, then, are a beginning point for spiritual and personal growth. They address the two fundamental issues of responsibility and empowerment. Your empowerment begins with an acknowledgment that you are able to choose those very templates, or beliefs, around which you build your world, starting with your self-image and moving on to your relationships, the culture, politics, and religion. Without a sense that you are in control of choosing those ideas you adopt as your own, or that choice is even possible, you may not begin to move forward in your development. You may believe you are stuck or trapped in the way things are, or in the way you have always been. You may believe you are not capable of growing or changing. You may believe growth is possible but is dependent on something outside yourself, such as a holy text, a spiritual practice, or a teacher.

We suggest that the journey of self-discovery and development as a Pagan begins by becoming aware of the power of belief, by acknowledging your power to choose the ideas you will accept as true, by accepting your responsibility for that choice, and by taking responsibility for how you act on your beliefs.

This chapter should be stimulating for you. If you find it threatening or uncomfortable, go to the section near the end called "If You Are Having Trouble" and work through the questions there with the help of a friend.

## HOW DO BELIEFS WORK?

Beliefs operate in much the same way a filter works on a camera.[1] We like to visualize the mind as a camera (Figure 2.1). The body of the camera is your physical

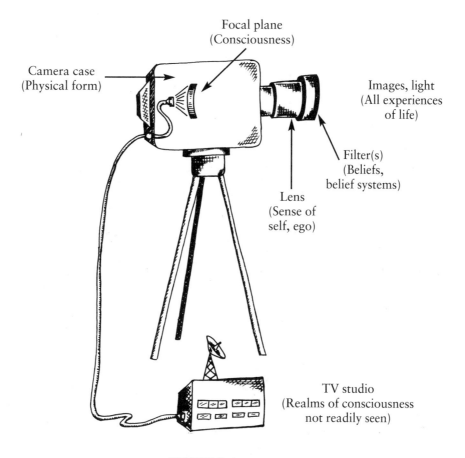

**FIGURE 2.1**
The camera of beliefs.

form. The mechanism within the camera, which enables the camera to work and have meaning, is your consciousness. The camera is connected through its wires and circuits to realms of consciousness that are not readily seen. In Figure 2.1 this is shown by the cable connecting the camera to a TV studio. We will focus on this connection further in chapters 5 and 6.

The lens of our camera is "us," the sense of self we carry through this lifetime. You could also refer to it as the "ego," for the lens acts as a processor or buffer between you and the "outer" world. Its job is to maintain the integrity of your sense of self and help you relate to your inner and outer environments in safe and productive ways.

Over your lens lies a filter. On a camera, light must pass through the filter before it can reach the lens and be captured as an image. There is no input received by the lens that does not first pass through the filter, and the light that passes through it is changed by it. It may enhance a color. It may make light appear pointed and starlike, or hazy and soft.

The camera's filter is not a permanent fixture. Each filter is created by someone, and the choice of which filter to apply belongs to the person using the camera. His or her choice will be based on the type of images and experiences he or she wants the camera to capture, and the purpose to which the pictures will be put.

Just as with a camera, you gather inner and outer information through the lens of your "self" or "ego" where it can be acted upon by your consciousness. The filter that lies over your lens is your beliefs. And just like a camera, your beliefs "color" how you see things. If your filter is pink, for example, you will see only a pink world even though the full spectrum of light hits your filter.

Why does this happen? The purpose of the filter is to screen out all input that does not match it. In the case of our pink filter, only light that matches the pink wavelength will be allowed through. In the same way, your beliefs filter out all experiences that do not match them. Any experience, concept, or idea that does not match the wavelength of your beliefs will tend to be rejected. The information simply will not be allowed through.

Who is in control of these filters? You are. You decide whether to adopt beliefs presented to you by governments, religions, cultures, friends, and family. Sometimes we lose sight of our power to choose because trends become strong and carry so much momentum that they seem to take on a life of their own. Even if you loan out the power of your beliefs to a cause or event, it is still your power to give.

The following visualization will help you see how beliefs shape your reality on a personal, day-to-day basis.

## visualization

## SELF-IMAGE AS A BELIEF FILTER

*If you are in a small group or class, the visualization should be read aloud for the group. If you are studying alone, we suggest you record the visualization so you can listen to it later. We find it too hard to read a bit, try to meditate, then read some more.*

*When reading or recording the visualization, please note that pauses are marked with a series of dots at the end of a sentence (. . .). These pauses are brief; say, between five and fifteen seconds, depending on what is appropriate. Longer pauses are marked as such, and should be given twenty seconds or so.*

*Although the word "he" is used later in this visualization, feel free to change it to "she" if you prefer.*

Get in a comfortable position. If you are sitting, put your feet flat on the floor. If you are lying down, put your arms down beside you and your legs out straight.

Close your eyes. I am going to lead your breathing for a few minutes, so breathe with me.

Breathe in through your nose: 1, 2, 3, hold, 1, 2, 3, hold; and out through your mouth: 1, 2, 3. In through your nose: 1, 2, 3, hold, 1, 2, 3, hold; and out through your mouth: 1, 2, 3. [*Repeat for five or six breaths. Time your words and numbering so that the breathing in, holding, and breathing out occur at equal intervals.*]

Now, in your mind, see yourself standing by a table. . . . On this table are three pairs of glasses. One of the pairs is yours; the other two belong to an imaginary person. . . . Ignore yours for the moment; you will come back to it soon. . . . Turn your attention to the glasses that belong to the imaginary person. One of the pairs is filled with a negative self-image, the other with a positive self-image. . . . Pick up the pair of glasses filled with the negative self-image and look at it. . . . When our imaginary person puts these glasses on, he believes that no one likes him, that he is an unlikable person, and he interprets everything that happens to him according to this belief. . . . You notice that the glass is tinted or filled with this belief. . . . It may have a color or be foggy or filled with swirls. . . . [*Remember that the purpose of the pauses is to give people time to imagine what you are saying.*]

Now put on this pair of glasses. . . . For the time you have them on you will be able to see your imaginary person and his negative beliefs in action. . . . Your imaginary person comes into view and you begin to follow him as he goes about his day. . . . As he walks to the car, he sees his neighbor outside cutting flowers. Your imaginary person calls a hello to his neighbor, but the neighbor doesn't even look up. . . . Unknown to your imaginary person, the neighbor has on a headset and can't hear him.

Now observe how you as your imaginary person perceives what happened. . . . What does he see about this situation? . . . Remember, you have his negative filter on right now. Perhaps he thinks, "My neighbor dislikes me so much she can't even say hello. No one likes me," . . . How does your imaginary person react? . . . Does his expression or body language change? . . .

Now your imaginary person arrives at work. . . . There is a meeting he is attending for a new marketing strategy. All previous ideas have been rejected and the team is desperate to produce something. Your imaginary person came up with an idea last night, but now that he's at the meeting, he can't bring himself to voice it. Looking through his negative filter, what might be going through his mind? . . . As he looks around at his coworkers, perhaps he's thinking, "My ideas are pretty dumb. No one wants to hear them anyway. Nobody likes anything I do. They'll just ridicule me." [*longer pause*]

Let this image fade. . . . You are standing again at the table and you take off the glasses with the negative filter. . . . Next to them are another pair of glasses that belong to your imaginary person, but these are filled with a positive self-image. . . . Hold them up and take a look at them. . . . Do they appear any different? . . . Put them on and look around you. . . . How does the world appear now? . . . Once again you see your imaginary person come into view and begin his day all over again. . . . He walks outside and says hello to his neighbor. . . . The neighbor doesn't respond. . . . What does this response look like when viewed through the filter of a positive self-image? . . . How might your imaginary person react? . . . How does his expression and body language respond? . . .

Again your imaginary person arrives at work and is sitting in the meeting. . . . How does he feel? . . . When it comes time to contribute his idea, what does he do this time? . . . How might he interpret his coworkers' reactions? . . . Take a look around and see the ways your imaginary person's world and his place in it appear different from when you wore the first pair of glasses. [*longer pause*]

Let these images fade, and take off the pair of glasses. . . . There is one pair left on the table. . . . This pair belongs to you. . . . Pick it up and take a look at it. . . . As you hold your glasses, ask yourself, "What is my self-image?" [*longer pause*] Think of a few words that describe your current image of yourself. . . . [*longer pause*]

Now see your beliefs flowing into the glass of the eyeglasses. . . . Watch the glass as you do this. . . . What are your beliefs doing to the glass? Are they giving it a certain shape, texture, or color? [*longer pause*] What do your beliefs about yourself look like? . . .

Now put on your pair of glasses and look out at your world. . . . What does it look like? . . . How does your self-image color how you see the world around you? How do you interpret what is going on around you? [*Long pause—up to a minute. You can go longer, but watch the body language of the group for shifting or otherwise losing concentration.*]

It's time now to take off your pair of glasses. . . . You take them off and put them back on the table. . . . You become aware of yourself again, and feel yourself coming back to your body. . . . Feel your arms and legs, and your body sitting or lying in this room. . . . Take a couple of deep breaths. . . . When you are ready, open your eyes.

*Give yourself a chance to get reoriented. If you are in a group, ask who would like to share his or her experience. Get a comment from everyone if possible. Whether you are studying alone or with a group, think about the visualization for a few minutes and ask yourself or the group the following questions.*

**questions to discuss**          **LOOKING THROUGH YOUR FILTER**

1. Were you able to see the images in the visualization? If you found it diffi-cult, don't give up. Visualizing is not a skill we use everyday, so it may take practice for you.

2. How did it feel to look out through another's filter? How did their world look and feel to you?

3. How did it change when it became your self-image and your filter? How does your self-image feel? Do you like the way the world looks to you through your pair of glasses?

4. Identify two or three things about your self-image that you like. What parts would you like to change? How will the changes affect your filter? How will the changes alter how you see and respond to the world?

**my journal**          **YOUR PLACE IN THE UNIVERSE**

• Five things I believe about myself and my place in the universe are . . .

• Are these beliefs my own, or did I pick them up from someone else? Did I hear them at home, at church, at school, on TV? The origins of each of my five beliefs are . . .

• How are these beliefs positive for me, how do they satisfy me and help me grow personally and spiritually? In other words, what do these beliefs *do* for me? This shows me how my beliefs help me grow.

For each of my five beliefs I will identify another belief I *cannot* have as long as I hold to my original belief. This shows me how my beliefs are limiting:

- If I believe in Belief #1, I cannot also believe . . .
- If I believe in Belief #2, I cannot also believe . . .
- If I believe in Belief #3, I cannot also believe . . .
- If I believe in Belief #4, I cannot also believe . . .
- If I believe in Belief #5, I cannot also believe . . .

As you can see from the above exercise, every belief is both expanding and limiting. The secret is to let your beliefs be your tools. They will help you make sense of your world and function well within it. They will provide you with a perspective absolutely unique to your filter, and therefore beautiful in its own way. Simply be aware that a belief, no matter how wonderful, draws a line and sets a boundary, and as a filter it automatically shuts out information that does not match it. With a little practice, you can catch yourself doing this and examine your filters whenever you wish.

**exercise**

**DRAWING YOUR SELF-IMAGE FILTER**

In the prior visualization involving eyeglasses you visualized your current self-image. Take a piece of paper and draw the pair of eyeglasses that represented your beliefs about yourself. Be as concrete or as abstract as you like. Using pens, markers, or crayons, draw or otherwise express the various aspects of your self-image that came to you during the visualization, and add any additional ones that occur to you now. Perhaps your beliefs suggest a certain color, picture, shape, words, or design. Draw them all onto your eyeglasses, even if the images blend together and the glasses get crowded. You can put the images next to each other or one on top of the other.

When you are finished, take a look at your drawing and see how it makes you feel. Do you like what you see? Does your filter look beautiful to you (we're not talking artistic ability here), muddy, dark, joyful, or out of balance? Imagine yourself having to look out through these glasses. Is this how you want to see yourself? Is this how you want to see the world? How is your filter shaping your life and your relationships; how you respond to the world and how it responds to you?

Now imagine words that you wish described your self-image. Write them down. Take another sheet of paper and draw another pair of eyeglasses. For each word of your preferred self-image, draw a picture, shape, or add in a color. How do you wish your self-image filter looked?

Now close your eyes and see yourself stepping into this new filter. Pick up your new pair of eyeglasses, put them on and look out on the world around you. How does the world look now? Do you feel any differently about yourself? What do your relationships look like, how do people respond to you, and what is your life like? In what ways is your life different than it was with the old filter?

## WHAT IS A BELIEF SYSTEM?

A belief system is a collection of beliefs that fit together to form a structure. Beliefs rarely travel alone; they tend to hang out in groups. Similar beliefs reinforce each other, and when added together can create very complex logical systems. Essentially, one idea builds on another, then another, and another, until a system is created.

Describing a belief system as a structure helps us see that, like a building, beliefs build one upon the other and rest on the ones that come before (Figure 2.2). If you move one of the foundational beliefs, the entire structure can collapse. Also like a building, belief structures contain related organizations, services, and governments that shape and create the society around them—sometimes to the good and sometimes not. As was stated earlier, beliefs do not stay self-contained, but provide a visionary blueprint around which people build the world.

If you were to stand inside a belief system and look around, you would see that the beliefs within it are generally internally consistent. By internal consistency we mean that systems are not built up arbitrarily with unrelated beliefs stuck together willy-nilly. Beliefs in a belief structure generally flow together smoothly and reinforce each other, with each additional concept supported by the ones that come before it. Just as with the United States's political philosophy,

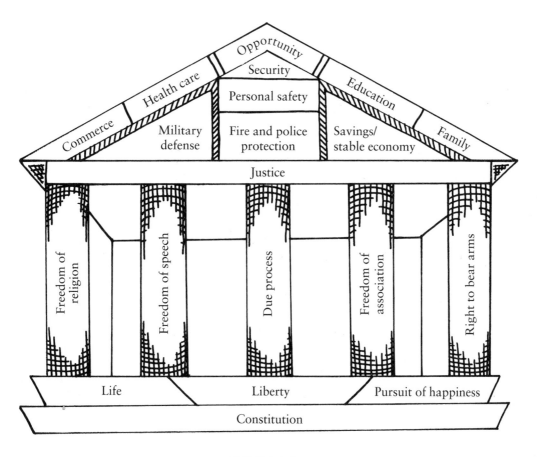

**FIGURE 2.2**
U.S. political philosophy as a belief structure.

the beliefs support each other in order to form a foundation, walls, ceiling, and doors. The ideas within one system are consistent with each other for the most part, and flow together in their own harmony.

Imagine that you are going on a tour of three religious buildings. One is a Christian church, one is a Muslim mosque, and one a Buddhist temple. In the Christian church you find sweeping arches and high spaces with paintings of angels on the ceiling designed to draw your mind upward to God. In the Muslim mosque you find more open floor space to allow people room to kneel and pray, and above you soars a minaret, which allows the caller of prayer to be heard for some distance. In

**FIGURE 2.3**
Three religious buildings.

the Buddhist temple you find clean lines surrounded by rocks, trees, flowers, and flowing water, arranged in a manner to impress you with calmness and harmony (Figure 2.3).

Now we ask you: Which of these buildings is correct? Or, stated the other way: which architectural concept is wrong?

Our point here is that all of these structures are beautiful in their own way. They are each constructed from a unique set of harmonious and consistent architectural principles, and each create a space of beauty suited to the belief systems they represent. Buildings make good examples because they are ideas in physical form. Belief systems are also structures, but since they exist primarily in the mental world they are not as easily seen. The shape of belief systems can only be observed through words, books, teachings, institutions, and the type of world created by those who follow them.

Pagans who take the time to develop their philosophy about how beliefs operate are more easily able to view beliefs and belief systems—including mythologies, religions, governments, cultural taboos, and corporate philosophies—with objectivity. When you are not emotionally bound to a belief, you are able to explore the direct relationship between it and the type of world that has been or can be built from it. Armed with this insight, you can then choose the beliefs that best work for you and the kind of reality you want to experience. Your objectivity will also allow you to examine your beliefs whenever you wish to see if they are meeting your expectations, and if not, to begin to change them.

Because belief systems are, for the most part, internally consistent, Pagans understand that to those within a given system the world makes complete sense from their point of view. Because Pagans understand that they do not have to adopt the beliefs of a system in order to appreciate its harmony, beauty, culture, and tradition, most Pagans are respectful and appreciative of other systems, and feel no need to change them. Because most Pagans honor diversity, they welcome a world filled with a variety of belief systems and are not interested in eliminating all but their own.

## exercise          IDENTIFYING BELIEFS

Take several sheets of paper and mark one "Childhood," another "Teenager," another "Young Adult," and the last "Me Now." If you are just now a teenager or young adult, eliminate whatever pages don't apply to you. Now put yourself in a quiet space and see yourself as a child. What did you believe as a child? Areas to include are beliefs about yourself, your body, your parents, God, religion, school, responsibility, guilt, sex, what makes you a good or bad person, and what is expected of you. Write down all the beliefs you can recall. Now do the same for yourself as a teenager, a young adult, and yourself now. Take a couple of days to do this if you don't have the time all at once.

After you have finished all the sheets, take a look at them. Are there any patterns? What beliefs haven't changed since your childhood? Pick one or two of the most important of these and write them down separately. Where did these beliefs come from, why do you believe they are true, and what influences brought you and now keep you with these beliefs? Do you think these beliefs are positive or negative for you? How do they free you and how do they limit you?

Now take a look at the beliefs that have changed dramatically from your childhood to now. Write them down separately. What happened to bring about these changes? What were the people, influences, and events that were relevant to these changes? How did you arrive at your current beliefs? Do you think they are positive or negative for you? How do they free you and how do they limit you?

## CLAIMING THE POWER TO CHOOSE YOUR BELIEFS

In the earlier self-image visualization you identified certain beliefs you hold about yourself. Your options were endless—I'm tall, I'm short, I hate my hair, I love my hair. I'm too thin, I'm not thin enough. I'm quiet, loud, intelligent, dumb, or pretty. Out of the entire universe of beliefs you could hold, you chose a particular set to be your self-image. Why did you choose the beliefs you did?

Ultimately, you control what you believe. The culture does not hold you hostage. Your upbringing does not hold you hostage. True, each of us was born and raised within a belief structure. We were raised within a family of some sort that had certain rules and expectations about how life worked. We grew up in a particular country in a given time and place whose culture shaped us and which we may have adopted automatically. But regardless of where we came from and how we were raised, what we believe today is up to us. It is also true that some of our beliefs and assumptions are not entirely known to us because they lie hidden, embedded within other beliefs, or in our subconscious. Even coming to an awareness of the existence of these beliefs can occupy a lifetime. Whether we choose to engage in such a journey of self-exploration and understanding, however, is up to us, and so is what we do with our beliefs and assumptions once we discover them.

Paganism on the whole tends to reject determinism when it comes to beliefs. *Determinism* denies that humans have free will and states that factors such as our genetics and environment determine our choices. According to determinism, even if it appears that you are making choices, you are actually only reacting to stimuli in a human version of Pavlov's experiment with dogs. Therefore, a person raised in a deprived environment has no choice but to become a prostitute or criminal. A person raised Catholic will always be a Catholic. A person raised in affluence will patronize the arts out of habit, not taste.

Life experience shows that this is not the case. We cannot predict what a person will do and outline the choices people will make based on their genetics and upbringing. There is no doubt that genetics and upbringing can create strong dispositions to do and believe certain things, but even determinists agree that their theory is not capable of predicting future behavior. Pagans generally stand for a belief in free will and the ability of persons to make independent choices in spite of internal and external pressures to the contrary.

Some of you may find these ideas about beliefs difficult. Others of you will feel right at home. If you are having difficulty, don't be discouraged. All of us struggle to one extent or another and at various times in our lives, River and I included. The following is the story of one of my own struggles with beliefs.

When I was around twelve years old I read *The Story of Philosophy* by Will Durant. This book follows the development of philosophy over many years and offers excerpts from key philosophers. Some ideas in the book support each other, but many are contradictory. As I read through the book, however, I began to get a sense of wholeness, a feeling that all of the philosophers were talking about the same truths and that all of them were "right," even though they contradicted each other. When I finished the book I closed the cover and sat and thought for a long time. The philosophers were obviously not in agreement with each other. How could my impression of wholeness be right? But the impression remained and was so strong that I had no doubt that the philosophers were each describing one part of a whole. It was as though I saw beyond the surface arguments and the surface contradictions and caught a glimpse of a river that flowed through them all. More than seeing it, I heard it, like a burst of singing.

Now this would be confusing for anyone, let alone a twelve-year-old. So I went about the business of growing up and didn't give this experience much thought. Even so, it changed me. Even from that early age, where others saw division, separation, and contradiction, I saw patterns, similarities, and interconnectedness. Not just in ideas, either, but in objects like myself, the sunlight, and a tree. I did not ask for these impressions; they were just there whether I wanted them or not.

By the time I was seventeen I was eager to test and integrate my experiences. Because I was raised by devout parents in a strict Protestant sect that is a part of Mormonism, I felt that the area of ideas as expressed in religion was an area in which I'd had the least exposure. So I began to ask, much to my parents' dismay, to attend other churches; and I did now and then, either with friends or on my own. I discovered that people had been writing about religion before the 1830s, when our church was formed, and not all of them were Christian either, a fact that had never been shared with me. So I read about Protestantism, Transcendentalism, several histories of the Catholic Church, writings by the saints and church doctors, and also the Sufi mystics, the Vedas, and the Bhagavad-Gita.

Eventually I decided I wanted to spend a weekend in a convent, and I befriended a nun in a contemplative order who invited me to stay as her guest. I was also hoping at some point to be able to visit a Buddhist monastery and a place that taught TM, or transcendental meditation. I thought the convent, being Christian, was a less shocking place to start. I was wrong! Upon making my request, a storm of opposition from my parents hit with full force. Hadn't I been taught that God was only in one church? Hadn't I been taught that He had given His authority to only one priesthood and that was ours? Since there was undeniably a spirit in all other churches, what was that spirit? Why, Satan of course. By going to these other places I was putting myself into Satan's clutches. Once I crossed the threshold of the convent, I would be within Satan's power. If the convent collapsed on me while I slept, my soul would be forever damned. My mother sobbed openly.

In my heart a terrible struggle began. On the one side was my intuitive knowledge, beginning with the strange insight upon reading the book of philosophy, that exposure to ideas that appear contradictory is okay because the contradictions are only on the surface. Underneath that surface lay a unity and a wholeness that spoke clearly to me. This wholeness calmed me, and when I listened to it I felt no fear at all. On the other side were the beliefs of others, the fears and warnings of others. These people were dear to me, their authority over me at that time in my life absolute. They were only repeating beliefs I had been raised with.

How do you balance, I wondered, what other people insist is true with what you *feel* in your heart to be true? If my inner certitude and inner perceptions were wrong, I asked myself, then how could I trust any perception I had? Could I trust my perceptions of love, honor, and integrity? Could I trust that I was seeing a green light instead of a red one? If I began mistrusting myself in one area, where would it all end? I felt as though I hung over an abyss.

I went on to the convent that weekend despite the dire warnings, but was so frightened that I couldn't eat a bite the first day. I didn't do much sleeping, either, and occasionally craned my neck out the window to see if the building showed any signs of collapsing on me. No heavenly choirs appeared during this first trip to the convent, and no major insights or breakthroughs resolved my doubts and questions. Yet the sense of wholeness remained, thereby continuing my struggles with the beliefs I was raised with in the years that followed.

Struggling with beliefs is not easy. You don't just find one that isn't true for you and—poof!—it's gone. Beliefs have power. Their filter colors you and colors your world. It forms you and it forms your world. If the beliefs fit into a structure or system, then the belief cannot be resolved until you no longer empower the structure. Taking back, or claiming, your power to choose your beliefs is sometimes a lifetime effort. For at least a decade following that brief weekend trip to the convent, I shook with fear and waited for buildings to collapse and Satan's armies to attack me whenever I stepped out into new territory. Over time, however, I discovered that other people's beliefs and fears are not my own, and I do not have to make them mine just because they come from my family or friends.

Eventually—and it was a process—I was able to release the beliefs and the fears of others over the years. Eventually the weight of many years of trusting my experiences and perceptions, combined with that sense of wholeness that came at odd moments, helped me find my way. The quiet assurance that my moments of connection left with me gave me the courage to continue and to dare. I believe that if you follow your inner knowing—whether it leads you to Paganism or somewhere else—you will find all the courage you need.

In our introductory Paganism classes, River and I found that the idea that we have control of our conscious beliefs and that beliefs are flexible is often the biggest sticking point for our students. The sticking point itself is a belief, or one of a cluster of beliefs, that the students bring in with them and have to sort through. We encourage our students to explore new beliefs and try to have a few encounters with them before they make up their minds. So we give you the same advice: see if a belief works for you before you accept or reject it.

If you are struggling with the material in this chapter, perhaps it is because you have a set of limiting beliefs that are troubling you. This will not come as a surprise if you consider that many of us were raised with the message that our culture in general, and our religions in particular, have all the answers. Not only are beliefs already decided for us, but there is no possibility of any beliefs existing outside of the established answers. We are punished and ridiculed in subtle, or not so subtle, ways if we disagree or question.

The threat of ridicule may be a source of real anxiety for some of you. You may be having trouble with this material, but are not able to put your finger on exactly why. You just know that thinking about these things feels wrong. This may cause you to experience anxiety and guilt, and perhaps a little fear. These feelings may come from messages impressed on you that it is wrong to question the status quo.

Now there are good reasons to maintain the status quo. Traffic lights work regularly, commerce flows smoothly, things are comfortable and predictable. The gift of predictability is that it frees all of us from having to think through ordinary choices every time we are faced with them. How long would it take us to go across town if at every block we had to decide which side of the road to drive on and what to do about intersections? Predictability allows us to move on to really interesting questions and ideas.

Questioning often brings new perspectives and change. Change feels threatening to the status quo, both inner and outer, as every major insight and invention can cause upheaval. The day automobiles began to be produced was a terrible day for buggy whip makers. How many buggy whip makers can you name now? And yet the internal combustion engine changed the face of industry and transportation and created much of the status quo enjoyed today.

The discomfort you may be feeling could be caused by your internal status quo resisting change. It may be a subconscious reaction to society's message to resist change. If so, you are in good company. All innovators are subject to this pressure, even those who are supposed to be pushing boundaries, say, in science and medicine. Both science and medicine routinely resist new ideas with as much vigor as any other part of the culture, despite their claim to impartial investigation.

Although our scientists no longer have to fear inquisition, excommunication, and burning at the stake, they face terrible pressures from their colleagues not to venture too far afield, sometimes in the form of threats of a ruined career and reputation. I have a cousin who is a doctor in the area of pain management, particularly chronic pain caused by injury or arthritis. Existing Western medicine doesn't have a lot of solutions for such patients. So, wanting to help them, he is pushing past what Western medicine currently believes to be true. He would not be in new territory if he viewed chronic pain and arthritis from the same perspective as everyone else. Despite his scientific methodology and publication in journals, however, he is ridiculed professionally because he is trying a new approach.

Someday his work may become the status quo and everyone will wonder why medicine didn't do it his way to begin with! But in the meantime, he may sacrifice his professional reputation. Society can and does put great pressure on us not to do new things, try new things, or think in new ways. It can take a lot of courage to stay with something only because it feels right to you.

**exercise**                                    **INTERSECTING BELIEFS**

Make a list of the various areas of your life, such as home, work, family, church, friends, clubs, hobbies, and so forth.[2] Identify the people in each category who are the most important in your life right now. You don't have to feel close to these people (such as a landlord), but list those who figure prominently. You can also name people you don't know personally (such as famous people) if they have had a big influence on you. The people you name are the ones you have chosen—at one level or another and for one reason or another—to bring into your life.

For each one of these people identify what you think are beliefs characteristic of that person that are beliefs you also hold. How do the two of you support each other in these beliefs? Then for each person identify what you think are beliefs characteristic of that person that are in conflict with one or more of your beliefs. How do these disagreements affect your relationship, what you discuss, the things you do, and how you support or not support each other?

Take another look at the people on your list and ask what would happen if you changed any of the beliefs you share with them. Would your relationship be affected, or would you lose their support? Are there beliefs you would change if you didn't fear losing their support? How would a change in your beliefs affect those relationships where you and the person have conflicting beliefs?

If you could change any of your current beliefs, what would it be? To hold that belief, what would you have to do that is different from what you are doing now? Did you identify any people above who hold the belief you are working toward or wishing to change? In what ways are they supporting you in this change? Have things occurred recently where you have drawn people to you who are supportive of your desire to change, grow, and learn?

## exercise                                        MAKING A BELIEFS BRAID

Take three strands of yarn, heavy string, or twine, each about twelve to fifteen inches long. You may choose strands of three different colors, or all three may be the same color. If you choose strands of the same color, you may find it helpful to tie a bead, charm, or stone to the end of each strand, or mark the ends with colored marker or paint to tell them apart. The three strands can also be of three different materials. The type of materials or the colors chosen are up to you. Choose one of the strands to signify your thoughts, ideas, and beliefs. Choose another to represent resources available to you. The third strand will represent opportunities.

Take the first strand of thoughts, ideas, and beliefs and, while holding it, say the following or similar words: "I open myself to new ideas and new ways of seeing the world. I open myself to becoming a new person. I open myself to having insights I've never had before, and allow myself to try on new perspectives of thought." Sit a moment in silent meditation. If you are doing this with a group, one person can read the words one phrase at a time while the rest repeat them.

Then take the second strand representing resources and, while holding it, say the following or similar words: "I open myself to meeting the friends, teachers, study groups, organizations, and books I need most right now. I open myself to find and welcome all the resources in the universe that are available to me and that I need at this time, whether they are physical, mental, or spiritual in nature." Sit a moment in silent meditation.

Finally, take the third strand for opportunities and, while holding it, say the following or similar words: "I open myself to create the opportunities I need to experience the new ideas and connections that are coming to me, to provide myself space and time in which to have insights and new experiences, and to see my beliefs in action. I open myself to personal and spiritual growth and to exercising personal responsibility. I open myself to all my gifts, even those I don't know I have, and to growing in unexpected and surprising ways." Sit in silent meditation for a moment.

Line up the ends of the strings and knot the group of strands an inch from the end. Put the knot under a heavy book or pin it to something so you can free your hands for braiding.

Begin braiding the three strands. As you cross the first string over say, "I am open." Then each time one string crosses another, repeat "open" until you are in a rhythm. Work slowly and steadily. Allow your breathing to match the rhythm of the braiding and your words. Let your mind calm and drift a little. As you repeat this exercise over the next month (see directions below), feel free to change the repetitive word to one that suits where you are on your journey right now. Examples might include "welcome," "weaving," "integrate," "growing," "searching," or "receptive."

As you are braiding, see yourself opening to new ideas and insights. As the threads cross each other, see yourself pulling together the resources of the universe in new and exciting ways to create opportunities for enriching experiences. Weave together the things you need for your growth at this time. See the people, teachers, friends, books, and ideas all coming together when you most need them.

When you have braided to within about two inches of the end, tie off your braid with another knot. As you tie the second knot, either say the following or similar words: "I give myself permission to be who I truly am. I acknowledge all my feelings, beliefs, questions, and uncertainties. I accept responsibility for my spiritual growth, my beliefs, and the actions that flow from them. I step courageously into the unknown that lies before me, because I trust myself, the universe, and my concept of the Divine to support me in my journey."

For the next several weeks carry your belief braid with you. You can put it in your purse or pocket, or hang it in your car or near your area at work. You can pin the knots together and wear the braid as a bracelet. Be sure to put it where you can see it frequently, but use your common sense. Don't put it where it might interfere with your job, with safety, or with getting your work done. You don't need to announce to everyone what you are doing and annoy them with it. If someone asks you what your braid is, you decide how much you want to share. A completely truthful answer is that it is a prayer braid, and seeing it reminds you of some important things you are working on spiritually.

Once a week take your braid home and untie it completely. Start again with the first knot and rebraid, repeating the words given earlier. Do this once a week for one month. After the month is over, you can keep the braid as a memento, pass it on to someone else, or transform it by fire or burying it in the earth.

## SEARCH: PAGANISM'S SPIRITUAL FOUNDATION

Your spiritual philosophy is the base on which you stand as you decide what your vision will be, the kind of life and world you want to create, and the beliefs that are best going to get you there. Because of the range and variety of Pagan beliefs, Paganism requires that each Pagan build his or her own personal spiritual philosophy. If you decide you are a Pagan, you are not going to be able to avoid thinking about what you believe and whether those beliefs will accomplish what you want.

We know Pagans who try to skip over this step. They give no real thought to their social, religious, and political philosophies. They have not pulled out and examined the images of God, heaven, and hell that they grew up with. They have not thought much about how the universe might work and cannot say much to you about magick, ritual, and energy work.

We're going to lay it on the line here. If you really don't want to question, think, and be responsible for your own spiritual philosophy, then Paganism may not be for you. If you're content to see yourself and the universe from established perspectives, then you should consider other religious systems.

If other religions aren't working for you, however, and you think Paganism is where you belong, then you're in the right place. This book will help you roll up your sleeves and begin to build your spiritual philosophy. Based on our experience, we believe that a spiritual philosophy addresses at least the following areas: the existence and nature of Deity; the relationship of ourselves and the universe with this image of the Divine; the nature of humanity, the nature of the physical and/or nonphysical universe and our relationship to it; questions regarding the nature of good and evil, ethics, and personal responsibility; and finally, what happens after death. We will be examining each of these areas from a Pagan perspective in this book.

First, however, you need a place to start. The foundations of other religions usually consist of a predetermined doctrine. This is not so in Paganism. Paganism has no established dogma.

It is our opinion that the foundation of Paganism can be summed up in the word "search." At the core of Pagan spirituality, whatever your particular beliefs and practice, lies an openness and a thirst for new knowledge, inspiration, and experience. In order for this kind of foundation to be successful it is important that you work your mental, spiritual, and ethical muscles so that they become strong. You will need your strength, because this kind of foundation carries a lot of responsibility with it. If you work your foundation properly, you will learn the skills needed to evaluate ideas, think critically, form your ethics, and then live by them the best you can.

As strange as it may sound, to those of you coming from religions founded upon dogma rather than search, it is our view that the beliefs a Pagan adopts are secondary! They are important because beliefs are the template around which reality is created, but they are not the primary spiritual goal of Paganism. As far as the particular beliefs you choose to hold are concerned, we assure you they will change over the years. If you are a Pagan, in your first year you may have an entirely different idea about how the universe works than you will in ten years. Right now you have ideas about spirits, Deities, energetic power, and magick that years from now will astonish you.

If your foundation is composed of a fixed set of beliefs, will you really be open to change and growth over time? We don't mean you can't find beliefs that work for you and hold them for a lifetime if you wish. We're not saying that growth only occurs if you change beliefs. The question is: Where is your starting point? A foundation based on a fixed set of beliefs usually does not allow the foundational beliefs to be questioned, and so in that sense growth is limited to certain acceptable areas. If your foundation is composed of a fixed set of beliefs or dogma, then you may eventually begin to view your set as the "right" set, and all others as the "wrong" set. Sound familiar?

For those of you having difficulty with this chapter, this might be a source of your anxiety. Many or most of us were raised believing that there is only one right set of beliefs, and that they can never be challenged or else, well, something terrible will happen. Since you now may be deciding to be open to examining everything, the old message may be telling you that you're going to be punished for it. You may even personify and project your fears and begin to encounter them in meditations or dreams. This is not unusual. It has happened to many of our students. Recognize the process, acknowledge your anxieties, and if you can, talk them over with a teacher or trusted friend. The following exercise may be helpful with this, and we suggest you begin to work through your anxieties now before going on.

## exercise                    IF YOU ARE HAVING TROUBLE

Make a list of all the ideas in this chapter that trouble you. Leave plenty of space between them. After each idea list the beliefs you currently hold about it. Study each one closely. Do your beliefs really conflict with the material in this chapter? If so, in what ways do they conflict? If not, in what ways do your beliefs and the ideas of this chapter agree? What is the source of your current beliefs? What are your current beliefs doing for you personally and spiritually? How will they take you to your next level of growth?

Next, write down how the ideas that trouble you in this chapter make you feel. If you feel uneasy, for example, which ideas are bringing up this feeling? What is this uneasiness like? If the uneasiness could talk to you about how it feels, what would it say? What do you think the origins of your feelings are? What is the message behind them?

If every one of your current beliefs were true, what picture do they paint of the world and your place in it? If every one of the ideas about beliefs we are presenting in this chapter are true, what picture do they paint of the world and your place in it?

If you open yourself to trying the ideas in this chapter, what is the worst thing that can happen to you? Why will it happen? Is this your belief or did you pick it up from someone else? What is its underlying message? If you could talk with the terrible things you have identified, what would you, as a rational adult, say to them?

Discuss your concerns with a Pagan, a teacher, or friend.

## keys to success

## OPENING TO NEW IDEAS FOR GROWTH

We offer the following points as keys to success in helping you work with the first two principles of Paganism.

**You are in control of what you believe.** If you have given away your power in the past, take it back now. Time to exercise those ethical and philosophical muscles for yourself!

**Take personal responsibility for your beliefs and actions.** No more blaming the culture, your parents, your first-grade teacher, a church, or the devil for who you are and what you have chosen to do.

**Allow others full responsibility for their spiritual choices and then be respectful of them.** If you expect this for yourself, then you must give it to others. You do so out of respect and the recognition that we are all unique and powerful, and together are learning how to cooperate to create the world we want.

**Stay objective.** You can decide that something works and is true for you without becoming emotionally entangled in it. You do not have to invest emotions in a belief in order to find meaning in it. You can continue to listen to and evaluate other ideas and beliefs in a calm, open manner because you know that doing so does not threaten or offend either yourself or the universe.

**Stay mentally flexible.** Try on new ideas from time to time, even those you disagree with, just to see how they fit and how the world looks. Try putting on your belief glasses with filters from other perspectives. Keep exercising your thinking muscles! Every idea that comes your way is an opportunity for you to try on a new perspective. Stay open to the possibilities, and test every idea for its soundness and usefulness to you. Take it into meditation with you, try it out at ritual, have energy experiences with it. Test it in the fire of experience if you can do so safely without violating your ethics or breaking the law. This includes ideas you find in this book, any other book, or that you hear from a teacher or workshop. Don't let the source determine your reaction, especially if the source is controversial. Always check it out for yourself.

**Put off the need to label experience.** This can be a toughie. What we mean by this is to resist the urge to label phenomena based on what you already know. You are going to experience many new things. If you are just getting started as a Pagan, you are going to witness and participate in a variety of energetic and spiritual phenomena. Even though you are going to have these experiences from your current frame of reference, resist pigeonholing them.

A story will illustrate our point. Some years ago River and I were asked to rid an apartment of a ghost that was bothering a young man. We were told that when the ghost appeared it would give various sinister messages to him or stand quietly staring. So we headed off to the haunted house to see what we could do for this unhappy spirit.

Once we arrived, the young man began telling us a rather disturbed tale about his life. He was confused, unhappy, and engaging in self-destructive behaviors, including drinking and driving. At this point our eyebrows went up and the situation began to look quite different. He told us that the ghost did not frighten him, that the ghost looked like himself, and that the "sinister messages" the ghost was giving him were warnings to stop drinking and driving. Now the goal of this young man was to make the "ghost" go away. If River and I had accepted the label of "ghost" for this phenomenon, then we, too, might have stopped there and decided to work on making it "go away."

What did we do? First of all, we urged him strongly and repeatedly to get professional counseling for his various personal problems and destructive behaviors. We urged him to stop his destructive behaviors, especially the drinking and driving. We respected his belief that a ghost was visiting him, though we were not convinced this was what was happening. We pointed out the possibility that the ghost was actually an inner portion of himself urging him to change. In support of this, we pointed out the resemblance between himself and the ghost, the ghost's concerned warnings, and the fact that the young man felt at ease with him. We offered the possibility that the ghost might leave on its own when his inner work was done. Because the ghost's message was obviously beneficial and constructive, and we believed it was in his best interests to take the message seriously, we refused to do anything to make the phenomenon go away.

If we had accepted the young man's label of the experience as a "ghost experience" and stopped there, we would have interpreted everything we saw and heard in a way that supported our belief. We would have missed other, and possibly critical, levels to this situation. Once you decide on a label, you attach a particular filter to your camera. Everything you see from that point forward only confirms your filter. All contradictory information will be screened out. So resist the urge to slap on that filter! Allow yourself to stand in the flow of possibilities and see things from many perspectives.

**Keep on growing.** You work does not end with this book or other classes. Building a spirituality is a lifetime process. The growing and the learning never stop. Give yourself permission to consider new ideas and try new directions when the time is right.

## exercise    **APPRECIATING YOUR SUCCESSES**

Sometimes we become so preoccupied with our failures and defects, or so focused on what we haven't yet accomplished, that we fail to appreciate our successes. If we stay focused on our imperfections, we reinforce the belief that we are incomplete, unhappy, or unworthy, and perpetuate this experience of ourselves into the future. Although there are times when we need to think about what dissatisfies us about ourselves and our lives, we also need to be sure to appreciate what we have accomplished and done well, and build on these strengths so that they become foundations for our future selves.

Take a sheet of paper and make a list of all the successes you have had in your life. Don't leave out the little things, like knowing how to cook, and don't overlook your health and body. Don't shortchange yourself when it comes to relationships either: Are you good with children, do your neighbors like you, do your friends confide in you? Take a look at your job, personality, appearance, skills, accomplishments, home, hobbies, relationships, sports and activities, money, possessions, and talents.

Take a moment and imagine what your life might have been like if you hadn't done the things you listed, acquired those skills, or had those experiences. Since you did, however, how is your life now the richer for it?

Go back over your list and choose a couple of items that seem most important to the quality of your life now. Take another sheet of paper and write one of these items at the top. Below it identify all the beliefs you can that went into its creation. Were these isolated beliefs or did they come in a cluster? Were you aware of them at the time or did they operate subconsciously? In what ways did your beliefs support you in the creation of this part of your reality? Next, while you were doing this item, what kinds of things did you think about? How did your imagination, thinking, and visualizations support your accomplishment? Did you see yourself being successful, and did you fantasize about it? In what ways did your mind support you in the creation of this part of your reality? Then think about how you felt while you worked on your accomplishment. What were your emotions and how did they support you being successful? Do this for each of the items you chose as most important to you.

Now take a look at the overall picture. Are there any patterns here? If you were going to give yourself advice on how to create success for yourself in the future using your beliefs, imagination, and emotions, what would you say? Make a note of these guidelines for yourself.

Hang on to this exercise, as you will need it in chapter 6.

## questions to discuss        ELEMENTS OF SPIRITUALITY

1. What issues has this chapter raised for you? How would your family and friends respond to this material? If you are a Pagan, how would a member of your prior religion respond?

2. What are the essential elements of spirituality to you? Do you think there is a difference between religion and spirituality? Where do you see Paganism fitting in?

3. What beliefs are important to you now? Why are they a part of your personal philosophy? Where do you think they will take you in the future?

## my journal        A PERSONAL TIMELINE

• Create a spiritual timeline of your life from birth to the present. On this timeline mark the events most memorable to you, including physical crises, and mental, spiritual, and psychic breakthroughs. Mark those times you experienced a noticeable change in your state of being, or a sudden change in beliefs.

- Ask yourself: How did my world shift and how did my perspective change after each of the events marked on my timeline? What did I believe before, and what did I believe afterward? What was I thinking and feeling before, and then after, the change?

- Did any of these memorable events or sudden shifts involve people who are or were significant to you? What role did these people play? What did they believe about the situation? Do you agree with them?

- How did these memorable events change you as a person?

# 3

# A PAGAN VIEW OF DEITY

Pagans usually approach the question of God with open-mindedness and flexibility. Pagans believe it's okay to ask questions about God, or Deity, it's okay to explore all images of Deity (both ancient and modern), it's okay to come up with unusual perspectives on Deity, and it's even okay to doubt that Deity exists.

Pagans tend to be flexible when it comes to ideas about God for several reasons. You will recall that Paganism is based in search, not dogma. Since there is no Pagan-wide dogma about Deity, there are no set or uniform opinions on the issue within Paganism as a whole. Most Pagans accept the likelihood that no two people will have exactly the same experiences of Deity.

Pagans are also flexible in their beliefs about Deity because most Pagans agree that God concepts are, if nothing else, just ideas. What do we mean when we say that Deity is an idea? We mean that all the theologies ever imagined—no matter how beautiful, powerful, or complex—are only descriptions. They are not the reality itself.

In other words, ideas about God are *not* God. Ideas about the ground of reality are *not* that reality. Furthermore, people may not even be having the same experiences of the Divine. Perhaps we each experience a different part or portion of the Divine, the part that speaks most deeply and personally to us alone. Since the point of contact each of us has with the universe is unique, our experiences of Divinity are probably not going to be the same as anyone else's. Even if we were able to pull together all the experiences of Divinity from all of humanity throughout all time, we would still end up with nothing more than a collection of experiences. We would not end up with the Divine itself, which exists independently from all our ideas about it.

When it comes to God, religions often get into trouble by stating that a particular idea *about* God actually *is* God. Once this happens, further questioning is discouraged and lines of orthodoxy are drawn. Those who describe and experience Deity one way become suspect to those who experience Deity differently. Those who define God to be a certain idea or experience may persecute, kill, or drive away anyone whose ideas and experiences differ. When Deity is declared to "be" a particular idea, all other ideas become suspect and even subject to punishment, no matter their validity. The God concepts of a culture become embedded into its belief systems and structures, and any additional or contrary information about Deity is rejected.

Such a belief system *is* literally a structure that houses God. When people make their ideas about God into God, they give Deity a permanent address. If the belief structure declares that God lives at 1 Almighty Drive, for example, then they will not likely look for God living even just next door at 2 Almighty Drive, and certainly not as far away as 7 Chakra Lane or on the Tao Freeway. From this perspective, if such a person encounters Deity on the Tao Freeway, then he or she must have the wrong Deity! They are at the wrong address! This point of view presupposes that the Divine resides at only one address and is therefore absent from all other addresses. We call this "address anxiety." You'll know you've encountered address anxiety the next time someone asks, "Aren't you afraid you'll worship the wrong God?"

In some religions, address restrictions are made explicit and members are required to dedicate, or covenant, themselves to one or more specific Deities. For the most part, this is not the case in Paganism. Pagans are not required, although they may so choose, to covenant with a particular Deity. They are free to hold whatever images of Deity are meaningful to them. As you will see in the discussion of the God Map below, most Pagans believe that Deity can have any number of addresses, and that all are equally valid.

What if religions resisted the urge to make ideas about God into God? What if they simply stopped making statements that Deity "is" this or that, and spoke only in terms of having an idea about or experience of Deity?

Speaking metaphorically now, let us say that a person has an experience of God as a mountain. Such a person could declare that God "is" a mountain, or he or she could simply describe their experience saying, for example, "I have an idea of the Divine as a solid mountain. I went looking for the Divine and experienced an eternal, unwavering presence that felt steadfast, strong, and immovable to me." Such a person might then encounter someone who says, "That's interesting, because my idea of the Divine is that of a mighty wind. I went looking for the Divine and was pulled into something that felt like joy, energy, and unlimited vitality to me."

As these two people interact they will have to choose how to interpret and describe their encounters. They can resist identifying the Divine with the images they experienced, and instead talk about the experiences. They can choose to discuss what the images of their encounters mean, how they are related, and how they differ. They can move away from discussions that go something like: "God is a mountain." "Is not." "Is so." Such arguments waste the valuable time and energies of both individuals and societies.

When we resist the urge to make our ideas of God into God, we are then left with the ideas themselves. This is harder. We are faced with the content of our beliefs, the merits of which are suddenly exposed to view. Why not insist that our God beliefs be as productive as our other beliefs? If we do so, we don't have to be afraid that we are offending the Divine or the universe, since none of our ideas *are* actually the Divine or the universe and do not adversely affect them. Destructive beliefs don't hurt the Divine, but they can hurt us, our society, and our world. We have the right to insist that the beliefs we adopt, even about Divinity, be healthy and productive and serve us well.

## questions to discuss          THINKING ABOUT GOD BELIEFS

1. When was the first time you questioned a belief about the Divine or the universe? What happened to bring on this questioning? How did you feel while you examined the belief? What did you end up deciding about it? What do you believe now about it?

2. Identify three or more beliefs about God held by the general culture or your religion of origin that you believe are unhelpful or destructive. How did these beliefs develop? What supports their existence now? In what way do you find them destructive? If you could replace them, what would you substitute in their place?

3. If you could design the Divine yourself, what would it be like? What qualities would it have? What kind of relationship between you would be possible?

## CONCEPTS OF DEITY

Over the centuries, similar concepts of Deity have been identified and grouped together as sharing certain characteristics. Some of the more common of these are monotheism, polytheism, pantheism, and animism.

A *monotheist* believes there is only one Deity. This Deity may or may not be alone in the cosmos, and may have a variety of spirit helpers. A monotheistic Deity may express itself in only one form, or its essence may be split across several forms, which still reduce back to only one Deity. The Trinity within Christianity is an example of the latter.

A *polytheist* believes in more than one Deity; that is, divine power that is spread and shared among several Deities.

A *pantheist* believes that all the created world together equals Deity. There is a little bit of the Divine in your arm, some more in the grass, and so on, and when combined all together, it adds up to Deity. In these systems, Deity may or may not exist as a separate being or personality.

An *animist* believes that every part of creation—both animate and inanimate—is filled with the Divine or has a soul. Deity is equally present everywhere, but is usually not divided into parts as with pantheism. Depending on the tradition, Deity may or may not also exist as a separate being.

There are some other terms you are likely to hear in a Pagan discussion about the Divine. These terms include *mythology, deity,* and *pantheons.*

A *mythology* is a collection of stories created by a culture to explain how and why things are the way they are. A religion's mythology tells the stories of the gods, deities, spirits, and important people that relate to that religion. Sometimes these stories are legend, and sometimes they are part history and part legend. From the Pagan perspective, the stories of the Greek gods on Mount Olympus are a religious mythology. From the Pagan perspective, the stories of Yahweh, Satan, Mary, Joseph, and Jesus also are a religious mythology.

*Deity* is another word for God or the Divine and describes any energy or being that is ascribed supernatural powers. Deity can be a catch-all word that includes gods, goddesses, angels, guardian angels, spirits, spirit guides, elves, fairies, elementals, higher selves, future or probable selves, and nature spirits, among others. Since the word "God" with a capital *G* is assumed by many non-Pagans to mean Yahweh, a specific Deity of the Judeo-Christian pantheon, Pagans tend to use the word Deity instead to avoid any confusion. In this chapter and throughout the book, however, we use the terms God, Deity, and the Divine interchangeably.

A *pantheon* is a collection of Deities connected by a common culture or mythology. You might on occasion hear Pagans refer to the "Roman pantheon," the "Norse pantheon," or the "Hindu pantheon." Pagans often study pantheons in order to learn about a philosophy more completely.

## WHAT DO PAGANS BELIEVE ABOUT DEITY?

It's not difficult to find statements made by both Pagans and non-Pagans that Pagans are polytheistic. This can be true, but it isn't necessarily true. What is true for Paganism on the whole is that Pagans may believe anything they wish about Deity. Certain Pagan traditions may adopt specific beliefs, but those beliefs operate only within that tradition and do not carry over to Paganism as a whole.

Many Pagans we know are indeed polytheistic, but some are monotheistic, some are a unique blend of pantheism and animism, and others avoid Deity concepts altogether. This diversity is not cause for alarm among Pagans. Differing views are seen as natural and healthy, since no two people have the same spiritual experiences and the same interpretation of them. The search for the Divine in its simplest terms is the search for that portion of the creative universe that intersects with you personally. It may be the portion from which you believe you spring, to which you feel the most drawn, or to which you feel the most directly, personally, and intensely "plugged in." Since this point of connection is uniquely personal, descriptions and experiences of it are naturally going to differ.

Most Pagans enjoy exchanging ideas about Deity and spirituality. The discussions we have been present for are usually lively and engaging. Rarely are there heated arguments or attempts to change someone's mind. Most Pagans are respectful of other views, and while open to learning about them, are not interested in trying to change them.

## THE GOD MAP

We developed the God Map for use in our introductory Paganism classes as a tool to help our students visualize the wide range of beliefs about Deity. It has helped our students gain a perspective not only of their own beliefs, but beliefs as they have been expressed throughout history.

The God Map consists of two continuums that can be plotted as a graph. The first continuum runs from top to bottom and indicates the degree to which people think of Deity as either a separate, *transcendent* force, or a nonseparate, *permeating* force. The second continuum runs horizontally and reflects the degree to which people think of Deity as either *abstract* or *concrete*. Figure 3.1 illustrates what the God Map looks like.

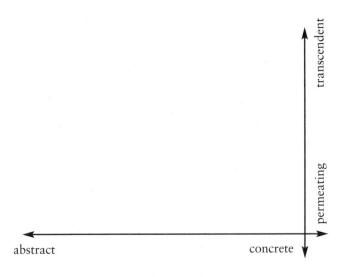

**FIGURE 3.1**
The God Map.

Let's take a closer look, beginning with the vertical continuum, which measures views of Deity from the transcendent to the permeating. The word *transcend* generally means to rise above or become separate. A transcendent Deity is one who is superior to everything else in the universe and is usually separate, or removed, from it. This separation may take the form of physical distance, in that the Deity lives far away, is remote, and difficult to approach. It may also take the form of spiritual distance, in that it is removed from all of us by its nature, which is in every way considered superior to our own. A transcendent Deity may be thought of as one that is "wholly Other." A large gulf usually exists, then, between us and a transcendent Deity.

Several years ago Joyce and I were walking around a popular night spot on a summer evening. In the street stood a young man with a chalkboard trying to attract a group to listen to his message. Out of curiosity we stopped to listen and this is what we heard: "Down here is man," he said, drawing a little stick figure at the bottom of the board. "And up here is God," he said as he went to the top of the board and drew a big sun (Figure 3.2).

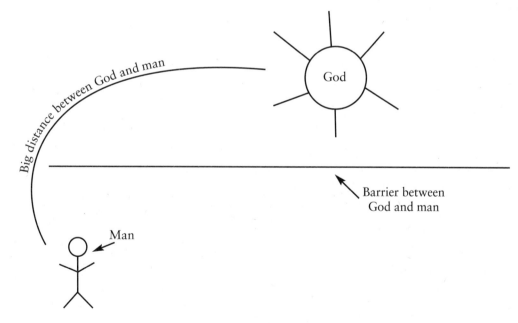

FIGURE 3.2
The chalkboard drawing.

He continued, "Man of himself is nothing, completely cut off from God." He drew horizontal lines between the stick figure and the sun. "On our own we could never reach God, talk to God, or even be noticed by Him. We are as far removed from Him as the stars are from Earth."

The man developed this idea further for a few moments, and shortly there-after we decided to move on and continue with our evening. What we had just heard, however, was a classic explanation of a transcendent Deity.

At the other end of the continuum is the concept of Deity as permeating. This concept is also called "immanence." To permeate something means to enter into it, to penetrate it, to become something totally or partly, and ultimately to share beingness or experience in some way.

A Deity that is viewed as permeating is not removed from creation. It is, in fact, wholly present with creation because it penetrates creation in some fashion. A pantheist, you will recall, believes that Deity so permeates creation that Deity has divided itself into pieces among it. Part of Deity is the grass, part is the wind, part is your little finger. An immanent, or permeating view of Deity does not have to be pantheist, however, as there are as many ways of visualizing a permeating Deity as there are people to visualize it. Permeating views can also include ideas of Deity as participating in lived experience with us, and of each of us participating in creation with the Divine.

Another way to describe transcendent and permeating is with the terms "without" and "within." A transcendent Deity can be visualized generally as living outside of you, or "without." Those who want to talk to a transcendent Deity address themselves to a being or energy "out there." A permeating Deity, in contrast, can be visualized as living inside of you, or "within." Those who want to communicate with this sort of Deity address themselves to the energies they feel most intimately connected with.

In the middle of our vertical continuum we place a blended concept we learned about from the Christian theologian Matthew Fox, called *panentheism*. This term was coined by K. C. F. Krause in the nineteenth century and developed further by Phil C. Hartshorne in the twentieth century. Matthew Fox adopted the term to describe his view of "creation spirituality" (see the recommended reading list for this chapter at the back of the book for one of his books on the subject). According to Fox, Deity is both a transcendent being and a permeating force;

that is, Deity is both of these things equally. Deity permeates without losing transcendence, and transcends all of creation while not losing its permeating presence (Figure 3.3).

Now let's consider the horizontal continuum of the God Map. This continuum measures the degree to which people see Deity as either concrete or abstract (Figure 3.4). Let's start with the concrete. People with concrete views of Deity have very clear images of what Deity is like. A concrete Deity has long, flowing blond hair, short dark hair, blue robes, white robes, no robes, is tall, is short, takes the form of humans, animals, or plants, and moves, talks, and acts in concrete ways.

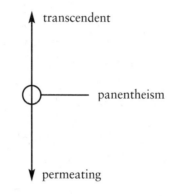

**FIGURE 3.3**
Panentheism blends ideas of transcendence and immanence.

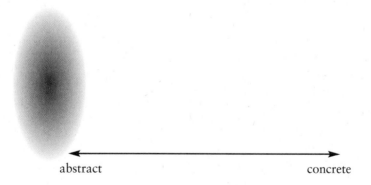

**FIGURE 3.4**
The horizontal continuum of the God Map.

Gods who are concrete take the form of beings and are assigned the characteristics of living things with which we are familiar. A Deity assigned human or animal characteristics is called "anthropomorphic." We both grew up, for example, with the view of God as a man with a long white beard who sits on a throne in heaven, who is jealous, who gets angry and punishes, and then, hopefully, forgives. Assigning this kind of human emotion, appearance, behavior, and character to a Deity is classically concrete and anthropomorphic.

At the other end of the spectrum is the abstract view of Deity. An abstract Deity will not be described as a being and will not be assigned physical characteristics and emotions. It may be difficult for a person with this sort of Deity image to express his or her ideas about Deity. Such a Deity may have no form or shape of any kind. Some people with abstract images see Deity as an energy, spiritual force, or movement perhaps similar to the concept of the Holy Spirit, or described as Love, the Life Force, or the Ground of Being. The "Force" of the *Star Wars* movies fits here.

As we near the left edge of the God Map we encounter a hazy region where abstraction blends into unknowing and, perhaps, unbelief. We know Pagans who are not sure that Deity exists at all, at least in conventional terms. The expression "All That Is" comes to mind here, a phrase that pulls together the animate and inanimate, and physical and nonphysical parts of the universe, but doesn't necessarily equate to a Deity. Some Eastern systems may belong in this region. For example, the Tao of Taoism is not a Deity but a term for "the way things are." The Jen of Confucianism is not a Deity but the ideal of benevolent action.

The third principle of Paganism given in chapter 1 states in part that, "We are responsible for deciding who or what Deity is for us." This principle can also be phrased as, "We are responsible for exploring ultimate questions." Ultimate questions are those that ask what the nature and construction of the universe is; how it operates; whether it is governed and if so, by what or whom; whether each of us or any other part of reality has a spiritual component; what the nature of spirit is; whether there is a god or gods, deities, or spirits with power; and whether there are any supernatural forces operating in our reality at all. Paganism's third principle, though couched in "Deity language," actually includes all these "ultimate questions," and our searching should address them all.

If you decide that Deity does not exist in a traditional form, or you doubt the existence of spiritual forces and entities altogether, this does not mean you have not successfully dealt with Paganism's third principle. All it means is that given your personality, level of growth, and type of spiritual experiences you have had so far, you have come to the answers that make the most sense to you. Because there is no requirement that Pagans agree on these issues, it does not matter if you are the only Pagan you know who believes as you do.

Like the blended idea of panentheism on the vertical continuum of the God Map, we also find blended ideas between the extremes of abstract and concrete on the horizontal continuum. These ideas include aspects of both a being and of energy. We have put these blended concepts in the center of the continuum. They include ideas such as archetypes, numinous energies, the collective unconscious, thought forms, and morphogenetic fields (Figure 3.5).

Blended ideas about Deity come from experiences people have with spiritual realities that seem to contain ideas from several parts of the God Map. Their experiences combine elements of beingness with elements of energy, thought, and consciousness. Mainstream religions often do not have concepts that describe these experiences and so some people may find themselves at a loss to understand them. How people who have these experiences decide to interpret them will depend on their belief system.

The concept of the *archetype* comes to us from psychoanalyst Carl Jung, and has become a familiar term in both psychology and religion. An archetype is an

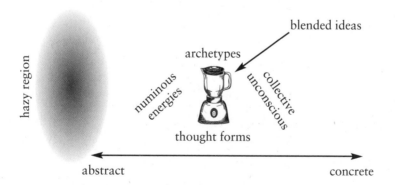

FIGURE 3.5
Blended ideas of a concrete and abstract Deity.

essence of lived experience that has recurred so frequently in human history that it develops an energetic "signature" or "presence," and may act as a blueprint for behavior. If we were to say that someone is living out the archetype of a Star-Crossed Lover or Hero, you would know what we mean.

Archetypes might be an aspect of the *collective unconscious,* which is a memory bank of lived experience that exists, according to Jung, in realms beneath our normal state of waking consciousness. Archetypes might be visualized as energetic data banks within the collective unconscious, which may have been infused with so much energy over time that they exist as independent entities. Archetypes sometimes act as if they have an "energy" or life of their own. When this happens, Jung says the archetype is a *numinous energy.*

Related to archetypes and the collective unconscious is the *morphogenetic field.* This word comes to us from Rupert Sheldrake, a physicist who theorized that living matter is interconnected by fields that transcend space and time. This includes inanimate objects, things, places, and even subatomic particles. These fields appear to act as blueprints around which particles and organisms form themselves, grow, and develop. Pagans often refer to the energies that build up in certain objects or places due to the focusing of thought and intention over a period of time as *energy fields.* People coming to such a place bring with them intense states of emotion, dreams, hopes, and fears. Over time, this energetic intensity builds until it is quite palpable, and again, in some instances may even seem to take on a life of its own. We have walked into churches, temples, centers of government, and old buildings, stopped, and said, "Oh gosh, feel that!" Venerated relics, springs, wells, and places of healing such as hospitals often accumulate fields of energy, as can natural landmarks, groves, monuments, cemeteries, and parks.

The deliberate creation of a field for a specific purpose or length of time is called a *thought form.* When a Pagan uses this term, he or she is referring to an energy being or force deliberately fabricated by those creating it. From the Pagan perspective, the thought form is a great example of how concentrated thought and intention can, by itself, create an apparently independent being. Thought forms are temporary energetic structures created for a specific purpose. We have witnessed the creation of thought forms to protect persons and places, to catch criminals, and to attract people interested in a certain work. When the purpose is accomplished or the period of time expires, the thought form is dissolved by those who created it.

If the form is not dissolved, or if the persons creating it are not aware they created a thought form and so continue to send it energy, then the thought form may continue on as an independent or quasi-independent force or being. What would be the consequences if an entire culture either accidentally or deliberately created a thought form and then supported it energetically for generations? What if they named this thought form God, or Satan?

Are we suggesting that archetypes, thought forms, and the collective unconscious *are* Deity? The experience of the Divine is deeply personal and not always easily expressed. Some people experience it in ways they can only describe with concepts like "collective unconscious" and "numinous energies." For others it is the "breath of life," the "great unknowable," and for still others "sister," "warrior," "father," or "mother." None of these experiences is more or less valid than any other. Every perspective on these "ultimate questions" allows us to glimpse yet another aspect of the Divine Ground; perhaps strange and unusual, but beautiful and intriguing in its own way.

Within specific Pagan traditions you will find a great deal of variety in how Deity is visualized, from the very concrete to the very abstract. Most Wiccans, for example, call Deity by the name of "the God" and "the Goddess." Some Wiccans see the God and Goddess as male and female beings who have a specific appearance and personality. Other Wiccans see the God and the Goddess as the essence of polarity, the opposing forces in nature that together form a balance that creates and sustains life. Both of these views are accepted within Wicca. We have discovered similar differences even within traditions that are considered more conservative, such as Asatru. The Asatru devote themselves to certain Nordic or Germanic Deities, which historically have quite traditional appearances, personalities, zones of power, and behaviors. Yet we have been present at discussions among Asatru who were debating whether the Deities are really anthropomorphic beings or are representations of spiritual forces. As we understand it, either view is accepted in Asatru.

Ultimately, you must decide for yourself what you believe about the Divine. Since your point of contact with the universe is absolutely unique to you, no one else's experience will be the same as yours. What you bring back and share from your explorations of Deity will enrich everyone.

## questions to discuss                     EXPLORING THE GOD MAP

1. What parts of the God Map do you find the most interesting? The most difficult? The most disturbing? Is there any part of the Map you don't like or understand?

2. Have you experienced change in recent months in terms of where you are on the God Map? If so, in what ways and why?

3. How do you think your friends, family, neighbors, and coworkers would react to the God Map? Where do they fall on this Map? How would they react to Paganism's flexibility concerning Deity images? Do you think Paganism's flexibility on this issue is a good thing?

4. Have you had a spiritual experience you find difficult to understand or describe? What happened in this experience? Describe your experience from each of the perspectives of the God Map: from transcendent to permeating, concrete to abstract, to blended. Do you find this difficult to do? Does the nature of the experience seem to change or feel different depending on which perspective you use to describe it? Which of these perspectives are you most comfortable with? Which are you least comfortable with and why?

## visualization                    ENCOUNTERING DEITY

*Take a moment to review the suggestions for visualizations given at the beginning of the visualization in chapter 2. Remember to pause where marked by dots (. . .) to give those participating time to visualize. You may want to bring a snack, warm drinks, and blankets to help reorient participants after the visualization.*

Get in a comfortable position. If you are sitting, put your feet flat on the floor. If you are lying down, put your arms down beside you and your legs out straight.

Close your eyes. I am going to lead your breathing for a few minutes, so breathe with me.

Breathe in through your nose: 1, 2, 3, hold, 1, 2, 3, hold; and out through your mouth: 1, 2, 3. In through your nose: 1, 2, 3, hold, 1, 2, 3, hold; and out through your mouth: 1, 2, 3. [*Repeat for five or six breaths. Time your words and numbering so that the breathing in, holding, and breathing out occur at equal intervals.*]

Starting with your feet, you will notice that you are being filled with a color—the color of relaxation. . . . Pick a color that is relaxation for you. . . . Whatever color relaxation is for you right now is beginning to fill your feet. This color is like fog or smoke, or perhaps a colored light, that fills and surrounds your feet. . . . As it fills them, you notice that your feet completely relax. Wiggle your toes, and then let them relax. . . . The color moves on up your legs and begins to fill your calves . . . then your thighs. As your legs fill with the color of relaxation, you feel them get heavy. Tighten your calf muscles, then relax them. . . . Tighten your thigh muscles, then relax them. . . . Your legs are now very heavy, and completely filled with your relaxing color. . . .

The color moves on up into your lower back. . . . You carry a lot of stress here, but as the color fills your back, you can feel it relaxing. . . . The color is now filling your stomach and your chest. . . . As it does, you can breathe perfectly fine. In fact, take a deep breath and let it out all at once. . . . Feel your stomach and chest relaxing. . . . The color of relaxation begins to flow into your shoulders and down your arms. . . . Wiggle your fingers and then let them relax. . . . Shrug your shoulders and then let them relax. . . . The color now fills up your head. . . . You can feel the little muscles around your eyes letting go . . . the muscles in your forehead . . . at your temples. . . .

You are now filled with your relaxing color as if you are a hollow vessel. . . . See this color completely filling your body and surrounding it like a cocoon. . . . In this cocoon, you are perfectly safe and comfortable. . . . In this cocoon, you can travel anywhere and return whenever you like. . . . Your cocoon is like your "flying carpet." . . . See yourself in your cocoon floating right up off the floor, through the roof of this room, and over the houses of the neighborhood. [*longer pause*]

You are now going to travel in your cocoon to your inner temple. . . . To get there, all you need to do is float up. . . . Let yourself float up and up. . . . If you need to, you can look back and see that there is a thread going from your cocoon to your body. . . . You don't need to worry about anything. . . . Let yourself float up as though you are smoke or the flame of a candle. [*longer pause*] Float up over the city and up into the clouds. . . .

There is a cloud ahead of you that you feel drawn to. . . . This is where you will find your inner temple. . . . Let your cocoon dock there. . . . . You can step out of your cocoon and right onto the cloud, which is perfectly solid. . . . You can leave your cocoon docked, it will be there when you come back. . . .

You are now beginning to walk across your cloud. . . . You are heading for your inner temple. . . . The mists are swirling around you and sometimes it is hard to see, but you know you are getting close. . . . The mists are beginning to clear. . . . Ahead of you you can see your temple taking form. . . . Now you can see it. . . . What does it look like? [*longer pause*]

Your temple might be a building, it might be a place, it might be indoors or outdoors. . . . It might be patterns, colors, or feelings. . . . Let your temple take shape for you. [*longer pause*]

You now enter your temple. . . . If there is a door, open it. . . . If it is a location, step into it. . . . If it is a pattern, color, or feeling, experience it. [*longer pause*] How does it feel to be here in your temple? [*longer pause*]

You become aware that there is someone here in your temple who wants to see you. . . . It is the point of contact between you and the creative power of the universe. . . . It is your idea of the Divine. [*longer pause*] Walk deeper into your temple, and you will find this point of contact, this deity, this energy. . . . What have you found? [*longer pause*] You can give it any appearance you like. . . . How does it appear to you? [*longer pause*]

It is very welcoming to you. . . . You can ask it anything you want to know. . . . What do you want to ask it, and how does it answer you? [*very long pause*] What does it want to tell you right now? . . . What do you need to know in your life at this time? . . . What does it tell you about your spiritual growth and what you need to be doing right now? [*very long pause*] [*In our experience, you need to give this pause a good three to five minutes, unless the group gets restless.*]

It is now time to leave. [*longer pause so they can break off their conversations*] Thank your energy or deity and say your goodbyes. [*longer pause*] Know that you can return to your inner temple anytime you wish. . . . Now, turn and leave the temple and walk back across the cloud to where your cocoon is docked. . . . Climb into the cocoon, wrap it around you, and begin floating back down to your body. . . . You can see the city coming into view . . . then this neighborhood . . . then this house. . . . You are coming through the ceiling of this room, and down into your own body. . . . Let the cocoon of color gradually leave your body, flowing back down your head to your feet and into the ground. [*longer pause*] You feel relaxed, peaceful, calm, loved, and invigorated. . . .

When you are ready, open your eyes.

*Let yourself get reoriented. If you are in a group, take a few minutes to be sure everyone is "back." If anyone has difficulty getting reoriented, offer the blankets and warm drinks. Share the snacks with everyone. Then ask who would like to share their experience. Get a comment from everyone if possible. Is the visualizing getting easier? You might wish to discuss the following questions.*

## questions to discuss     SHARING YOUR ENCOUNTER

1. What color was relaxation to you? How did it feel? How did you visualize it covering your body? Was the cocoon comfortable for you?

2. Did you have any trouble "floating" up and away from yourself? Was doing so comfortable, fun, difficult, exhilarating? Did you have any anxieties?

3. What form did your inner temple take? How did you visualize Deity, or your personal point of connection to the universe? Did it take a tangible form? Did you feel any emotions or sensations?

4. What did you and your idea of the Divine discuss? Was it difficult or easy to communicate? Was it hard to leave when it came time to say goodbye? Would you ever want to go back to your inner temple?

## exercise        WRITING A LETTER TO THE DIVINE

If you could write a letter to your idea of Deity, what would you say? Take a few minutes and think of all the things you've always wanted to say to your concept of Deity if you found yourself face to face with him, her, or it. Then take a sheet of paper and write a letter. It doesn't matter what you say or how you say it, as long as it authentically captures how you feel. You can express any sort of feelings you wish: happy ones, grateful ones, even angry and sad ones. If you want to write this letter all at once, that's fine. If you want to work on it over several days or weeks, that's fine too. After you've written it, you might want to put it with your journal or some other place to keep for awhile; or, if you'd like the feeling of "sending" your letter to the universe, then think of a way that most feels like sending to you. It might be burning the letter in your fireplace, throwing it into a river or the ocean, flushing it down the toilet, or burying it in your backyard. Make a little ritual of sending your letter to your Deity, either by yourself or with friends. If you'd like to keep your letter to refer to in the future as well as send it, then make a photocopy of it first.

# A GOD MAP STORY

This is a story about one person's experience in exploring the God Map. We chose this particular story because it occurred fairly recently, and because it involves a person already mentioned in this chapter: Matthew Fox, the theologian responsible for applying the term *panentheism* to "creation spirituality." We are not telling his story in order to pick on any person, group, or religion, but to illustrate how precious the freedom to explore Deity images is.

In the 1950s, Matthew Fox decided to devote his life to God after suffering from polio as a youth.[1] He entered a Dominican college, eventually joined the Dominican Order, was ordained in 1967, and went on to become a well-known Catholic theologian.

Unfortunately, Fox was also known as a dissenting theologian. He did not always agree with approved Catholic teachings. He proposed, for example, that Deity is both Mother and Father, and suggested that the feminine, dark, hidden, sexual, creative side of Deity has been too long neglected. He approved of the women's spirituality movement and believed it helped bring a necessary balance to an overly male theology. He was in favor of ordaining women to the priesthood.

Fox also proposed that the human story should begin with the idea of Original Blessing, not Original Sin, and that humanity is endowed by God with a nature highly blessed and gifted. What we do with these gifts is up to us. We can ignore them, abuse them, or enjoy and develop them. In his opinion, the story of the Fall (Adam, Eve, and the Garden of Eden) is a story of what happens within our natures when we reject the divine gifts and attributes that are ours. He did not agree that the Fall proves human beings to be flawed, cursed, or damned. He also adopted the term *panentheism* to describe God, which shifted him away from the Catholic Church's stridently transcendent view of Deity and toward one more permeating and immanent.

In 1977, Matthew Fox founded the Institute of Culture and Creation Spirituality, which eventually came to be located at Holy Names College in Oakland, California. His institute explored all kinds of spiritual perspectives. One of the members of his faculty was Starhawk, a Wiccan author who is well-known in Pagan circles.

As you would expect, the Vatican's eyebrows shot up once it caught wind of Matthew Fox's ideas and activities. It sent him a warning through the Sacred Congregation for the Doctrine of the Faith, headed at that time by Cardinal Ratzinger. (This congregation, by the way, used to be known as the Office of the Holy Inquisition.) Cardinal Ratzinger ordered Matthew Fox to cut off all ties to his institute because it taught unorthodox ideas and had a Wiccan on its faculty. Matthew refused, and in 1988 was silenced for one year. This didn't mean he couldn't talk for a year, but that he was forbidden to preach or teach publicly. Matthew obeyed the year of silence, and then promptly went back to doing what he did before.

Tensions continued to mount between the Vatican, Matthew Fox, and the Dominicans. Eventually the pressures grew to a point in 1993 when Matthew was expelled from his order. The following year he left the Catholic Church entirely and became an Episcopalian, where he remains today.

Let's put this story onto the God Map and see how it looks. First, where should the Catholic Church go on the Map? Along the continuum of transcendent to permeating, the official position of the Catholic Church has historically been one of transcendence. The old *Baltimore Catechism No. 3* tells us this clearly in lesson 2, question 8: "When we say that God is the Supreme Being we mean that He is above all creatures." As between abstract and concrete, question 8 tells us that God is a supreme *being* who, as we can see throughout the Bible, has been assigned a personality, behaviors, and other anthropomorphic characteristics. It is true that the catechism tells us in question 8 that God is a spirit, but then it defines a spirit in question 9 as "a *being* that has understanding and free will, but no body" (emphasis added). Although the concept of the Holy Spirit can be considered abstract, lesson 3, question 28 calls the Holy Spirit a "Person" of

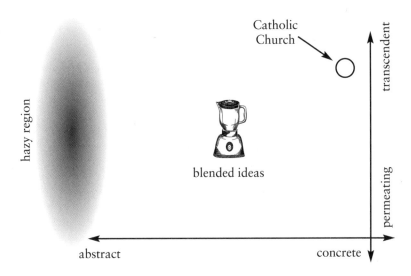

**FIGURE 3.6**
The Catholic Church's position on the God Map.

the Trinity. Sticking with this traditional view of things puts the Catholic Church in approximately the position on the map shown in Figure 3.6.

Matthew Fox's position regarding panentheism clearly moves him down the vertical continuum to a point directly between transcendent and permeating. We can debate whether his views on the nature of Deity and man are more or less concrete than the church's, but we can probably safely edge them toward the group of blended ideas that occupy the middle ground. For these reasons, we put Matthew Fox—at least at the time of his silencing—in the position shown in Figure 3.7.

Matthew Fox moved in his thinking from point A to point B. It doesn't look like much on the God Map, does it? Look how much of the universe of ideas about Deity hasn't even been touched! Yet Fox's change in perspective caused him to be publicly shamed, ridiculed, silenced, forced from his order, and eventually from the Catholic Church itself. His experience is, unfortunately, nothing new as many people throughout history have suffered similar or worse fates. Depending on the time and the culture, even small deviations from orthodoxy have resulted in humiliation, exile, and death. This is address anxiety in its most extreme and destructive form.

In contrast, modern Pagans have the freedom to explore the entire universe of beliefs we call the God Map, and even beyond it into ideas that fall completely

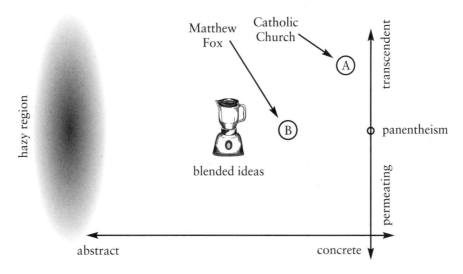

FIGURE 3.7
Matthew Fox's position on the God Map.

off the Map. We enjoy a degree of freedom that most others never experience, that some have suffered and died for even in our own time, and yet we may not even give our freedom a thought.

It's time to change that. Go back to the last diagram and draw the God Map on to a small card or piece of paper. Mark points A and B, and then mark your own spot on the Map. Put this paper where you meditate or hang it up at work. When you have free moments, study your drawing. Think about the price some have paid for unorthodoxy and then think about the freedom you enjoy, whether you are a Pagan or not. If you are a Pagan, and if you did not live in a free society, what might be happening to you? Give some thought to what you can do to ensure that this freedom continues not only for Pagans, but everyone in your city, country, and ultimately, the world.

## exercise                                   **THE GOD OF YOU**

This exercise is designed to help you connect with the portion of your concept of the Divine that intersects with you personally, and then to express that connection as you directly and individually experience it. Joyce and I were inspired in this exercise by Jane Roberts, who wrote the following in her book called *The God of Jane:*

> We share the world with others, but portions of it carry personal significance. We see them as no one else does. So it was for me that morning. No one else was watching what I watched from my own personal viewpoint. I felt as if I were being privileged to view a beginning of the world—or my edge of it. Or, I thought suddenly, it was like seeing a new corner of your own psyche transformed into trees, grass, flowers, fog and sky—a hopeful, magical, ever-coming-into-existence part of the psyche that we'd forgotten or I'd forgotten. I felt as if I were viewing that part of myself that I'm always pursuing, the part that is as clear-eyed as a child, fleet, at one with its own knowing; the part that exists apart from daily concerns; the part that was my direct connection with the universe; the part that represented that section of the universe from which I emerged in each moment of my life. And in that moment I named it the God of Jane. . . .[2]

At first this concept seemed shocking to Jane, being quite different from what she had been taught in her strict Catholic upbringing. But the more she worked with the idea, the more she resonated with it. She liked the idea that there might be an intimate connection between each of us and the universe. She goes on to say:

> . . . when I use the phrase "the God of Jane," I'm referring to or trying to contact that portion of the universe that is forming me—that is turning some indefinable divinity into this living temporal flesh. I'm not trying to contact the God of Abraham, for instance, or the Biblical Christ, or the inexplicable power behind all of reality. My intent is more humble than that, more personal, more specific: I want to contact that tiny portion of All That Is that forms my image, that transforms itself or part of itself into my experience . . .[3]

Take a moment then, as Jane did, to put yourself in contact with that portion of the universe you feel is most intimately connected to and supportive of you. Then try and put into words what you experience. At the top of a sheet of paper write "The God (or Goddess) of _____" or "The Deity of _____" or "The Divine _____" and fill in your name. Let the images and thoughts begin to flow and then begin to journal or write a poem about your experience of the Divine. Go with your flow of consciousness. You don't have to write in complete sentences. Use whatever imagery comes to mind and allow yourself to be playful and creative. Your perspective is absolutely unique and special and no one else shares it. It may seem ordinary to you, but your link to the universe is yours alone.

## keys to success

## BUILDING A CONNECTION WITH DEITY

Working through Paganism's third principle is a necessary part of building and strengthening your spiritual foundation and identity. To help you in this process, we offer the following suggestions.

**Establish a home base.** Your home base is where you start from; in other words, where you are right now in your beliefs. It is also where you will return as you explore other ideas about Deity. As your ideas change, so will your home base.

What do you believe about Deity right now? Take some time to identify your ideas and express them. You may already have a sense of where you fall on the God Map. If not, make a list of your ideas and see if you can identify their connecting themes. Ask a friend to help if you can't spot them yourself. Knowing your place on the Map will help you identify your current perspective. Then—beginning with where you are—study, learn, and experience all you can about your current beliefs.

**Make a connection.** After you've studied and learned for a time, give it a rest. Let all that knowledge and theory percolate awhile. In the meantime, focus on opening yourself to connecting—if you haven't already—with your concept of Deity. This is the point where you and the Divine meet and intersect. Go find it.

Heroic measures are not required here. You don't have to prove yourself by performing feats of endurance, ingesting questionable substances, meditating in strange postures, or engaging in harsh forms of penance like heading a Pagan festival committee. You already have the attention of the universe. It is keenly aware of you, and you intuitively know the point where you intersect with it. Give yourself some quiet space and time, and trust that you will find your connection.

**Develop a relationship.** Once you have a connection with your concept of Deity, you need to begin forming a relationship with it. How does Deity interact with you, and how do you interact with it? If you are a Pagan, you have most likely come to Paganism with beliefs in place regarding how you and Deity are supposed to relate, beliefs which you may discover you no longer hold. After all, there's really only one relationship possible with a transcendent Deity (at least according to convention), and that is one of "worship" flowing from you, the subordinate, upward to the Deity.

Paganism stands for the proposition that there are more ways to relate with Deity than just worship, and that it is in fact possible for a relationship with Deity to involve no worship at all. Many Pagans form relation-ships with Deity that focus on being partners and cocreators of reality in a manner that is more fraternal. These cooperative and participatory rela-tionships may seem strange at first. Be open to the possibility that your relationship with Deity, whatever your concept of it, may become some-thing completely different than you expect. Some good ways to develop your relationship with Deity are prayer, meditation, magick, ritual, div-ination, dancing, drumming, quiet listening, and active service.

**Flex your ethical muscles.** Allow your Deity concepts and your ethics to develop together. Your ideas about Deity and your philosophy of life should be in harmony with each other. There is no reason for your ethics and your Deity images to conflict. If they do conflict, something is wrong and you need to take a hard look at both of them.

Unfortunately, some religions promote the belief that a person can, and even should, act against his or her conscience if Deity, or someone claiming to speak on behalf of a Deity, commands it. This position is unacceptable in Paganism. You have the right and the responsibility to act in accordance with your conscience and what you believe to be right. There is no need to do anything you believe to be unethical in your reli-gious practice. Keep your ethical muscles healthy by working them for yourself and insist that your Deity beliefs and your ethics support each other.

**Keep exploring.** When you feel ready, venture away from your home base and explore as many other perspectives for which you have time and interest. Being an explorer is a lifetime process, so pace yourself. Don't let your other responsibilities slide because you're going a hundred miles an hour in your studies! Keep all aspects of yourself in balance.

As you go, give yourself permission to try on new ideas. Go sit in other places on the God Map and check out the view. Don't form your opinions on a perspective until you've tried it on. It's even okay to try on an idea you don't agree with. Be open to learning from unexpected sources. Good ideas and insights can come from anywhere. It's okay to agree with an idea originating from someone no one has heard of or who is unpopular, and it's okay to disagree with an idea even though it comes from someone famous. Evaluate an idea based on its substance, not its source.

**Be respectful.** You are going to encounter a lot of different ideas about Deity throughout your life. Be respectful of what works for others, even if you disagree with them. Sometimes we learn the most from what makes us uncomfortable. While you're respecting the views of others, don't forget to include yourself. Don't bash where you came from or what you used to believe. For whatever reason, you needed to be there then, and where you came from got you where you are today.

**my journal**                    **BELIEFS ABOUT DEITY**

- I currently believe the following about Deity . . .
- Three things I used to believe about Deity but don't now are . . .
- Why did I change these beliefs? Why do I think my current beliefs are better?
- The Deities I am most interested in studying right now are . . .
- Why do I want to study these Deities?
- Where do I want my studies about Deity to take me in terms of my personal and spiritual growth?

# WHAT ABOUT SATAN?

Sooner or later someone you know is going to give you an earful about how Pagans worship Satan. Not that they're telling you anything new. You've heard it before.

Since the association of Pagans and witches with Satanism is deeply embedded in our culture, you are not going to be able to avoid addressing the issue of Satan as you grow spiritually. If you choose to become a Pagan, at some point you will have to reconcile who you are with who others say you are. This means you'll need to find a new vantage point from which to see society and yourself in relation to it, to form more clearly your ideas about good and evil, to sort through your understanding of what makes you afraid, and understand what this society fears about itself. This means you are going to have to come to terms with Satan.

In this chapter we take a look at how the concept of Satan developed historically, how society's negative views of Paganism developed, and then ask questions such as: What social and religious functions does Satan serve? What is Satan's role in mythology? Who are Satanists? Can a Satanist be a Pagan?

This chapter should be stimulating for you. If you find it threatening or uncomfortable, go to the section near the end called "If You Are Having Trouble" and work through the questions there with the help of a friend.

Our purpose here is to challenge you and help you grow spiritually; and if you are a Pagan, to work the principles of Paganism as sincerely and authentically as you can. To that end, we believe there is no idea you should be afraid to look at. There is no concept—from God to Satan and back again—whose merits cannot be held up to thoughtful examination. This chapter will give you a lot of things to think about. We encourage you to think them through for yourself until you arrive at what is comfortable and makes sense to you right now. In a few years, you may find yourself coming back to this chapter and going through the process again.

## HOW DO PAGANS VIEW SATAN?

This is a question not easily answered since every Pagan has his or her own opinion on the subject. Most Pagans will agree that whatever else Satan may be, he is at least a Deity of the Judeo-Christian-Muslim pantheon.

Because Satan is specifically a Judeo-Christian-Muslim Deity, and since many Pagans choose to retain no connection to the Judeo-Christian-Muslim pantheon unless they consider themselves Christopagans or Judeopagans, most Pagans do not believe in Satan or give him any energy or homage. Since most Pagans do not believe in Satan, they do not worship him. As we explored in the previous chapter, Pagans don't necessarily describe their relationship with Deity as one of worship, so the idea of worshipping Satan is a foreign concept for many Pagans in any case.

Do Pagans believe Satan exists or not? Again, a Pagan's point of view is going to reflect his or her view of Deity in general and will derive from where he or she puts him- or herself on the God Map. Remember that, as it is used by many Pagans, the term *Deity* can refer to any supernatural or spiritual being, force, or power. Therefore, Pagans generally consider Satan a Deity. If a Pagan believes that Deities are anthropomorphic beings, for example, then he or she will view Satan as an anthropomorphic being. If a Pagan believes that Deities are archetypes, then he or she will view Satan as a psychological or energetic pattern. If a Pagan believes that Deities are currents of power, then he or she will probably view Satan as one or more specific energy currents. If a Pagan views Deity as a thought form, then he or she will likely take the position that even if Satan didn't exist before, he does now because of all the energy that millions of minds have fed into him over the centuries.

Let's take a deeper look at Satan as a Deity, and in particular, how he became associated with Pagans.

## PAGANS, WITCHES, AND BAD REPUTATIONS

Pagans and witches are frequently labeled "devil worshippers" despite the fact that Satan or the devil is a Judeo-Christian-Muslim concept. How did this mislabeling happen? A quick tour of history will provide some answers.

Our story begins with the early Hebrews. As a people, the Hebrews struggled to create and then maintain their social and religious identity in a harsh environment during a period in which they were embroiled in repeated wars. The Hebrews believed they were a people chosen by their Deity, called Yahweh, as we can see, for example, in Genesis 12:3. Before Moses leads the Israelites out of Egypt, he tells Pharaoh that the plagues are coming "so that you may know that the Lord makes a distinction between the Egyptians and Israel" (Exodus 11:7). From Moses' perspective, Israel is favored by Yahweh, and those outside of Israel (the Egyptians) are not. We can characterize this perspective as an "insiders and outsiders" or "us and them" worldview.

This worldview develops as a prominent theme throughout the collection of Hebrew writings we know as the Old Testament. The sixth- and seventh-century B.C.E. prophets carry the theme even further. These prophets suddenly substitute descriptions of Israel's enemies with the enemy's Deities, specifically their monsters and demons. That is, instead of referring to their enemy as this or that tribe or city, they refer to them as monsters. Their enemies are no longer people, then, but demons who must be crushed.[1] This process is called *demonization*.

In that same period, the Jews characterize the religious beliefs and observances of their non-Jewish neighbors as "abominations" (Deuteronomy 18:9), and describe them as "fortune telling, soothsaying, charms, divining, casting of spells, oracles, and consulting with ghosts and spirits of the dead" (Deuteronomy 18:10–12). The Jewish writers overlook the fact, however, that their own religious practices involve prophesying by oracles who frequently consult dead leaders and prophets, and who do indeed tell the fortunes and futures of others. What would be labeled as the casting of spells—such as sending a plague of locusts—when done by an outsider, is considered a miracle from God when accomplished by an insider. One problem with the "us and them" worldview is that it frequently condemns the behavior of outsiders and glorifies that of insiders, even when the behavior is exactly the same.

One of the first ways Satan is portrayed in Hebrew literature is as the principle of opposition, or an obstruction to a goal. For example, in Numbers 22:22–25, we are told the story of Balaam who gets on his donkey and heads in a direction Yahweh doesn't want him to go. Yahweh sends Satan, his loyal servant, to stand in the road and turn the animal aside, which Satan does. Many versions of the Bible mistranslate "Satan" as "angel," but the Hebrew word used in this story is *le-satan-lo*.[2]

Keeping with the theme of opposition and obstacle, Satan is used again in 1 Chronicles 21:1 when King David orders the taxation of his people. The scripture says, "The Satan stood up against Israel and incited David to number the people." Here we see an unpopular action demonized even though performed by Israel's own king.

By the first and second centuries C.E., we see the formation of a few separatist Jewish sects who remove themselves from mainstream Jewish culture, usually to live Jewish laws more "purely." The Essenes are an example of such a group. The writings of these separatist groups characterize Jews not belonging to the sect as "satans," accuse them of being in apostasy, and of being seduced by evil.[3] For the first time we see Jews demonizing other Jews. The more these sects separated themselves from mainstream culture, the more extreme they became. In time, their writings give Satan more prominence, make him into a personified figure, and assign him several different histories. These histories often place Satan in the position of an angel who engages in combat with heavenly forces and loses.

Not surprisingly, the tendency to describe the world as a heavenly combat zone continues into the Christian gospels. The early Christians are, after all, considered by some historians to have initially been a Jewish separatist sect. The Gospels, particularly Matthew and Luke, portray Jesus' life and ministry as a cosmic struggle between the forces of good and evil. Satan and his forces are at war with Yahweh and Jesus, and they conspire to bring about Jesus' destruction and crucifixion. Satan is also given as the cause of conflict between Jesus and the Jewish leadership.

In John 8:44, Jesus denounces the Jews as "children of the devil," an extremely unfortunate comment that supported anti-Semitism for centuries. By the end of the Gospels, then, the demonization of outsiders is focused toward all Jews and any others who oppose Jesus and the new church.

The persecution of Christians in the first centuries C.E. heightened the Christians' sense of combat between the forces of good and evil. Although Christianity may have begun as a sect of Judaism, by the time of the persecutions, most members were Gentiles, or non-Jews. During this period, Christian writing shifted the focus of the combat, or the demonization, from other Jews to the Roman authorities.

It may come as some surprise to you that by the end of the second century C.E. and the reign of Marcus Aurelius (161–180), most Roman philosophers were monotheists. Although Deity was addressed by many names, the hymns and anthems began to identify the Deities with one divine being. By the time of Marcus Aurelius, many Romans took for granted the unity of all gods, and demons, in one divine source.[4]

Part of what upset the Romans about the Christians was not their monotheism, which both groups shared, but their concept of Satan. As Platonic philosopher Celsus wrote in 180 C.E., he believed that Christians showed their ignorance in "making up a being opposed to God and calling him 'devil,' or in the Hebrew language 'Satan.' It is blasphemy to say that the greatest God has an adversary who constrains his capacity to do good."[5]

Celsus accuses Christians of inventing a heavenly rebellion in order to justify an earthly rebellion. His accusation has some merit since early Christians used their belief in Satan to justify cutting themselves off from a society they saw as enslaved to demons (the Roman Deities). Those who became Christian were required to cut off association with their family and stop supporting their city. They were taught that all ties of nation, society, and family were unholy.[6] Celsus asks what else one can expect ". . . of those who have cut themselves off from the rest of civilization. For in saying this, they are really projecting their own feelings onto God."[7]

Remember that freedom of religion as we know it did not exist at this time. Deviations were considered blasphemy and were strenuously persecuted by many cultures, the Romans included. Unfortunately, Christianity developed in this same intolerant environment.

In 180 C.E., the Christian writer Irenaeus produced his massive five-volume work on heretics titled *Against Heresies*. A heretic, according to Irenaeus, is a fellow Christian whose views differ from the consensus and is therefore an agent of Satan.[8] For the first time, we see the word "heretic" in Christian literature and the beginning of demonization of Christians by other Christians. Tertullian, a contemporary of Irenaeus, points out that the word *heresy* (*hairesis*) literally means "choice" and a heretic is "one who makes a choice."[9] He states that making choices is evil, and suggests that church leaders who want to eliminate heresy not allow people to ask questions, for it is ". . . questions that make people heretics."[10]

So far in our story, then, Satan has been used to describe a variety of "outsiders"—again, as a part of an "us and them" worldview—beginning with non-Israelite tribes, then other Jews not part of certain sects, then the Roman authorities, and finally other Christians. St. Anthony (250–355 C.E.), a renowned desert monk who greatly influenced early monasticism, takes Satan one step further when he teaches his monks that Satan is their own *self*. According to St. Anthony, Satan is our thoughts, imagination, and impulses. Now even the most intimate presence, that of our self, is demonized.

## WHY WITCH-HUNTS?

By the eleventh and twelfth centuries, actions taken against heretics begin to accuse them of witchcraft and devil worship. In 1320, witchcraft was added to the Inquisition's list of heresies.[11] In 1484, Pope Innocent VIII issued his famous Bull, or proclamation, which granted Inquisitors full authority to capture, torture, and punish "witches."[12] Two years later, the Inquisitors Heinrich Kramer and Jacob Sprenger, both Dominican priests, published their book *The Malleus Maleficarum*, or *The Witches' Hammer*. Their book sets out methods for identifying and torturing "witches," and it became the standard text for witch-hunters for the next three centuries.

How history got to this point makes an interesting study that fills many books, but here are the highlights: St. Thomas Aquinas, also a Dominican and who died in 1274, came to the conclusion after studying Aristotle and others that women are defective men; that is, women exist because of a mistake in the conception or gestation process.[13] In Thomas's day it was believed that men were the sole active agent for causing pregnancy and that women contributed nothing to conception, save being passive vessels. Thomas firmly believed that an active element can only produce something like itself, therefore only men should be born from the act of sex; stated another way, the energy of semen aims to produce something as equally perfect as itself, but owing to unfavorable circumstances—such as moist, south winds—women are occasionally produced (187). Therefore, a woman begins her life as a biological failure—a "developmentally retarded man" (188)—who is obviously "defective in her reasoning ability."[14] According to Thomas, because of the influence of these moist, south winds, women have a higher water content than men and are more easily seduced by sexual pleasure and temptation.[15]

Kramer and Sprenger, the writers of *The Malleus Maleficarum,* are quite impressed with Thomas's reasoning and quote him frequently. They share his view of women, as we see from the following:

> All wickedness is but little to the wickedness of a woman . . . What else is woman but a foe to friendship, an inescapable punishment, a necessary evil, a temptation of nature, a calamity of desires, a domestic danger, a delectable detriment, an evil of nature, painted with fair colors![16]

Also, because Kramer and Sprenger agree with Thomas that those darn moist, south winds make women more susceptible to sexual temptation, they believe there must be more female than male witches, as we see from this passage:

> All witchcraft comes from carnal lust, which is in women insatiable. According to Proverbs 30: "There are three things that are never satisfied, yea, a fourth thing which never says, It is enough; that is, the mouth of the womb." Wherefore for the sake of fulfilling their lusts they consort even with devils . . . And blessed be the Highest Who has so far preserved the male sex from so great a crime: for since it was in this sex that He wished to be born and to suffer for us, therefore He has granted to men this privilege.[17]

So there you have it. The witch-hunts were the product of several centuries of nonsense about women and sex rooted in biological ignorance, ideas that today seem so ludicrous we cannot fathom anyone believing them, let alone acting on them. These beliefs illustrate very well, however, how beliefs build upon each other, concept by concept, until they form a belief system. This system becomes a template around which people act to create a certain reality. The type of reality that is created shows us the merits of the beliefs that support it.

## WHAT HAPPENED TO THE ACCUSED?

The witch-hunt process normally went like this: An accused witch was first urged to confess. If she refused, she was put to torture. As she was tortured, the Inquisitor asked a series of questions and a clerk took down her answers. The torture continued intermittently—usually for days and weeks—until the accused confessed. For this, the torturers were paid from the victim's funds. Expenses included the costs of torture, the torturers' meals, lodging, entertainment, and travel. The estates of confessed "witches" and heretics were confiscated. After confession, most victims were condemned to death, though some were released.[18]

It is unclear how many people were killed in the Inquisition, but modern historians often put the number between 40,000 and 200,000, most of whom were women and German.[19] The Inquisition reached its peak in the sixteenth and seventeenth centuries, the same period in which the first English translation of the Bible—the King James version—was completed (1611). The witch bias of the English translators becomes clearer when certain passages of the King James version are compared to the earlier Greek and Hebrew manuscripts, manuscripts which were considered lost and therefore not available at the time the English translation occurred.

## A LOOK AT THE BIBLICAL WITCH BIAS

Let's look more closely at the witch bias in the King James version of the Bible, beginning with the Hebrew word *kashaph*. It means to whisper or mutter incantations, prayers, or possibly even gossip, but it was translated into English as "witchcraft" and "sorcery"[20] (see Exodus 22:18, Deuteronomy 18:10, 2 Kings 9:22, 2 Chronicles 33:6, Micah 5:12, Galations 5:20, and Nahum 3:4). The earlier Greek translators, on the other hand, felt that the root of the word *kashaph* meant "poisoner," as their texts tend to use the word *pharmakeia*. This literally means "medicine" or "drug" and is the root of our word *pharmacy*. The scripture in Exodus 22:18, then (in some versions it is verse 17), which King James's antiwitch translators wrote as "Thou shall not suffer a witch to live," should instead have been rendered to refer to a poisoner, gossiper, or person praying non-Jewish prayers.

Other examples of the antiwitch bias found in the English translation include 1 Samuel 15:23, in which the Hebrew word *qecem* is translated as "divination" or "witchcraft," but which literally means to distribute by drawing lots or chances—that is, gambling. Another is found in Acts 8:9, in which the Greek word *existemi* is translated as "bewitched," but which actually means "to amaze or astound."[21] These Biblical witch statements came along at a good time since they helped justify the actions of the Inquisition.

## A FABRICATED IMAGE

Inquisitors approached an accused witch with ideas already in mind—strange though they were—about what a "witch" was and what a "witch" did, and they asked their questions accordingly. As the accused was tortured, the Inquisitor asked his questions one at a time. The torture continued until the Inquisitor got the answers he wanted. As we know today, people being tortured will say anything. If a poor peasant woman is asked if she killed and ate babies at a satanic mass while a hot poker is being shoved into her eye, what do you think she'll say? Do you think she won't "confess"? Wouldn't you?

We realize we're being blunt about this, but this process *is* how the image of "witches" was created. As the decades turned into centuries and the Inquisitors shared information, the picture of what a "witch" was changed and grew. Witches ate babies, had sex with Satan and animals, kept cats as familiars, cast curses on their neighbors, poisoned water and food, ruined crops, blighted cattle, attempted to assassinate priests and kings, drank blood, performed black masses, blasphemed God, desecrated holy objects, called up demons, flew on brooms, and so on and so forth. This progression is chronicled in an enormous body of case histories, such as the bibliographies of Graesse, the catalogues of the Abbé Sépher, the three volumes of the *Manuel Bibliographique,* the two thousand sources contained in the bibliography of Yve-Plessis, and the forty-six volumes of Dr. Hoefer, Schieble, and Stanislas de Guaita.[22]

Not only did the church and civil authorities promote this fabricated information as being true, but the common person, who was not only illiterate but by now terrified as well, believed them. Thus the antiwitch bias continued for nearly four hundred years and into the present, extending even into Hollywood. Let's be absolutely clear: Every popular image of witches and Pagans is a fabrication based in torture and a misinformed biological view of women. People who repeat these images today and claim they are true demonstrate their ignorance of history. They also give their support—even if unknowingly—to the torturing of human beings and to the ludicrous views of women that began with Aristotle and were repeated by St. Thomas and others.

If a news commentator went on the air at Hanukkah and proceeded to make misinformed statements fabricated by the Nazis about Jews, how do you think the public would react? Yet people routinely assume the fabrications of the Inquisition are true and apply them to modern Pagans. They don't even give it a second thought. Not too long ago a paper in our city ran an article about Halloween and quoted a Christian minister who said, among other things, that Halloween and all things Pagan are demonic and an abomination to God. River and I called the newspaper to discuss running a rebuttal article, and spoke directly to the authoring journalist who said to us, "What is it with you people? I've been bombarded with e-mails, letters, and phone calls from both Pagans and non-Pagans complaining about the article! Why are you guys so sensitive?"

We responded, "You mean you wouldn't object if your religion were labeled demonic and its members accused of abominations? Where is the evidence to support your statements? Tell you what, why don't you run this article again next week, word for word, except this time change the word 'Pagan' to 'black people' or 'Jews.' We have a good idea of what the reaction would be. Don't you?"

Silence reigned on the other end of the phone. "How about an interview tomorrow?" he asked, and the following week the paper ran a very fair and accurate rebuttal.

It is our experience that most people adopt the cultural bias against Paganism without giving it any thought. Most people are not trying to be malicious about it, they're just ignorant of the facts. Once they become more aware of how things developed, however, they usually go on to grant Paganism the same respect they give any other religion.

**questions to discuss**

**YOUR IMPRESSIONS OF PAGANS**

1. What were the first things you learned about Pagans and witches growing up? Where did you learn this information? How was the information being used?

2. Do you think this culture continues to fear witches and Pagans? If so, why?

3. What can you do to correct false information you hear concerning witches and Pagans? If you've had experience with this already, what reactions did you encounter? How might you respond?

4. If you used to believe misinformation about Pagans and witches, or even fear them, what caused you to change your mind?

## THE SOCIAL ROLES OF SATAN

As our brief journey into history shows, Satan is a useful social concept. Below we identify some of the social roles he has played and then give a response from the Pagan perspective.

**Insiders versus Outsiders.** Possibly the most central social role that Satan has played is that of distinguishing between those who belong to a specific group and those who do not.

Distinctions can be useful. Because we are each capable of making distinctions, we know the difference between "my" side of the road and "your" side, "my" bank account and "yours." Because we distinguish, we understand and appreciate differences such as "liberal" and "conservative," "capitalist" and "socialist," "pro-choice" and "not pro-choice." If you are Pagan, you may be so because of the distinctions you drew between Paganism and other religions. We each make decisions all the time based on distinctions.

The problem comes when distinctions become adversarial, or follow an "us versus them" principle. In this worldview, "we" are here and "you" are out there, and we're against you. It's a short step from this position to demonizing those who differ from us.

Pagans stand for the principle that demonization is an unacceptable way to relate to others. Having differences is fine. Disagreeing with others is okay. Drawing distinctions that are unique to you is dandy, but there is no need to turn others into the enemy.

On the whole, Paganism embraces diversity. The richness that results from human beings expressing themselves fully—both in their similarities and their differences—is a thing of beauty to Pagans. It is a human treasure. Demonization of others has no place in the Pagan worldview and the type of society Pagans wish to build.

**Control through fear.** What better way to gain control of people than to make them afraid—afraid of the boogeyman, afraid of being damned, afraid of asking questions, afraid of themselves? As we saw from the desert monk St. Anthony, Satan is not only the boogeyman "out there" somewhere; he is your very self. The boogeyman is *you.* Your thoughts, feelings, and desires are demonic forces pulling you down to damnation.

From this perspective, the world is so utterly dangerous that even your own self betrays you as an agent of Satan. Where can you possibly turn to be safe? The voices—whether of civil or religious authority—have an answer for you. You can trust only them. The only solution is to hand over your power to them and they will keep you safe.

As you know from your study of Pagan principles, Pagans choose to retain their power to decide their beliefs, form their ethics, and take responsibility for their life and their choices. The idea of giving away one's personal power is completely unacceptable to most Pagans. Paganism, then, stands opposed to the concept that you cannot trust yourself, and is opposed to attempts to control through fear.

**A rallying point.** When a group succumbs to fear and demonizes "outsiders," Satan often becomes a rallying point. An experience we had will serve as an example. Some years ago a friend who recently graduated from a seminary and was beginning his ministry in a Christian church shared an interesting story. He told us he recently attended a conference for ministers. At this conference he went to a workshop where the ministers discussed the distressing trend of low church membership. The speaker leading the workshop suggested a strategy being tried by some churches that might help. The strategy was to create an enemy to blame for attacking the church—specifically, Satan. His attempts to destroy the church were centered on cultural influences, some of which included the rise of Paganism and "New Age" beliefs. Our friend said this strategy was encouraged because, "Having an enemy has always strengthened Christianity, from the time of the martyrs forward. Creating an enemy now might help increase membership." Even though this idea is not a new one, we were still astounded.

Later, as part of an Introduction to Paganism class we were teaching, we encouraged our students to attend several different types of worship services and report back to the class on their experiences. One of the churches we recommended was one we believed to be fundamentalist and pentecostal. Just to be sure, River and I went to services there ourselves. We happened to attend on a Sunday when the preacher informed his congregation that Pagans are part of Satan's army and are planning to kill all Christians everywhere. This was news to us! Based on this sermon it appears that some groups may be trying the strategy offered at the ministerial conference.

These stories are examples of how Satan can be used as a rallying point. When people feel threatened, they circle the wagons and join together more closely as a community. Most Pagans, however, are not attracted to this type of community building. A community built around fears, threats, and demonization of others is neither healthy, respectful, nor sustainable. Maintaining a battle-ready stance is exhausting. Pagans would rather use their energies to gain an appreciation of other beliefs and cultures, and to promote dialogue and cooperation among the peoples of the world.

## THE MYTHOLOGICAL ROLES OF SATAN

In addition to social functions, Satan plays several roles within his mythology. Understanding these roles will help you identify "satanic" qualities and characteristics and recognize them in other mythologies and even the culture. Satan represents certain behaviors and qualities experienced throughout human history, regardless of belief system. What is Satan's role, then, as a mythological archetype?

**Satan as the principle of opposition and obstacle.** This is the first archetypal role we assign to Satan because this is one of the first ways he is encountered in Hebrew literature. As was discussed in our brief history, we first meet Satan when he stands before Balaam's donkey and physically blocks his path (see Numbers 22:22–25). You will recall that Satan is a servant of Yahweh at this point, and he blocks Balaam at Yahweh's request.

Instead of being evil, the principle of opposition can be viewed as divinely inspired and supported. Looking at opposition from an energetic perspective shows that it is, in fact, a necessity of life. Without opposing forces, the Earth would not turn on its axis or follow an orbit, species would not reproduce, plants would not germinate, airplanes would not fly, and none of us would even be able to walk. Without finely balanced forces in opposition, life and growth would be impossible.

Satan, then, stands as an archetypal figure for these forces. Since life itself is subject to opposition and resistance, you can choose to view Satan and these energies as lessons and opportunities that, in the end, create an environment in which all of us can grow.

**Satan as a questioner of authority.** This may well be Satan's most flamboyant and controversial role. It is, however, an extension of his role as the principle of opposition and obstacle. In this case, however, the object of opposition happens to be an authority figure. Depending on your view of authority, individualism, and choice, this role of Satan may make you more or less uncomfortable.

Examples of Satan playing this role can be found in the story of the Garden of Eden (Genesis 3:1–24) and in several encounters with Jesus throughout the New Testament. Remember that the New Testament was written by writers who, for the most part, saw the events in Jesus' life as part of a cosmic battle between the forces of good and evil. To make a worthy opponent, Satan needed to be adversarial and defiant.

From an archetypal perspective, the pattern of a weaker opponent questioning, challenging, and defying a more powerful authority figure is a familiar one. Many of you experienced this archetypal energy personally during your adolescent years. Some of you saw it and admired it in the marches led by Martin Luther King, Jr. protesting racial discrimination, or heard about it in the life of Gandhi and his struggles with the British government. You see it today on bumper stickers that read "Question Authority," as well as in the picket lines of those demonstrating outside abortion clinics. This archetypal energy fired the defiance of colonists in the eighteenth century, which escalated into the Revolutionary War and led to the creation of the United States.

Even today churches and schools encourage the questioning and defying of authority when dictated by conscience. Joyce has memories of sitting in Sunday school learning about those who stood up for their faith against great odds, and being asked by the Sunday school teacher if she would proclaim her faith even if faced with a firing squad. When River was in school studying those Nazi officers who defended themselves at trial by claiming they were only following orders, he was asked if he would follow orders he knew to be wrong, even if resisting meant he would go to a concentration camp and die.

As a society we have mixed feelings about the satanic archetype of questioning authority. On the one hand, we condemn it and are frightened by it, and on the other hand, we admire those with the courage to stand by their principles no matter what the pressure or consequences.

**Satan as trickster.** A trickster is a Deity who teaches by means of tricks, surprises, and unexpected lessons. Many mythologies have trickster Deities, such as Hermes, Discordia, Loki, Eris, and the American Indian Coyote. When you interact with a trickster, you think you are headed in one direction, but to your surprise and chagrin discover yourself somewhere else. Often you will end up the "better" for it, or at least the wiser, even though trickster experiences are not necessarily pleasant.

We see Satan playing the role of trickster in at least two biblical stories. The first occurs in the Garden of Eden (Genesis 3:1–24) where, in his form as a serpent, he convinces Adam and Eve to eat the forbidden fruit. Much to their dismay, this action catapults them out of their quasi-animal state and puts on them the burden of making choices and deciding right from wrong. The second occurs in the Book of Job when Satan takes Job—with divine approval—through a series of horrible experiences. These experiences become a means of growth for Job, and an opportunity to talk with Yahweh about the meaning of life, suffering, and spirituality. Job's experiences are certainly not ones he would have chosen for himself, but he comes out the other side of them a completely different man than he would have been without them.

**Satan as tempter.** Closely related to the role of trickster is Satan's role as tempter. In the story of Job, for example, Satan not only takes Job through certain transformative experiences, but he tempts Job to despair, to give up his faith, and be destroyed by what is happening to him. As Job resists these temptations, he moves forward spiritually.

The tempter, then, helps us clarify what is important to us. The temptation serves as a point of evaluation. As an example, look at the story of Satan tempting Jesus in the desert (Luke 4:1–13). Luke tells us that before Jesus began his ministry, he took himself into the desert to fast and pray. No doubt this was a time of preparation and purification for Jesus, and a time to think hard about choices that lay ahead. Satan comes to Jesus in the desert and tempts him three times. The first time, Satan encourages Jesus to turn stones into bread, thereby satisfying his physical or carnal needs. The second time he offers Jesus worldly power if he will abandon his devotion to Yahweh. The third time Satan urges Jesus to test his spiritual power by casting himself from a height and having the angels catch him.

Throughout these temptations Jesus had to ask himself, "How important is my ministry to me right now? Is it more important than power? Is it more important than physical satisfaction?" Each temptation was a way for him to evaluate his goals and sort out his priorities. After his desert experience, he knew what mattered to him.

Temptation serves this same function for each of you. If you want to be a concert pianist, for example, you will have to decide if paying for lessons and practicing every day are priorities for you. If you find yourself buying a TV with your lesson money and visiting with friends when you should be practicing, then you need to re-examine your goal. The temptations may be stronger than your desire to be a pianist. This isn't necessarily a bad thing to discover. It's better to find out upfront that your values and priorities lie somewhere other than where you thought they did.

As you move forward in your life and search for those interests, relationships, and life projects that fire your passion, temptation will come to you and it will ask, "Is this thing over here more important to you than your goal?" You will have to decide how to answer. Satan as tempter represents this process of evaluation. His testing and prodding bring you to a level of empowerment and clarity you might not otherwise reach.

**Satan as suffering hero.** This one may take you by surprise, as we don't usually think of Satan as a hero in the Garden of Eden story. Heroes are characters who perform extraordinary tasks or feats, often for the sake of others, and who take risks and bring about changes that affect the lives and destinies of one or more characters in the story. As the mythologist Joseph Campbell puts it, the journey of the hero consists of a separation, initiation, and return.[23] Heroes begin their tasks by leaving their normal environment—the *separation*—and traveling to the site of the task or conflict, which may be another country, the underworld, or a supernatural realm. Once there, heroes are *initiated* into their roles; that is, they engage in their tasks and performs their feats, which Campbell describes as the "penetration to some source of power."[24] A consequence or change results from the heroes' actions, which can have both beneficial and detrimental effects on others. The saga ends when heroes *return* from their tasks, either to their prior state or to some new condition brought about by their heroic conduct.

While heroes are frequently rewarded for their accomplishments, occasionally a myth ends with a hero's punishment. We call such a character a *suffering hero.* Who or what punishes the hero? Generally, the ruling powers of the mythology. Occasionally the hero's task involves going head-to-head with authority, and to succeed against that kind of power the hero, as Campbell says, must "trick" the authorities "out of their treasure."[25] If the hero succeeds, he or she becomes the "carrier of the changing," and releases from the control of the authority figures the "vital energies that will feed the universe."[26]

To help understand Satan as a suffering hero, let's take a look at the story of a similar hero: the Greek Prometheus. According to Greek mythology, Prometheus was the son of the Titans Iapetos and Klymene. The Titans were the reigning gods before the emergence of the Mount Olympus gods you are probably more familiar with. Zeus, in fact, who came to be the ruling Deity of the Olympian pantheon, was also a son of a Titan (Kronos). Zeus eventually overthrew the Titans and confined them to an abyss.[27]

After Zeus took charge, Prometheus became aware of the condition of the human race, which was living in an animal-like state. Zeus refused to give humans even the most basic gift of fire so that humanity might improve its situation. Prometheus decided a change was in order, so he steals fire from Zeus. To Zeus, who is the keeper of lightning and thunderbolts, fire *is* the essence of his godly power. Prometheus brings this god-like gift to the earth and gives it to humanity. Because of this gift of fire, humanity is changed forever. In Campbell's words, Prometheus tricked Zeus out of his treasure of fire, became the carrier of this treasure to humanity, and released a new and vital energy into the universe. As punishment, Zeus orders Prometheus to be chained to a mountain where an eagle comes and eats his liver and causes him great agony. Eventually his liver grows back, and the eagle eats it again, and so his torment goes on forever. Not satisfied, Zeus then creates Pandora—considered the first mortal woman—who is so curious that she opens a box filled with every form of vice, suffering, and disease, and releases them into the world.[28]

In the Garden of Eden story, humanity also exists on the earth in an innocent, quasi-animal state. Like Prometheus, Satan is aware of a god-like quality that would change humanity's condition. Satan gives this god-like gift to humanity through the active cooperation of Adam and Eve. In this case the gift is not fire but the knowledge of good and evil—the ability to distinguish, form value judgments, and make choices. As Yahweh says of this gift, speaking to another unidentified Deity, "See! The man has become like one of us, knowing what is good and what is bad." (Genesis 3:22). Receiving this gift marks a sudden shift in the development of humankind. Again using Campbell's words, one could say that through his cunning as a trickster (see above for a discussion of Satan as a trickster Deity), Satan tricked Yahweh out of his treasure of a god-like knowledge, became the carrier of this treasure to humanity, and released a new and vital energy into the universe.

As with Prometheus, Satan is then punished for his actions. Yahweh curses Satan, bans him from the company of other animals, and condemns him, in his form as serpent, to crawl on his belly forever (Genesis 3:14). Like Zeus through Pandora, Yahweh goes on to punish humanity by making childbirth painful for Eve and requiring Adam to toil for his food (Genesis 3:16–18). Yahweh also banishes them from the Garden of Eden in order to keep them from eating of the tree of life and becoming even more god-like by not experiencing death (Genesis 3:23–24).

As this comparison of the two stories shows, both Prometheus and Satan defied a more powerful Deity in order to bring a gift to humanity, and both were punished for doing so. From an archetypal perspective, then, we can say that Prometheus and Satan represent the pattern of those who benefit humanity at great cost to themselves. For this reason we identify both Deities as suffering heroes.

**Satan as the embodiment of evil.** This is a later development and, in our opinion, a result of using Satan as a means of demonization. Satan has been used as an archetypal cesspool, if you will, into which is dumped all the things people fear, despise, and repress. Rather than looking at these things head on, people label them evil and satanic and let the label do their thinking for them. Once a person or activity is identified with this label, it is feared, shunned, and persecuted. Those who use the label "satanic" tend to become quite emotional about the things that have been labelled. Calm, rational thought collapses before the terror and hysteria inspired by this cultural boogeyman.

Anything can be labeled as satanic and evil if it suits the purposes of those doing the labeling. We have seen the label attached to politicians, public figures, religious denominations, spiritual movements, modern conveniences, books, movies, technology, toys, and television characters.

As history has shown, demonizing what you don't like or understand is nothing new, but it doesn't help you become more culturally and spiritually mature, especially in a world that is increasingly diverse and global. For the most part, Pagans try to avoid using emotional labels and instead evaluate an idea on its merits. Pagans also try to avoid shifting blame away from themselves as a means to avoid personal responsibility for their actions, an idea we'll look at in chapter 7. Dumping your misbehavior onto Satan—"the devil made me do it!"—doesn't cut it in Paganism.

We think it's also clear from our examination of the mythological figure of Satan in this chapter that Satan is a far richer and complex character than we often suppose. This is probably because society has become so afraid of him as the cosmic boogeyman that many of us cannot study him objectively, even though we do so for more malignant characters of other mythologies.

**questions to discuss**

**YOUR VIEW OF SATAN**

1. When someone mentions Satan, what comes to your mind? What feelings come with the images? Where did you learn the views you currently have of Satan?

2. Can you think of any additional roles Satan has played socially or mythologically? If so, what?

3. Do you find it difficult to approach the issue of Satan from different perspectives? If so, which one is causing you difficulty? Which of the perspectives covered above is the most unusual or different from your own?

## WHO IS A SATANIST?

Are there Satanists out there or not? If the label doesn't apply to Pagans in general, who does it describe, if anyone? We identify three primary groupings of people we consider "satanic," though for different reasons.

The first group consists of those who truly worship Satan as a Deity of the Judeo-Christian-Muslim pantheon. People in this group are not Pagans and would not likely identify themselves as Pagans. Frequently, they identify mythologically with their religion of origin, which in the United States is probably Christianity. To members of such a cult, Satan acts in his role as the embodiment of evil, a principle which these Satanists claim to serve and worship. The wild tales that occasionally circulate about human and animal sacrifice and ritual abuse—if they have any factual basis at all—would be related to these destructive cults. The movie *Rosemary's Baby* gives us Hollywood's version of them.

The next group of Satanists are those who belong to the Church of Satan, founded by Anton LaVey in 1966. LaVey wrote *The Satanic Bible,* which sets out the essentials of his satanic beliefs. In the Church of Satan, Satan is viewed primarily as an archetype representing a variety of specific energies. It is these energies that interest the members of the Church of Satan, not Satan himself per se; they do not worship Satan. In fact, they do not worship any Deity, since one of their guiding principles is autonomy and self-determinism. They look to Satan as an archetype of how to think for themselves, act from the center of their own power, and avoid the "herd mentality."

The third group of Satanists are those who belong to the church of the Temple of Set, founded by Michael Aquino in 1975. Setians consider themselves an offshoot of the Church of Satan. This group does not focus on Satan at all but on the Egyptian god Set. Setians are mixed on what Set is; some view him as a concrete being, others as an archetypal energy. However, he represents to both views the principle of intelligence or consciousness, especially when it is "isolate" or acting independently, relying solely on its own conscience and taking full responsibility for its actions.

You may hear both the Church of Satan and the Temple of Set described as "left-hand" paths. This term is not meant as an insult to lefties, but commonly refers to something that differs or dissents from the norm. A left-hand path is one of spiritual dissent and one that tends to look to the seeker's own efforts rather than for help or "salvation" from Deities and other authority figures.

When a Christian or other religious commentator makes a statement about some person or group being "Satanist," ask which type of Satanist. Are they referring to renegade Christians, or do they mean a member of the Church of Satan or Temple of Set? When we use the term "Satanist" in this book, we are referring only to the LaVey and Setian groups, or individuals who have adopted portions of their philosophies.

## CAN A SATANIST BE A PAGAN?

As we stated in the beginning, most Pagans generally agree with the seven principles of Paganism outlined in chapter 1. We find it highly unlikely that a renegade Christian who worships the principle of evil would be attracted to Paganism; we have not met any such people ourselves. Members of the Church of Satan and Temple of Set are free to associate with whomever they wish, and we know several members of left-hand paths who participate in Pagan events. Whether or not members of left-hand paths describe themselves as Pagan will depend on their individual philosophies.

A question that is raised from time to time among Pagans is, *"Should* members of left-hand paths be allowed to call themselves Pagan?" Since anyone may call themselves Pagan, that really decides the question. Part of the controversy, however, seems to be centered on the use of the word "Satan" by followers of left-hand paths. Some Pagans have gotten so tired of having the label "Satan worshippers" attached to them by the general culture that they just don't want the *S* word associated with them in any way. It doesn't matter that the word is used archetypally, or that there are aspects of that archetype to which they themselves relate. It doesn't matter that they have a "Question Authority" bumper sticker on their car, that they were arrested for protesting the World Trade Organization, that they helped the Discordians hide the firewood for the main ritual last night, and that they worked through personal issues over the winter with the help of Deities associated with darkness, death, or loss, such as Hecate. Forget all that! It's that darn *S* word!

When you have an informed understanding of Satan's mythological role, you can see him in his proper context just as you do Hecate and a dozen others. It is okay to be completely objective about the issue of Satan even if everyone else reacts emotionally to it. If you allow yourself to panic when you hear the *S* word, then you are letting others define the issue and your response to it. We want to be clear that we are neither promoting nor discouraging Satanism as a spiritual path, though it is not our path. We are, however, encouraging you to approach this issue as you would any other, and Satanists as you would any other person.

Another part of the controversy seems to surround the "darkness" of left-hand paths. Members talk about the Prince of Darkness, black magick, working with chaos, and so forth. We suggest you get into a discussion with one or two members of a left-hand path sometime and ask them what they mean by these terms. They may or may not be using them in the way you assume.

In and of itself, Pagans don't have a problem with "darkness." Life is conceived in the dark, seeds sprout in the dark soil, and half of the year—from the Fall Equinox to the Spring Equinox—is dark and ruled by the dark forces of coldness and death. Each of our own lives have seasons of darkness, such as times of rest and recuperation, aging, grief, dying, moving, changing jobs, and so forth, as explained in chapter 1. Roughly half of each day (depending on the seasons) is dark and half is light. A Pagan knows that balance is important and that the dark is as important as the light.

Pagans do not associate "dark" with evil and "light" with good. This association comes to us from ancient Middle Eastern religions, particularly Zoroastrianism. Zoroastrianism, which emerged sometime around 1400 B.C.E. and still exists today, believes that the forces of good and evil are fighting for control of the world.[29] The forces of good are symbolized by light, and specifically fire, an element which the Zoroastrians venerate and keep in their temples.[30] The Zoroastrians had a great deal of influence on the Jewish peoples during their Babylonian captivity, and several of their beliefs were incorporated into Jewish thought, and eventually into Christianity and Islam.[31] Zoroastrianism is generally considered a dualistic religion, one which divides the world into black and white.[32] The dualistic worldview became firmly rooted over the centuries and is very engrained in the culture from which modern Pagans emerge. Of course, Pagans are going to tend to retain this perspective unless they become aware they have it and decide to examine it.

If you hear Pagans talking about "light" and "dark" energies or Deities, they most likely do not mean "good" and "bad." Since the light half of the year, which occurs in spring and summer, is associated with new projects, growth, and abundance, then spiritual work with "light" energies and Deities usually relates to these themes. Such "light" themes may include starting a business, becoming pregnant, finding romance, building a home, making new investments, signing up for college courses, planting a garden, appreciating gifts, growing in ways that are visible and tangible, and in general dealing with issues focused in the outer world or on external things.

The dark half of the year, as was explored in chapter 1, occurs throughout the fall and winter, and its themes relate to change, disintegration, ending of cycles, and transition. Spiritual work involving "dark" energies and Deities may include issues of rest, harvesting and storing, reflection, wisdom, letting go of what is not needed, courage, faith, accepting change, leaving a legacy, losing a job, moving to a new city, having children leave home, losing a loved one, illness, and in general dealing with issues and processes that are internal or hidden.

We have friends who insist that creativity, in whatever form, is a "dark" energy. Some Pagans believe there is no such thing as a "dark" or "light" energy, but that energetic power is all one thing and is only categorized for convenience. For some Pagans, "dark" and "light" are terms that help describe the flavor or feeling of an energy and are just two of many terms that could be used. Other terms we have heard include "heavy," "tingling," "dense," "pulsating," "singing," "rich," "colorful," "demanding," and "gentle."

If you wonder what Pagans mean when they use words such as "dark" and "light," ask them. Every Pagan has his or her own vocabulary for describing personal spiritual experiences. Pagans and non-Pagans who panic at the use of the words "dark" and "light" are again letting others define the issue and their response to it. Part of Paganism's gift to the world is in offering a new way of seeing things. While others see "dark" and "light" as referring to good and bad, Pagans see such terms as part of the natural cycle that forms a healthy and balanced whole. This wholeness includes spiritual dissent as well as conformity.

Another part of the controversy among Pagans concerning Satanists relates to this sense of balance. Some Pagans are critical of members of left-hand paths for overemphasizing the individual at the expense of group effort, and individual power at the expense of assistance from Deities and other universal forces. Some Pagans criticize followers of left-hand paths for being overly focused on dissent and losing sight of cooperation.

Anything can be taken to an extreme, of course. Balance is the key. Sometimes people feel they need to focus for a time on an aspect they believe is missing in order to bring it into more prominence, and hopefully, greater balance. A primary example of this within Paganism is found in the women's spirituality movement, of which Dianic Wicca is a part. This movement arose from a sense of imbalance; that religion had been male-oriented for so long that the feminine aspect was degraded or missing entirely. To overcome this imbalance, Dianic Wiccans focus exclusively on female Deities, celebrate only female mysteries, and often don't allow men to attend their circles. Is this one-sided? Yes. Can it be taken to an extreme? Yes. Are there some Dianics who do, in fact, take it to an extreme? Undoubtedly. Even so, does the women's spirituality movement serve a useful purpose? Yes.

We suggest to you that the left-hand paths serve the same function with regard to issues of power and authority as the Dianic Wiccans do with regard to issues of gender. The people we know who are Pagan and also followers of left-hand paths, Discordian, or are focused on chaos and dissent, believe that the aspects they represent have long been neglected in religion. They believe they are helping to restore a balance by emphasizing the role of the individual and critical thinking, and diminishing the importance of authority figures, including Deities. Is this one-sided? Yes. Can it be taken to an extreme? Yes. Are there some members of left-hand paths who do, in fact, take it to an extreme? Undoubtedly. Even so, does the left-hand perspective serve a useful purpose? We believe so.

## questions to discuss     ISSUES SURROUNDING SATANISTS

1. Do you know any Satanists, that is, those who follow a left-hand path? What are their general beliefs and philosophy? Do they consider themselves Pagan? Do you think they should? What issues do you think this raises for Paganism, if any?

2. Do Satanists benefit Paganism in any way? If yes, in what ways? If not, why not? Is there anything about their perspective that is unique and perhaps beneficial? Would you ever study the satanic movement and its philosophy?

3. Why might a person become a Satanist? What would you say to a person interested in a left-hand path?

4. How would you explain Satanism to someone who knows nothing about it?

## exercise     IF YOU ARE HAVING TROUBLE

Make a list of all the ideas in this chapter that trouble you. Leave plenty of space between them. After each idea, list the beliefs you currently hold about it. Study each one closely. Do your beliefs really conflict with what troubles you about the material in this chapter? If so, in what ways do they conflict? If not, in what ways do your beliefs and the ideas of this chapter agree? What is the source of your current beliefs? What are your current beliefs doing for you personally and spiritually? How will they take you to your next level of growth?

Next, write down how the ideas that trouble you in this chapter make you feel. If you feel uneasy, for example, which ideas are bringing up this feeling? What is this uneasiness like? If the uneasiness could talk to you about how it feels, what would it say? What do you think the origins of your feelings are? What is the message behind them?

If you challenge your current ideas on the subject of Satan, what is the worst thing that can happen to you? Why will it happen? Is this your belief or did you pick it up from someone else? What is its underlying message? If you could talk with the terrible things you have identified, what would you, as a rational adult, say to them?

Discuss your concerns with a Pagan, a teacher, or friend.

## DEALING WITH UNCOMFORTABLE IDEAS

As you move forward on your spiritual path, you will find yourself dealing with controversial and difficult ideas. If you are a Pagan, you will also have to face your fears and the fears this culture has of you. To help you in this process, we offer the following suggestions.

**Don't fear ideas.** As was stated at the beginning of the chapter, we believe there is no idea you should be afraid to examine. People who tell you to fear certain ideas and not ask certain questions probably have an agenda. Find out what it is.

An idea is a mental construct and in and of itself cannot hurt you. We have never, in all our years of teaching, seen an idea come swooping down out of the sky and injure anyone. You are not going to be punished in Paganism for thinking any thought you want to think, asking any question you want to ask, and exploring any idea you want to explore.

**Be prepared to face your fears.** Despite what we just said, we know you are going to bring your fears with you. You may very well have some anxiety about thinking the things you do and feeling the ways you feel. This is natural and a part of making the transition from where you used to be to where you're headed. Your old beliefs, which said you would be punished if you rocked the boat, are still giving you grief. Even worse, now we've gone and made you think about Satan and all that "scary" stuff.

Don't be surprised if during this transition period you encounter some of your fears. All of our students have gone through this at some point, as River and I did ourselves. The mind is a powerful tool and it takes you literally. When you go up to your inner door marked "Boogeymen" and open it saying, "I want to see what I've got stored in here," your subconscious will take you at your word. Whatever things you fear, whatever you've repressed or disowned, whatever your boogeymen are, were put here by you. The fact you've acknowledged these things and opened this door might in itself make you afraid.

It is very, very common to encounter your fears while you go through transition periods. Your fears may come to you as sensations, feelings, dream images, and figures, or even play themselves out in people who come across your path. The most common places our students encounter their fears is in dreams, meditation, and rituals. Whenever you are more open to the subconscious, your fears may appear to you. When they do, they are trying to tell you something. Listen to them. It's possible they've been trying to get your attention for years!

If you don't like how your fears are expressing themselves, ask them to change or lighten up. You are in control of this whole process, after all—a fact we tend to forget! If you begin to feel overwhelmed, seek professional counseling or psychiatric help. You may have tapped into a deep-seated psychological issue or problem that needs to be worked on.

Normally, however, this initial processing of fears and repressed material doesn't last forever. It will run its course. In fact, the more open you are to hearing what your inner self has to say, the quicker it usually goes.

**Judge an idea by its merits, not its source.** This can be difficult to do, especially when the source is controversial. Let an idea step forward, show itself, and stand or fall on its own merits. Sometimes great ideas and insights come from unexpected or reviled sources. What do *you* think of the idea? Does it speak to you? Do you feel comfortable with it? When you try it on does it work for you? Resist the urge to judge an idea based on who said it. This mental flexibility will serve you well in your spiritual growth.

**Don't give in to hysteria.** This means not letting the opinions of others determine your own. Mass hysteria on any subject is almost always driven by fear and ignorance and is usually not well informed or sensible. Many of history's worst atrocities arose from mass hysteria. The sheer momentum of the group mind can be almost overwhelming, both in terms of its energy and its physical and emotional force, but at these times in particular you need to keep Paganism's first two principles in mind. According to these principles, *you* are responsible for what you believe and how you behave. If you let peer pressure decide your beliefs and behavior, you are handing your personal power and responsibility over to others.

**Evaluate belief systems by how well they work.** We're not going to tell you that you shouldn't form judgments about other philosophies, religions, paths, and traditions, because evaluating ideas is a part of growing spiritually. What we do strongly recommend is that you put aside labels as a means of evaluation. Labels are almost always prejudicial and inflammatory and impart no useful information.

Instead, form your judgments about Pagans, groups, covens, movements, and teachers based on actual behavior, values, beliefs, and ethics. Do their ideas seem sound, healthy, and workable? What kind of a reality can you build using their ideas? How do people in this path or tradition behave? How do they treat others? How do they treat themselves? Is their life working well or are they always in some kind of crisis? What about their ethics and values—do you like what you see? Is their behavior ethical and honorable? Can you count on them? Are they honest? Would you want this person as a friend?

## SATAN, EVIL, AND YOUR SPIRITUAL FEARS

- The things I believed about Satan as I was growing up were . . .
- My beliefs about Satan now are . . .
- My beliefs about demons and evil spirits now are . . .
- Three beliefs I cannot hold while believing the things I do about Satan, demons, and evil spirits are . . .
- The things I fear spiritually are . . .
- The things I believe can harm me spiritually are . . .
- How did I acquire these beliefs and fears?
- What can I do to determine whether my beliefs and fears are well-founded?
- What do I need in order to feel safe spiritually?
- Three things I can do to help correct prejudice and misunderstanding about Paganism are . . .

# 5

# THE LIVING UNIVERSE

As was explored in an earlier chapter, beliefs are very powerful. What you believe about the universe shapes what you think is possible in the universe. What you believe is possible determines to a great extent what you experience. If you believe that you cannot interact with the universe at deeper levels, then you will never try to do so. If you believe that the universe is made up of isolated bits of matter, then you will not try to feel interconnected. If you believe that God or the forces of evolution control the universe in a manner that makes your involvement irrelevant, then you will never engage with the universe as a cocreator. If you believe that the universe is inert and passive, then you will think it impossible to enter into a relationship with it. If you believe that consciousness is an accident of nature unique to humanity, then you will not experience the living face of the universe.

To help you appreciate Pagan philosophy in this area, we begin with those beliefs about the universe that are currently in effect in Western culture. From that perspective you can then more clearly see how Paganism differs from the accepted view. Following this is a look at other sources of inspiration that Pagans use to help them understand and relate to this magickal, living universe. These sources are mysticism, science, and personal experience.

# THE CURRENT WESTERN MINDSET

Our current Western mindset regarding the universe is called the *mechanistic* or *classical* view, initially developed by the renowned scientist Sir Isaac Newton. In the late 1600s, Sir Isaac Newton proposed the idea that all events in the universe are governed by a consistent set of rules, or laws. Newton's laws do not explain why the universe behaves as it does, only what it will do under certain circumstances.

Newton saw the world as being composed of bits of matter that move predictably around the universe, like billiard balls on a pool table. These bits or "particles" exist in a three-dimensional space and move in an orderly fashion through time, from the past and into the future. The result of Newton's three laws of motion and the law of gravitation is that matter is viewed as inert and passive, unable to act on its own, unable to change its condition without the action of an external agent or force. Newton's laws were considered universal and eternal, making the motion of every piece of matter predictable. According to Newton's view, if you were to compute all of the positions, velocities, and masses of all pieces of matter, then you could determine those same characteristics into the future. This is called *determinism*, and it leaves no room for free will or the activities of consciousness. With only three simple laws and gravitation, it seemed as though all behavior of the material universe could be explained. Human beings were considered subject to these same laws, and the universe was seen as a giant machine, that was indifferent to human desires and goals and went its way without direction or purpose.

For three hundred years, Newton's mechanistic view remained virtually unchallenged. During that time it shaped science, medicine, religion, philosophy, and psychology. For the most part, these disciplines formed themselves into a coherent belief system that supported the mechanistic view. Much of psychology, for example, was built around the concept of acceptable and unacceptable experiences of reality, the acceptable ones being those, of course, that conform to the Newtonian consensus of objective reality.[1] In the area of religion, the Newtonian belief system portrays the universe as an orderly, predictable machine, created and run by God, the great machine maker. This God is himself orderly and immutable, as is demonstrated by the laws that he created to run the big machine. Medicine and biology portray people as another type of machine, and until recently have tended to treat the body and not the person, sometimes describing life and intelligence as accidents caused by the interactions of matter, and consciousness as a waste product of the brain.

Most Pagans will agree that there is a place for Newton's view of the universe, especially when dealing with everyday reality and the world of objects. The mechanistic model does a good job of explaining surface reality, but does not go below the surface into deeper levels.

Paganism is one of the first modern Western religions that consciously breaks from the mechanistic Newtonian view of the world. It is one of the first modern religions to integrate, or at least give serious consideration to, a variety of mystical and scientific perspectives. Paganism offers a range of worldviews and an opportunity to create a different relationship with the universe than many of us knew growing up. This new relationship is summed up in three of Paganism's principles.

**Principle #4: Everything contains the spark of intelligence.** Many Pagans believe that everything, from the smallest subatomic particle to the largest planetary system, is alive, contains a spark of intelligence, or has some type of consciousness. As we will explore later in this chapter, mysticism, science, and magickal experience suggest that consciousness is multidimensional and that it folds and unfolds into physical reality from unseen realms. Its expression in the physical realm is only a part of its greater reality.

**Principle #5: Everything is sacred.** The concept of sacredness means different things to different people. However, many people, including Pagans, use the word to mean one or more of the following:

- something has been blessed or approved by a Deity
- something is rare and precious and should be treated carefully
- something inspires awe and wonder
- something is good and wholesome
- something inspires feelings of kinship and respect

Most Pagans would feel comfortable with one or all of these meanings. Most Pagans see the universe and all its parts as rare, precious, and worthy of appreciation, respect, and careful handling. Pagans are filled with awe and wonder at the mysteries of the universe and believe that its sacred nature imposes a burden of stewardship on humanity. Because of their views on magick, which are explored in the next chapter, Pagans also frequently feel a sense of kinship and connection with the universe. Depending on their Deity beliefs, Pagans may also believe that Deity permeates the universe and therefore see the universe as holy and blessed. They may also believe that Deity's presence in creation shows that it is good, wholesome, and unflawed in its nature.

**Principle #6: Each part of the universe can communicate with each other part, and these parts often cooperate for specific ends.** Herein lies the heart of magick. Magick is a natural, not supernatural process, which, in its simplest form, is the communication and cooperation of many consciousnesses. Magick is a byproduct, if you will, of the natural functioning of the universe. As the sparks of intelligence, or consciousness, that make up the universe interact, they communicate. Based on this communication, they respond to each other and adjust their behavior, and can choose to cooperate toward a common end.

---

## questions to discuss

### FEELING INTERCONNECTED

1. What does the word "sacred" mean to you? How does it apply to your relationship with Deity, with others, and with the universe? Does it have any practical meaning or application for you?

2. Do the statements "Everything is alive," or "Everything has the spark of intelligence in it," mean anything to you? Have you ever had a sense that the universe is alive? If so, what was your experience and how did it affect your view of the universe?

3. What does consciousness mean to you? Do you believe it's possible for everything in the universe to be "conscious"? How does consciousness express itself? Do you think it's possible for its form to be different on levels other than this physical world? If so, what might consciousness look like in these other levels?

4. Have you ever had the experience of feeling connected to everything? What was it like? What insights did you come away with? What effect, if any, did this experience have on you?

# UNBROKEN WHOLENESS: SCIENCE AND A MAGICKAL UNIVERSE

As we covered earlier, the Pagan mystical view of the universe can be summed up as follows: Everything is sacred and alive (that is, shares the spark of consciousness or intelligence), and each part of the universe can communicate with each other part. One of the last places you might expect support for the Pagan view is from science, and yet recent discoveries in quantum physics point to a magickal universe. Many Pagans find these discoveries to be a source of inspiration. However, Paganism's view of a magickal, living universe is not in any way dependent on the findings of science.

This chapter provides an overview of scientific development as it relates to the existence of a living universe. Those readers who desire more technical and detailed information than what we provide here should check out the recommended reading list given for this chapter, and particularly *The Hidden Domain* by Norman Friedman and the additional sources he references. Even if you're not a big science fan, we think you will gain a lot from reading the following sections. You may be surprised by the recent and remarkable developments in science and the spiritual implications of some of these developments. If you wonder what science can possibly have to do with magick and spirituality—particularly Pagan spirituality—then you certainly should take a closer look at the next several pages.

## Newton's View Is Challenged

It didn't take long for the mechanistic view of the universe to run into difficulties. One problem with Newton's theory is action at a distance. How can the law of gravitation operate if the space between pieces of matter is a vacuum? Various theories were advanced, but generally took one of two positions: Either forces in the universe, such as gravitation and electromagnetism, are particles that travel through the vacuum of space, or space is not a vacuum but is filled with some mysterious substance that carries these forces on it like a wave. Thus began the wave-particle debate. Those scientists who favored the wave view postulated that the universe was filled with ether, an invisible fluid that carried the waves of gravitation and electromagnetism. However, the existence of an ether was experimentally disproven by Albert Michelson and Edward Morley by 1887. In 1864, James Maxwell established that electromagnetic energy was transmitted from one point to another by a mysterious agent called "fields."

The wave-particle debate spilled over into discussions of the nature of light. Classical physicists wondered, "Is light a particle or a wave?" Newton was of the opinion that light is a particle. In 1801, the issue of the nature of light seemed to be put to rest by the scientist Thomas Young, who conducted what has come to be known as the "two-slit experiment." His experiment established the nature of light as a wave. Young put a light beam behind a screen with a small slit in it. In front of this screen he placed a second screen containing two slits. In front of that he placed a third screen to catch the light emitted from the two slits of the second screen. The light beam traveled through the first slit, then split to go through the two slits, and then illuminated the third screen with two areas of light, each partially overlapping the other.

Young knew that if light is a particle, the overlapping area would be brighter than any other area as it would receive particles from both slits. This didn't happen. Instead, the third screen showed a pattern of light and dark bands. This result occurs only when light acts as a wave; the phases of the light waves reinforce or cancel each other. Where they reinforce each other, the light is brighter. Where they cancel each other, the light is dimmer. These patterns of light and dark bands are called "interference patterns." Interference patterns will be discussed later in the chapter in regard to holograms.

## Quantum Theory

For nearly one hundred years the idea that light is a wave went essentially unchallenged. This changed in 1900 with Max Planck's studies of the absorption of light by black bodies, that is, objects that do not reflect back any frequency of light. As Planck ran his experiments, he observed that as the temperature of a black body is raised and lowered, it emits radiation at various frequencies. He expected the radiation to flow continuously, as one would expect from a wave, but it did not. Instead, it came in discrete batches that behaved like particles. He called these batches "quanta." Einstein, a contemporary of Planck, was intrigued by his discovery, and went on to show mathematically that light is absorbed, as well as radiated, in batches of quanta. Thus, "quantum theory" was born.

Due to Young's earlier experiments, most physicists of Planck's day thought of light as a wave. Thinking of light as a particle was more difficult. Although many scientists were uncomfortable with the idea that light could be both a particle and a wave, the idea stuck and eventually light "particles" came to be called "photons." If light can act as a particle, would something we expect to act as a particle act like a wave?

## Those Pesky Particles

In Newton's time, the smallest bits of matter known were atoms. Since then, scientists have discovered that atoms are composed of even smaller bits, such as the electron, proton, and neutron. These subatomic bits have classically been viewed as particles, similar to marbles or billiard balls. If we were to substitute electrons for light in Young's experiment, what would happen? If electrons really are particles, the overlapping areas of the third screen will be more heavily hit. When the two-slit experiment was conducted using electrons, however, the electrons created the same sort of interference pattern as light. This remained true even when the electrons were fired one at a time so that they could not interact with each other. Scientists were so confounded by this development that they decided the single electron must be breaking in two, going through both slits at once, and then interfering with itself. To decide this question, a measuring device was put at each slit. As the electrons were fired one at a time, they went through only one slit or the other, just as we would expect from particles. So what happened? The interference pattern on the third screen then ceased to exist! The electrons stopped acting like waves altogether when they were measured. Scientists were left with the conclusion that when we look directly at an electron, it acts like a particle, but when we don't, it acts like a wave.

This paradox was summarized by the scientist Niels Bohr in 1927 in what became known as the "Copenhagen interpretation," now accepted by a majority of physicists around the world. Bohr stated that at the quantum level a particle has no properties unless it is being observed and measured. Particles of matter exist only as potentialities that become fixed, or *develop into particles,* when they come into contact with a measuring device. The scientist Werner Heisenberg postulated that beneath physical reality is a deeper level filled with what he calls "potentia." At this level, matter does not exist, but only has *tendencies* to exist, and all possible events—even contradictory ones—reside together in potential. The act of measurement causes one of the potential states to come into being.

## The Wave Function

In the early 1900s, a scientist named Louis de Broglie went beyond the issue of the characteristics of light and proposed that *all* matter has wave-like characteristics.[2] These wavelike properties can be described as a wave field or wave function. The wave function is not something you can see, nor does it exist in three-dimensional space, but its effects can be observed. Every particle of matter has its own wave function (39), which can be visualized as a "smear," or a representation of all the paths it may take.[3] The scientist Richard Feynman theorized that the potential particle takes *all* possible paths as its wave moves from point A to point B, so that when the wave reaches point B, it contains information from every path it could have taken to get there.[4] When the particle is observed, however, its wave function collapses and only one path becomes actualized.

Why does one probability get chosen for the particle rather than another? Who or what makes these choices, and at what level are these choices made? Many of the scientists who study the nature of reality theorize that levels of reality exist underneath or parallel to this one and are where these choices are made.[5] If such levels exist, how are they connected, and how is information passed between them?

## Bell's Theorem and Non-locality

In 1964, the scientist John Stewart Bell proposed in what is known as Bell's theorem that after two particles meet, they continue to influence each other. The influence is not caused by nuclear forces, gravity, or electromagnetism, but exists because each particle leaves a part of itself with the other, thus allowing them to communicate instantaneously.[6] What do they leave? Not a piece of matter, but a piece of *information*. Particles are less like balls of stuff and more like information packets. Instantaneous communication is theoretically not possible in a universe limited by the speed of light, so Bell proposed that this connection between particles occurs outside of space-time. His theory was later proven by laboratory experiment, and instantaneous communication between particles, also called "non-locality," became a provable fact.

Already we have moved quite a distance from Newton. Instead of an empty, three-dimensional space filled with billiard-ball-like pieces of matter, quantum physics portrays a universe that acts as a seamless whole, where each part communicates instantaneously with every other part, and is filled with waves of information that arise from levels outside of space-time. In a Newtonian world, the whole is the sum of its parts. In a quantum world, the whole oversees, and perhaps even creates, the parts.

## Is the Universe a Hologram?

The hologram may offer a way to visualize the wholeness of the universe (Figure 5.1). A hologram, as you may know, is a three-dimensional image of an object that is created by means of a particular photographic process. During this process, light beams that strike the image being photographed are later reunited, and when this occurs they create an interference pattern on a photographic plate. This interference pattern doesn't look like a photograph at all, but a complex pattern of concentric rings. However, when a laser beam is later shined through the plate, a three-dimensional image of the object appears again. You can walk completely around a holographic image and see it from every angle. If you try to touch it, however, your hand will pass through it.

Holograms are further remarkable in that if you take the holographic plate, break it in two, and shine a light through the pieces, you will see a complete image of the object in each half of the plate. If you continue to break the plate into pieces, each piece continues to produce a complete, three-dimensional image of the object.

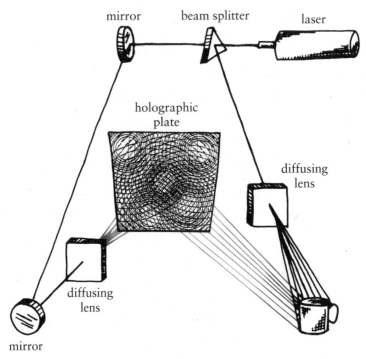

**FIGURE 5.1**
The production of a hologram.

Unlike a regular photograph, there is no one spot on the plate that corresponds to one part of the object. Rather, every part of a hologram embeds within it the entire image. Stated another way, the picture of the image is *enfolded* into the interference patterns. In this enfolded state, the image is essentially invisible, but when laser light hits the plate and the image reappears, we say that is has *unfolded* into reality.

## The Holomovement and David Bohm

In 1980, the physicist David Bohm theorized that the universe continuously enfolds and unfolds itself from waves to particles and back again. He called this activity of the universe the *holomovement*. The process of enfolding and unfolding may occur many billions of times a second—so quickly that it is not discernible to us.

Bohm compared the holomovement to a demonstration he saw while watching TV.[7] In this demonstration, a jar was filled with glycerine, a heavy clear liquid. In the center of the jar was a cylinder connected to a crank handle on top. A drop of ink was added to the glycerine and the handle of the cylinder slowly turned. As the cylinder turned, the ink drop began to smear and mix into the glycerine until it was no longer visible. Yet as the handle was turned back in the opposite direction, the smear reversed itself and the ink reformed into the original drop.

Like the ink drop, Bohm theorized that the universe diffuses as it enfolds and appears not to exist. Then, as the cycle reverses, the universe unfolds into existence again, into something that can be seen.

Bohm theorized that the ink drop disappears into what he calls the *implicate order,* and that it unfolds, or becomes visible again, in what he terms the *explicate order.*[8] Within the implicate order, consciousness and matter are not distinct from each other, and therefore cannot be interacted with independently. The material world, in effect, acts as a tool that separates matter and consciousness so they can interact in creative and meaningful ways while still experiencing the stability of a physical world. It is possible that the implicate order needs the display of physical reality in order to function and express itself. How would you, for example, be able to check your e-mail or play a computer game if you had no monitor on which to see what is happening inside your computer? As Bohm said, "Life-energy is more than just biological organization; it reaches into intelligence. Guided by a display, it can do almost anything, but without a display it has nothing to do."[9]

## String Theory

String theory, which was first proposed in the 1970s, suggests that the universe is not composed of particles as we think of them, but of very small loops of string that vibrate at certain frequencies. As Brian Greene, a string theory physicist, says in his book *The Elegant Universe,* the universe consists of "loops of strings and oscillating globules, uniting all of creation into vibrational patterns that are meticulously executed in a universe with numerous hidden dimensions capable of undergoing extreme contortions in which their spatial fabric tears apart and then repairs itself" (386). The frequency at which the strings vibrate determines what the string is; that is, electrons vibrate one way, photons another. These strings are so small that we currently cannot see them, being only $10^{-33}$ centimeters long, also called the Planck length. String theory postulates that the Planck length is as small as things get in this physical universe. String theory does not attempt to describe what might exist below the Planck length.

Our study of string theory has not yet revealed how it explains non-locality (i.e., simultaneous communication between separated particles that seems to exceed the speed of light) as proven in Bell's theorem, nor does it directly address the hierarchy of levels proposed by Bohm. This may be because string theory is silent on these points, or because we have not studied string theory long and hard enough. However, our initial impression of string theory is that it does not conflict with either non-locality or Bohm's hierarchy of levels, since both of the latter are postulated to occur outside of space-time, or below the Planck length. String theory may one day address these deeper levels, as Brian Greene tells us on page 387 of *The Elegant Universe:* "We have seen glimpses of a strange new domain of the universe lurking beneath the Planck length, possibly one in which there is no notion of time or space. At the opposite extreme, we have also seen that our universe may merely be one of the innumerable frothing bubbles on the surface of a vast and turbulent cosmic ocean called the multiverse. These ideas are at the current edge of speculation, but they may presage the next leap in our understanding of the universe."

## Paganism's Perspective

For the most part, Pagans are at ease with recent scientific discoveries and its retreat from a Newtonian, mechanistic view of the universe. Most Pagans we have met seem to understand intuitively that this reality is a physical display and that a lot more than we readily perceive is going on at other levels. Pagans use magick, meditation, dance, singing, ecstatic sex, and shamanic journeys, among many other things, to reach an altered state of consciousness from which they can sense the hidden levels of the universe and actively participate in them. Science's recent discoveries act as a source of inspiration for many Pagans who are seeking to understand how and why magick works on a practical level, and to find ways in which they can cooperate better with the universe. It also gives Pagans a starting point from which to speak to those who dismiss Paganism, particularly Pagan magickal practice, as superstitious and irrational.

Quantum experiments are confirming what Pagans already know: That *all* parts of the universe—from the smallest to the largest—are alive with a spark of intelligence, and that the universe communicates, responds, and shares information instantaneously among all parts of itself.

## questions to discuss

### YOUR VIEW OF THE UNIVERSE

1. Before you heard of Paganism or became a Pagan, what did you believe about the function and organization of the universe? Has studying Paganism caused you to change or reconsider any of those beliefs?

2. Is the Pagan view of the universe as sacred, alive, and communicative more appealing to you than the current Western mindset? Where do you think you fit into such a universe? How might Paganism's view of the universe change how we behave in it?

3. How does your view of the universe impact your spirituality?

## visualization

### FEELING THE SPACE IN AND AROUND YOU

*Take a moment to review the suggestions for visualizations given at the beginning of the visualization in chapter 2. Remember to pause where marked by dots (. . .) to give those participating time to visualize. This visualization[10] is very quiet and internal and plenty of time should be provided to follow your directions. For this visualization we suggest ten or fifteen seconds for the pauses marked by dots (. . .), and thirty seconds for those marked with "[longer pause]," though these should be adjusted to fit the pace of the group.*

Get in a comfortable position. If you are sitting, put your feet flat on the floor. If you are lying down, put your arms beside you and your legs out straight.

Close your eyes. . . . Let go of the concerns of the day. . . . Feel yourself beginning to relax. [*longer pause*] As you relax you become aware of the beating of your heart. Listen to your heart beating. [*longer pause*] Feel your heartbeat throughout your body. . . .

Now gradually turn your attention from your heartbeat to your breathing. . . . Feel yourself breathe in . . . and breathe out . . . breathe in . . . and breathe out. . . . Relax into the rhythm of your breathing. [*longer pause*] Notice the quiet point that exists in the space between your breaths. [*longer pause*]

Begin to expand your awareness so that you feel this quiet point of space all around you. . . . Notice the space around your body. . . . Feel the space that is above you. . . . Feel the space to your left . . . to your right. . . . Feel the space that is beneath you. . . . Feel this space on the outside of you. . . . Feel it on the inside. [*longer pause*]

Notice that the space inside of you feels the same as the space outside of you. [*longer pause*] What you call the inside of you, and what you call the outside of you is only a distinction you have chosen to make. [*longer pause*] Notice that what you call you, and what you call not-you is a subjective decision you have made. [*longer pause*] [*If the group is not restless, this pause can last a minute or two.*]

Now find that point of you that is aware of itself. . . . This is your consciousness. [*longer pause*] See yourself as being made up entirely of consciousness; . . . not just the part of you that is aware of itself, but every cell of your body. [*longer pause*] Focus your consciousness into the space you call the inside of you. . . . How does this feel? [*longer pause*] Now focus your consciousness into the space you call the outside of you. . . . Does this feel different or the same? [*longer pause*]

Now bring your consciousness back into your body and become aware again of your breathing: . . . in . . . out . . . in . . . out . . . [*match this to their breathing*]. Gradually become aware of the rest of your body: your head . . . your arms . . . your back . . . your legs . . . your feet. . . . Feel the chair (or floor) beneath you. . . . Feel yourself coming back into the room. . . . When you are ready, open your eyes.

*Let yourself get reoriented. If you are in a group, take a few minutes to be sure everyone is "back." If anyone is having difficulty reorienting, keep them warm and offer a warm drink or snack. Then ask who would like to share their experience. Get a comment from everyone if possible.*

## THE GROUND OF BEING: MYSTICISM AND A MAGICKAL UNIVERSE

Another source many Pagans use to understand and connect with the magickal universe is the writings of mystics, both ancient and modern. A mystic is a person who has direct, personal contact with the Divine or the universe, usually within a religious context. Mystical experiences, however, can occur in all times and places, even to those people who are not particularly religious. These experiences are not limited to persons of a particular faith, age, or spiritual development. Mystical experiences can happen without warning or any preparation on the mystic's part.

Despite their occurrence in every time, place, and religious setting, mystical experiences are uncannily similar in their messages. This phenomenon was initially articulated by the historian Aldous Huxley, who described what he called a "perennial philosophy" underlying the writings of mystics. The primary message of this perennial philosophy, according to Huxley, is that there is an Absolute Principle or Ground of Being, and that all of us and all of creation are one with it.[11] Also, this Ground exists outside of time in an eternal now and in a realm where traditional language is inadequate. As Roger Walsh, a professor of philosophy and anthropology and a mystical scholar, puts it, "This domain is not limited by space or time or physical laws, since it creates space, time, and physical laws, and hence it is unbounded and infinite, timeless and eternal."[12]

Mystics also tend to perceive that the material world flows from and is supported by this Ground, and that all of physical reality is interconnected through it. As Andrew Harvey, a mystical scholar, describes it, "We see that we are all parts of a whole, elements of an universal harmony, unique, essential and sacred notes in a divine music."[13] Mysticism, then, also points to the universe as magickal—sacred, alive, and interconnected. Although mystics tend to express themselves in the language of their faith, the magickal universe is still clearly visible.

The mystics of ancient and primitive peoples tell of our interconnectedness with nature. They speak of the web of life. They view the material world as saturated with the presence of the Divine, urge us to respect all things, and to accept our responsibility to act as guardians of the natural world. As an example, see the poem below from a speech given by Chief Seattle to Governor Isaac Stevens of the Washington Territory in 1855.

> Teach your children
> What we have taught our children—
> That the earth is our mother.
> Whatever befalls the earth
> Befalls the sons and daughters of the earth.
> If men spit upon the ground,
> They spit upon themselves.
> This we know.
> The earth does not belong to us;
> We belong to the earth.
> This we know.
> All things are connected
> Like the blood which unites one family.
> All things are connected.
> Whatever befalls the earth
> Befalls the sons and daughters of the earth.
> We did not weave the web of life;
> We are merely a strand in it.
> Whatever we do to the web,
> We do to ourselves. . . .[14]

The mystics of the Eastern traditions encourage us to "wake up" and know ourselves, and not to let the desires and pains of human experience act as a block to our enlightenment. Taoism describes the Tao as the infinitely mysterious Oneness from which all things spring, are sustained, and to which they return at death. The Tao is described as the creative force and the ordering principle of life. The Tao is also a way of living life that is in tune with the mystery and is peaceful, balanced, and joyful. See the passage below from the *Tao Te Ching*.

> Something exists which was born before heaven and earth,
> Which stands still, silent, and alone.

It does not change or end
And yet is mother to the world.
I do not know its name, but I call it The Way.
If I must give it a name, I will call it Great.[15]

The Hindus call the ultimate reality that is nameless, formless, and beyond definition, *Brahman.* The Hindus conceive Brahman as a Presence of Pure Being, Pure Consciousness, and Pure Bliss. Hindu mystics assert that humans are one with Brahman in their *atman,* or soul. The following passage comes from the *Svetasvatara Upanishad* (c. 800 B.C.E.).

If you come to know the One hidden in all things,
Like cream hidden within butter,
The One who embraces the universe,
Then you will be released from all fetters.
The Great Soul is found in the heart of creatures;
Framed by the heart, by the thought, by the mind,
With this One there is no day or night,
No being or non-being, only It alone.
It is Imperishable, the choicest splendor of the Sun,
Created from primeval Intelligence.
This One has no above, below, or middle where It can be grasped,
There is no likeness of It, whose name is Great Glory,
Its form cannot be seen with the eye.
Those who know It with their hearts and minds,
Who know that it is within them, become immortal.[16]

The Jewish mystics see God as inhabiting every part of nature and every aspect of human life. They believe this life should be a mirror of God's holiness and justice. The Jewish mystics introduced God as an agent actively involved in human history. They also envisioned the principle of Shekinah, or Wisdom, a female energy that was seen as ". . . the emanation of the utterly unknowable Source in reality and the glory of God within both creation and the individual soul."[17] This is clearly expressed in the passage from Proverbs below.

Does not Wisdom cry? and understanding put forth her voice?
She standeth in the top of high places, by the way in the places of the paths.
She crieth at the gates, at the entry of the city, at the coming in at the doors.
Unto you O men, I call; and my voice is to the sons of man.
Counsel is mine, and sound Wisdom:
I am understanding; I have strength.

The Lord possessed me in the beginning of his way, before the works of old.
I was set up from everlasting, from the beginning, or ever the earth was.
When there were no depths, I was brought forth;
When there were no fountains abounding with water.
Before the mountains were settled, before the hills was I brought forth;
While as yet he had not made the earth, nor the fields,
Nor the highest part of the dust of the world.
When he prepared the heavens, I was there:
When he set a compass upon the face of the depth:
When he established the clouds above:
When he strengthened the fountains of the deep:
When he gave to the sea his decree,
That the waters should not pass his commandment:
When he appointed the foundations of the earth:
Then I was by him, as one brought up with him:
And I was daily his delight, rejoicing always before him.[18]

Islamic mystics, the Sufis, speak of the grandeur of God, and see the relationship between people and the Divine as very intimate and mysterious, even passionate. This relationship is beautifully expressed in the following selections by Rumi and Mahmud Shabestari, respectively, both of whom were Sufi mystics in the thirteenth century.

Wondrous is the moment we meet in the palace, you and I,
Two bodies, two faces, and yet one soul, you and I,
The flowers are ablaze, birdsong surrounds us with immortality
As soon as we enter the garden, you and I.
The stars gaze down on us
And we shine as if we were the full moon itself, you and I.
Heaven's fiery birds are consumed with envy of us,
Exhilarated we laugh, you and I.
Such a miracle, entwined together, you and I,
Such a miracle, one lover, one flame, you and I,
We are together now and in the world to come,
In a rapture without end.[19]

The world is a mirror.
In each atom blaze a thousand suns,
In each droplet gush a hundred oceans,
Within a grain of sand is the promise of future beings.
The ant looms larger than the elephant.
In its heart, one droplet is the Nile,

Within the seed live a hundred future harvests,
Within the corn the entire cosmos,
On the wing of an insect, a sea of wonder,
In the center of the eye, heaven eternal.
Even though the human heart is small,
The Lord of earth and heaven has made it His home.[20]

The Christian mystics frequently focus on love in action. When we are transformed, we mirror God's overwhelming love for humanity. This is not a fluffy love, but one that demands all of one's self. Christ's sacrifice on the cross is an example of this complete giving of one's self. Hadewijch, a nun of the fifteenth century, describes the demands of this divine love in the following passage:

Those of you who wish to enjoy the divine here on earth,
Dancing with it in ecstasy and delight,
Dwelling in it with pleasure,
Must adorn yourselves with virtues
Or this whole course of study will be lost on you.

Arrange your lives for the pursuing of divine love,
And you shall be enlightened by reason and insight.
Love will place you in her school
Where you shall become a master and receive her highest gifts,
Which wound beyond any cure.

Those of you wounded in this way shall be shown
The knowable and unknowable vastnesses within her.
You will sometimes feel great hunger,
Sometimes great satisfaction.
Your longings shall keep you unhealed,
But this should not surprise you.

For is not nature cut down and reborn,
Wounded, and then returned with even greater growth?
So it is also with yourselves.
Neither blossoming nor withering can harm you,
No season deter you.
Every season can be one of advancement in Love.[21]

Thomas Traherne, an Anglican minister who lived in the seventeenth century, offers another perspective:

The whole world is the theater for our love.
We are made to love, both to satisfy this necessity within us
and also to answer the love of creation around us.
By love our souls are joined and married to the world around us.
If we focus upon only one part of creation,
we are not loving it too much, but the other parts too little.
Never was anything in this world loved too much.
What a treasure is a grain of sand when it is truly understood!
All infinite goodness and wisdom and power are in it.
What a world this would be if everything were loved as it should be.[22]

## visualization

# THE CONSCIOUSNESS IN ALL THINGS

*See the visualization earlier in the chapter for instructions. As before, this visualization is very quiet and interior, and plenty of time should be given to picture the images. Don't start this visualization unless you have plenty of time; it should not be rushed through.*

Get in a comfortable position. If you are sitting, put your feet flat on the floor. If you are lying down, put your arms beside you and your legs out straight.

Close your eyes. . . . Feel yourself beginning to relax. [*longer pause*] As you relax, you become aware of the beating of your heart. . . . Listen to your heart beating. [*longer pause*] Feel your heartbeat throughout your body. . . .

Now gradually turn your attention from your heartbeat to your breathing. . . . Feel yourself breathe in . . . and breathe out . . . breathe in . . . and breathe out. . . . Relax into the rhythm of your breathing. [*longer pause*] Notice the quiet point that exists in the space between your breaths. [*longer pause*]

Begin to expand your awareness so that you feel this quiet point of space all around you. . . . Notice the space around your body. . . . Feel the space that is above you. . . . Feel the space to your left . . . and to your right. . . . Feel the space that is beneath you. . . . Feel this space on the outside of you.

. . . Feel it on the inside. [*longer pause*] As before, you notice that the space inside of you feels the same as the space outside of you. . . . What you call the inside of you, and what you call the outside of you is only a distinction you have chosen to make. [*longer pause*]

Now notice that what you call "you" is made up of a bundle of consciousness. . . . See the part of you that is aware of itself. . . . See that it is made up of consciousness. . . . See that every cell of your body is alive with its own consciousness. [*longer pause*] Greet the consciousness of your body and acknowledge it. [*longer pause*] Hear its greeting back to you. . . . Feel the tremendous cooperation that exists among the cells of your body . . . and between your body and the point of focus you call "you." [*longer pause*] What is the consciousness of your body like? . . . How does it feel or show itself to you? . . . Does it feel like a dance . . . or a song? . . . Does it have its own rhythm or frequency? . . . Do you see images or pictures? . . . What does it feel like to you? [*long pause—up to one minute*] Is there anything your body wants to tell you at this time? [*another long pause*]

Begin now to turn your attention away from your own consciousness and toward that space you consider to be outside of yourself. [*longer pause*] Notice that the space outside of you feels the same as the space inside. . . . Notice that this space contains the whole universe. . . . You can now see that everything in the universe is made up of consciousness. [*longer pause*] What does this consciousness feel like? [*longer pause*] How does it show itself to you: . . . as a vibration or frequency? . . . an energy? . . . a movement or sound? . . . Do you see images or pictures? . . . Do you feel any emotions? [*long pause—up to a minute*]

See that the consciousness of the whole universe surrounds you and flows away from you in all directions like a vast sea. [*longer pause*] See yourself as a part of this vast living ocean of energy. . . . Understand that what separates you from the vastness is your point of focus. . . . What you call "you" and what you call "not-you" in this ocean is a function of your focus. . . . It is a function of your will and intention aimed at one certain point and expression of being. [*longer pause*] Even though it is vast, this living ocean will not overwhelm or consume you. . . . You are a valid and meaningful part of the whole. . . .

Now greet the consciousness of all things and acknowledge them. . . . Let them greet you in return. [*longer pause*] Feel the tremendous cooperation that exists among all the parts of this sea of consciousness . . . and between the universe and the point of focus you call "you." [*longer pause*] Is there anything this living ocean wants to tell you at this time? [*long pause—up to a minute*]

Know that you can connect with this sea of consciousness whenever you wish. . . . Know that you can connect with the consciousness of your body whenever you wish. . . . Bid them farewell for now, and begin to bring your consciousness back into your body. [*longer pause*] Become aware again of your breathing: . . . in . . . out . . . in . . . out . . . [*match this to their breathing*]. Gradually become aware of the rest of your body: your head . . . your arms . . . your back . . . your legs . . . your feet. . . . Feel the chair (or floor) beneath you. . . . Feel yourself coming back into the room. . . . When you are ready, open your eyes.

*Let yourself get reoriented. If you are in a group, take a few minutes to be sure everyone is "back." As before, provide warm drinks and a snack for anyone having trouble getting reoriented. Then ask who would like to share their experience. Get a comment from everyone if possible.*

## questions to discuss

## CONNECTING TO THE SEA OF CONSCIOUSNESS

1. Were you able to connect with and sense your own consciousness and that of your body? Were you able to connect with the living ocean of the universe? What visualizations or impressions came to you? Is this visualization starting to get easier? Did your body or the universe have something to say to you? What was it?

2. What do you think that scientists and mystics are trying to say about us and this universe? What is Paganism saying? What does all of it mean to you? Does it have any impact on your life or spirituality?

3. Have you ever had an experience you would consider mystical? What was it like and what happened? How did it affect you?

## EXPRESSING YOUR EXPERIENCE WITH THE UNIVERSE

This exercise contains a variety of methods for expressing your recent experiences in meditation. Give them all a try, though you may find that some work better for you than others. If something is really working for you, stay with it, and eventually come back to the others.

Take a sheet of paper, a drawing pad, or canvas, and draw your experience either of your own consciousness or the universal consciousness. How did it appear to you? What did it feel like? Draw what you saw and felt. It can be as concrete or abstract as you care to make it. You can write words, pictures, symbols, or other images. You can use pencils, pens, charcoal, or paints. Be creative. There is no right or wrong here. Your artistic ability doesn't matter. You don't have to show this drawing to anyone if you don't want to. However, if you wish to share it, that's fine. If you're doing this in a group setting, it can be very helpful and enlightening to see everyone's drawings and hear what they mean.

Once you have finished with your drawing, you need a noisemaker. If you have a drum, tambourine, or rattle, go get it. If you don't have one, you can borrow one or make one. Improvise. A kettle or metal trash can turned upside down makes a fine drum. A jar with some popcorn kernels in it makes a great rattle. Once you have a noisemaker, put your picture in front of you and sit quietly for a moment. Put yourself mentally back into your recent visualization. Find the feeling again of what it was like to experience the vastness of the universe, the cooperation of consciousness, or the consciousness of your body. Get in touch with what moved you most.

When you are there, ask yourself how your experience felt rhythmically. What was its beat, its pulse, its frequency, its rhythm? Begin to drum or rattle in time with this rhythm. Allow yourself to float into the experience and become one with this rhythm. This *is* the pulse of the universe as it expresses itself to you. It can be loud, it can be soft, it can be very simple, or more complex. There is no right or wrong here either. Relax into your drumming or rattling and go with it for as long as you like—five minutes, fifteen minutes, a half an hour. Let it become a meditation for you. Let your mind relax, as this is not a thinking meditation but a vibrational one. You may find yourself getting flashes of things—insights or feelings—that you didn't in the earlier meditation. Go with it. If you are in a group setting, each person should be given the opportunity to drum or rattle his or her rhythms individually while the rest of the group listens. Be respectful and supportive. The group can then drum together for a time and go into a meditative space together. We recommend you do this exercise on your own, even if you have done it with a group. If there is a drumming circle in your area, try this exercise again with them.

After your drumming or rattling has ended, and while you are still in your meditative space, stand up and get in touch with the consciousness of your body. Find the sound or tone that represents the vibration or frequency of your body. If your body could sing itself, what sounds would it make? Make those sounds. You can shout, laugh, sing, or hum. You can sing one note or a whole tune. If you are in a group, let each person make his or her sounds one at a time. We know this can make some people uncomfortable, but give it a try; it won't be as bad as you think! Then let everyone in the group make all their sounds together for about five minutes. It doesn't matter if they harmonize or clash.

The final method of this exercise is to feel your consciousness and connection to the universe in your body. If you could dance the living universe, what would that be like? If you are alone, you can put on music or move to silence. If you are in a group, everyone can dance at the same time, preferably to music. If people are embarrassed, you can lower the lighting in the room, blindfold everyone, or ask them to close their eyes. That way everyone can move without worrying about how they look. You can use taped music or a live drumming group if you have access to one. If a drumming group is meeting or performing in your area, this can be a good opportunity to go dance. Best of all, if you can attend a Pagan festival known for its drumming and dancing, go and be sure to set aside an hour or so one night for this exercise.

Before you begin, get quiet and mentally put yourself back into your recent visualizations. Feel your self, the intelligence of your body, and the pulsing of the vast and living universe that surrounds you. Feel how all these things cooperate and respond to each other. Feel yourself as a part of it. Then begin to move. You can move slowly, you can move fast, you can walk, you can dance, you can whirl, you can wave your arms in the air, you can lay on the ground, you can crawl. It doesn't matter. Relax into your dance. Let it become a meditation for you. This is not a thinking meditation, but a kinesthetic one. Your mind can be quiet. Let all parts of your body join in the dance; let them express themselves. You will probably find yourself going into an altered state and that's fine. You may find yourself getting flashes of things—insights or feelings—that you didn't in the earlier meditations. Be open to whatever comes to you. We suggest you not dance longer than an hour or two at most. No need to overdo it your first time! If you think you may lose track of time, ask a friend to come get you in two hours.

At the end of all these exercises, write down what happened and what it meant to you. What methods of expression did you like best? Did any not work at all for you? What might that tell you about the best ways for you to connect to the universe? What further insights, feelings, or images came to you through these exercises? You can repeat some or all of these exercises from time to time as you wish, or create your own.

## THE UNIVERSE AS A COSMIC TV

In order to help our students pull together the various spiritual, scientific, and mystical concepts we cover in this chapter, Joyce and I developed a model of the universe that we call the Cosmic TV. Television is a good model because most people are familiar with it, and the way in which TVs function happens to offer a nice analogy to the workings of the magickal universe. You may find that viewing the universe as a TV helps you make sense of the ideas in this chapter and understand how they work on a more practical level.

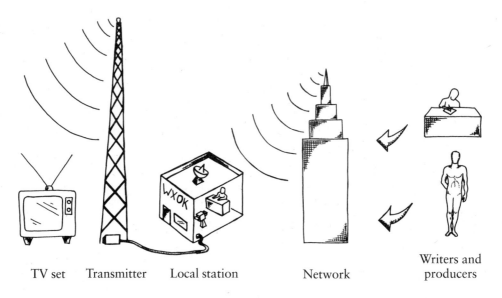

**FIGURE 5.2**
The Cosmic TV.

Notice in Figure 5.2 that the Cosmic TV is composed of several parts. First is the TV set, which displays a picture. The picture comes from a signal that the TV set picks up through its antennae. (For the purposes of our illustration we're sticking with a no-frills, low-budget TV complete with rabbit ears, although cable and satellite would fit the analogy just as well.) The signal travels to the TV after it has been broadcast from a transmitter tower. The transmitter receives its signal from a station. The station creates the signal and then adds some programming. What programming it does not create it receives from a network. The network creates programming and also receives programming from producers who are independently creating movies, documentaries, and the like.

The first part of the Cosmic TV is the TV set. This is the display of physical reality. Without it, none of what is occurring at the transmitter, station, network, or producers would ever be known or seen by any of us. The TV is equipped, by means of its antennae and internal components, to take the invisible signal it receives and turn it into a graphical display. In the same manner, the three-dimensional world takes the wave functions permeating the universe and breaks them down into physical reality. David Bohm, as you'll remember, called the display the "explicate order."

The TV displays its pictures from information that comes to it as a signal. This signal is produced at a station, carried to a transmitter tower, and then broadcast by the tower as radio waves that travel through the air. The transmitter's job is to change the station's signal into a form the TV can perceive. The transmitter must "unfold" the signal before it can be perceived successfully.

David Bohm saw the physical universe—the explicate order—as arising from a hidden reality he called the "implicate order." Just as with the station signal, the information coming from the implicate order is not immediately useable by physical reality. The information has to be "unfolded" in order to be experienced. The TV transmitter and signal, then, is in many ways equivalent to David Bohm's implicate order (Figure 5.3).

Like the implicate order, the transmitter exists in a realm not immediately perceived by our TV set. The transmitter and the implicate order are the first point of contact between the physical display and deeper levels of reality. You will notice that the transmitter and implicate order do not create the content, or programming, that is transmitted. To find the source of the content you must look to deeper realms, or as David Bohm would say, to more "subtle" realms, such as the station and network.

The station creates local programming, such as newscasts and advertising, which it combines with programming received from the network. The station then translates its programming into an electronic signal, which it forwards to the transmitter. One part of the station is oriented toward the transmitter, or the physical realm. If the station did not create a signal and did not see to it that the transmitter received this signal, our TV screen would always stay blank. The station is also oriented toward more subtle realms, such as the network. The station, then, participates in an exchange of meaning and information between a more physical realm on the one hand, and a more subtle one on the other.

Bohm believed that the universe may be ordered in increasingly subtle levels as we move away from physical reality. You can see this at work with the TV. The transmitter is a step removed from the TV set, the station is a step further removed, and the network and producers are even further removed. The TV set

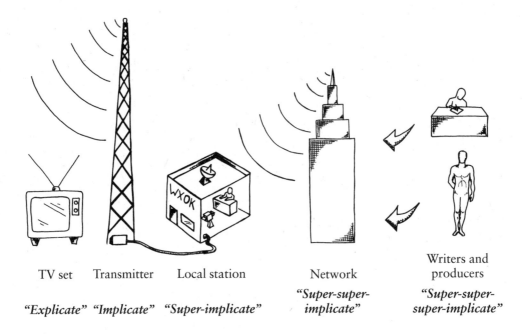

**FIGURE 5.3**
Bohm's subtle levels of reality in the Cosmic TV.

cannot communicate directly with the network. It cannot, in fact, even perceive that it exists. In order for the TV to function properly, each level must interact meaningfully with the levels on either side of it. Following the implicate order comes the next deeper level, which Bohm calls the "super-implicate order." Like our station, the super-implicate order gives input into the purpose, form, and meaning of what will be experienced in the physical realm. The will and intentions of the super-implicate order determine what will eventually be seen on the TV set of the physical world.

As the station creates and controls the signal sent to the transmitter, so the network controls some decisions and programming of the station. The network, using Bohm's terms, would be another level deeper still, or a "super-super-implicate order." Then, behind the network lies a powerhouse of producers who create additional programming for the network to use as it sees fit. These producers are a "super-super-super-implicate order." Bohm suggests that the levels of order in the universe may be infinite.

While Bohm's orders go on to infinity, our analogy ends here. Still, you can see from the Cosmic TV how one level leads to and interconnects with the next, and how each level exchanges information through it to the levels on either side. This flow is similar to Bohm's holomovement. The levels of orders do not exist as a hierarchy but as a continuum, with the holomovement occurring constantly as a flow of information from the more subtle to the more physical and back again. The TV display, which you know as physical reality, is just one expression of the universal flow that operates on many levels.

There is another interesting aspect to the Cosmic TV, and that is the way in which the TV set creates the picture on its screen. You may think that the picture on a TV appears completely formed. This is true with a motion picture, where each frame of the film contains a complete image, which the projector simply illuminates; by running the frames quickly, you see the illusion of movement and action. Not so with a television; unlike a motion picture, the TV draws each screen one dot at a time. It starts at the upper left corner of the screen and, going back and forth, draws a picture with colored dots until it reaches the bottom of the screen.

When the picture is complete, the TV goes back, checks the signal, and begins drawing the next screen based on what the signal tells it to do. You do not see this occur because it happens too fast to notice. With each passing second the TV draws sixty complete screens, one dot at a time. At this rate of speed, you are left with the illusion that the picture is always there and that one image flows seamlessly into the next.

In the same way, quantum physicists believe that the physical display of the universe is "drawn" many times a second. Bohm called this enfolding and unfolding. Other scientists refer to it as "blinking on and off." Although it's not known precisely how fast the universe does this, some scientists believe it may be as fast as $5.3 \times 10^{-44}$ seconds (derived from "Planck time"[23]), which is pretty darn fast. Because the universe blinks on and off so rapidly, our experience of physical reality is constant. None of us ever notice when it blinks off. We believe it is always there. Just as with the TV, we see one seamless image.

This particular aspect of the universe has some interesting implications for magick. If, as you saw with Bohm's ink drop, the universe blinks off or enfolds and disappears from this reality, where does it go? Bohm suggested that the universe enfolds back into the implicate order; and since the implicate order is also blinking on and off, it enfolds itself back into the super-implicate order. The super-implicate order then enfolds itself back into the super-super-implicate order, and so on, perhaps infinitely. On its return trip, the ink drop unfolds itself from the super-super-implicate, to the super-implicate, to the implicate, and finally to the explicate, where it "blinks on." As it makes this journey, the ink drop is exposed to all the information available at every level it passes through. So if the universe is indeed holographic in nature, this means it is exposed to all information known everywhere, not only what it encounters directly.

Our Cosmic TV works the same way. Sixty times a second a picture is drawn on the screen by the TV set; and sixty times a second the screen is also blank. The TV set goes back into *its* implicate order—the signal—and gathers from it the information the TV needs to draw the next screen. This signal contains information created by deeper levels, such as the station, network, and producers. In a manner of speaking, then, our TV set also travels all the way back to its super-super-super-implicate level and gathers the programs or information conceived and created at these deeper levels. Each level is connected to the next, interfaces with the levels on either side of it, and passes information along.

If all of us, along with the entire universe, are blinking on and off billions of times a second, then we are *not* here as much or more as we *are* here. If we travel through an infinite number of orders to the deepest levels of our reality and back again, then each of us are also in contact with all information everywhere. As we travel through the various levels of reality, we are exposed to all the information in them. Just as those levels share their information with us, we share our knowledge, dreams, and desires with them. By the very nature of reality, in other words, each of us have the entire universe at our fingertips. This doesn't mean we *control* the universe, as we are only one of many parts, but our presence is felt and our voice is heard just as we hear and respond to others. Every time we "blink" back on into existence, we re-draw or re-create our physical selves and our physical world. This creative potential gives us and the universe nearly unlimited opportunity to bring experiences to us, and allows us to cooperate in the experiences of others. Magickal practice is a recognition of this aspect of the universe and a willingness to work with it consciously and deliberately.

# PERSONAL EXPERIENCE
# AND A MAGICKAL UNIVERSE

As noted at the beginning of this discussion, what you believe about the universe shapes what you think is possible in the universe. Newtonian physics shaped what was believed possible for over three hundred years not only in science, but also in social structures, religion, biology, psychology, and medicine. What might happen to the culture if the universe were no longer viewed as a big machine, but the unfolding of consciousness or intelligence into physical expression? What might happen to medicine and biology? What might happen to religions and social structures if the society comes to believe that the will and intention of the parts create the whole? What becomes of God? What becomes of you in this interconnected living flux?

Since Paganism has no set dogma, it offers no one set answer to these questions. Different groups and traditions have their own perspectives. How you decide to answer these questions will depend on your beliefs. You must decide for yourself what kind of universe you live in. Your personal experience is as significant a source of instruction and inspiration for you as anything else. As helpful and thought-provoking as science and mysticism are, they are only aids. They can never substitute for your experience. They are, really, no more than the record of *someone else's* personal experience. Paganism supports the view that your experiences are every bit as valid and authoritative as that of others. Put the universe to the test in your meditating, ritual work, and magickal practice over the next several years. See for yourself how the universe responds to you, what works, and what doesn't work. Try new things that challenge your beliefs and push your envelope a little bit. Then, when you speak to others about this topic in the future, you will be speaking from your experience, not just your intellect.

## exercise          FINDING YOUR POINT OF POWER

The point of power is the here and now. You create yourself anew each moment. Your focus of consciousness is delicately poised between its expression in the physical universe on the one hand, and all of unmanifest reality, such as the implicate and hidden orders, on the other. Because the unmanifest is timeless and spaceless, the past and future are equally available, or simultaneously present there. It is from your point of power in the present that you make choices and navigate your way through past and future as they appear to spread out in a linear sequence on either side of you.

Sit quietly and let yourself relax. Take several deep breaths. Your point of power is that instant in which you create yourself and your reality; it is that eternal moment in which you step from the unmanifest to the physical and give shape and form to your world. Find this moment, this eternal now. Feel the energy and vitality that surges between your inner and outer worlds in every instance. Place yourself in this moment of power. Accept only as much as you can and let the rest flow through you unimpeded as you observe it. This is not fluffy stuff; it is nothing less than the enormous creative vitality of the universe.

After a few moments, move back into your awareness of yourself in everyday life. As you go on with your day, see if you can catch glimpses of this point of power and the creative force of the universe at work in you. Repeat this exercise periodically.

 **BELIEFS ABOUT THE UNIVERSE**

- The things I believed about the universe and my relationship with it as I was growing up were . . .
- My beliefs about the universe now are . . .
- The things I find the hardest to accept, that make me sad, or that I doubt are true about the universe are . . .
- Is there anything about the universe I fear?
- The kind of relationship I want or wish I could have with the universe is . . .
- The experience with the universe I most want to have right now is . . .

# 6

# MAGICK

In the previous chapter we laid the groundwork for understanding what magick is and how it works. The principles of Paganism affirm that all parts of the universe, large or small, are alive with a spark of intelligence, that they are interconnected, and can communicate and cooperate with each other. Surprisingly, mystics from all faith traditions and scientists have made discoveries or had insights that also seem to support Paganism's view.

When a Pagan speaks of magick, he or she is not referring to illusion or sleight of hand. You will notice that "magick" has been spelled with a *k* throughout this book. Pagans frequently use this spelling to differentiate the magick of their spirituality from stage tricks. When a Pagan refers to "performing magick," he or she is not referring to performing illusions, but to the process of stepping into the universal flow and choosing to participate with it in a deliberate fashion. Other religions describe much the same process and its results using other names, such as prayer, meditation, inspiration, bliss, contemplation, communion, synchronicity, visions, revelation, prophecy, and miracles.

One of the standard Pagan definitions of magick comes from Aleister Crowley, who states in the introduction of his book *Magick in Theory and Practice*, "Magick is the Science and Art of causing Change to occur in conformity with

Will."[1] We find this definition, though descriptive, to be only partly helpful. We would define magick as *the actions of many consciousnesses voluntarily working together within an aware and interconnected universe to bring about one or more desired results.* Our definition neither requires nor excludes the involvement of a Deity. Our definition also encompasses many activities you may at first glance not think of as magickal, such as walking across a room or healing a cut on your finger. These more ordinary activities, however, still require the organization, communication, and cooperation of multitudes of consciousness—even if only at the cellular level—to bring about a desired end.

The following are some general points about magick to remember.

**Magick is natural.** Magick is a natural act—not a supernatural one—in that it arises out of the structure and nature of the universe. However, many people of various faiths throughout the world, including some Pagans, believe that their forms of magick arise from or are controlled by supernatural forces. Their experience of magick is no less real or powerful than those who believe it to be a natural process.

**Magick is rational.** Many magickal systems, particularly those grounded in scientific principles, are logical and based in reason. The conclusions drawn about what magick is and how it works proceed logically. This does not mean that magick is not also intuitive. Any time you deal with concepts or phenomena that are below the level of physical reality (i.e., that are in the implicate and super-implicate orders where space and time do not exist), you are by definition outside of the objective world. Translating experiences that occur at these deeper levels can be difficult and by their nature involve intuition and subjectivity. However, the subjective nature of some experiences does not make the underlying principles of magick irrational.

**Magick is cooperative.** Most Pagans will agree that magick is a voluntary and cooperative process. We call this *cooperative magick.* However, there are Pagans who maintain that magick can be used to command or force an action or result through either natural or supernatural means, or that the magick user can dominate another intelligence (such as a spirit, elemental, energy field, or being) and bend it to their will. We call this the *command mode* of magick. Persons who believe in the command mode of magick can be as successful with magick as those who don't, and their experience of magick is no less real and powerful for them as those who practice cooperative magick. In this book, however, we approach magick from the cooperative point of view.

**Magick works regardless of what you believe about it.** You don't have to adopt a particular set of beliefs for magick to work for you. We have seen magick work for secular humanists, Christians, Pagans, and agnostics, among others, regardless of what they called it or believed about it. Beliefs are critical, however, when it comes to what you believe is possible magickally, since a limiting belief will block experiences that do not match it.

**Magick can be performed by anyone.** Not only is magick *capable* of being performed by everyone, it is *already* being performed by everyone.

# THE MECHANICS OF MAGICK

There may be times in your life when you want to connect with the universe. Maybe you want to make that connection in order to feel closer to your idea of that which forms and sustains the universe. Maybe something is happening that's important to you and you want some input about it. Maybe there is something you would like to have happen in your life and you want to help draw it to you. Magick is not, however, necessarily limited to this sort of conscious interaction since magick can be performed subconsciously while participating in the creation of physical reality that "blinks on" as the explicate order. When discussing magick here and throughout the book, however, we are referring to a deliberate and conscious, not subconscious, interaction with the universe.

The mechanics of conscious magick are actually fairly simple. In essence, magick is performed by putting yourself into a receptive state, forming your concern or intention clearly, projecting this intention into the universe, and then letting it go to do its work.

## Becoming Receptive

The first step is to put yourself into a *receptive state*. This means freeing yourself of distractions and allowing your focus to move toward your point of connection with the universe. If you're tense from your commute home and are replaying that meeting with the boss over and over while the kids yell for dinner, you may find it difficult to sink into that space of quiet awareness where you see yourself in the flow of things.

Most meditation techniques provide good means of quieting yourself and becoming receptive. The quieting can be mental, rather than physical, as many people have success with yoga, t'ai chi, walking meditations, tantra, and other techniques that engage the body. One of the simpler methods we find effective is sitting quietly and listening to the beat of our heart and observing our breath. You have already tried this technique in the last two visualizations of chapter 5.

The term *altered state* is an expression frequently used by Pagans to describe becoming receptive. The altered state is so called because the speed of our brain waves is slowed down (Figure 6.1). For the purposes of focused magickal work, there is usually no need to go deeper than the alpha state. If you have ever gotten lost in a daydream, you've been in an alpha state. If you've arrived at a destination and don't remember the drive there, you've been in an alpha state. Most of us tend to think of our waking consciousness as a static thing, but actually we pass through many states of consciousness in a day.

A common Pagan practice that helps persons get quiet, become receptive, and move into the alpha state before rituals and magickal workings is called *Grounding and Centering*. We briefly touched on Grounding and Centering in chapter 1 in the discussion of ritual. There are many methods and definitions of Grounding

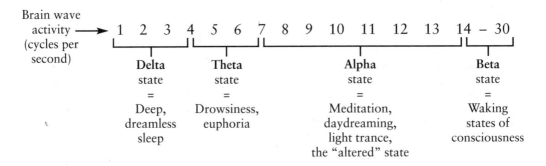

FIGURE 6.1
States of brain wave activity.

and Centering, depending on which Pagan tradition you consult. However, Grounding is essentially the mental act of aligning your energy centers so that you are connected to both the mental and physical realms. Getting grounded can involve feeling "plugged in" to what Pagans may refer to as *earth energies,* which are usually thought of as the energies of the physical world, and the corresponding *sky energies,* which are typically seen as the energies of mind and spirit. When grounded, a person feels whole, complete, and balanced. Centering is the mental act of placing your focus. In Pagan practice this focus is frequently placed at a point in the energetic body that corresponds to the type of energies being engaged. The energetic system most often used to visualize this placement is the chakra system, which comes to us from Hinduism.

Hindu mystics believe that energy flows through the body in a certain pattern (a belief found in other Eastern systems as well), and that these energies meet and cross at intersection points called *chakras* (Figure 6.2).

The seven chakra points are associated with certain functions and energies. The seventh and topmost chakra, located above the head, connects you energetically to the universe and those spiritual energies you believe sustain you. Its vibration or frequency is considered to be quite high and light, and the color associated with this chakra is white. A halo painted around the head of a saint is the Western rendition of this chakra.

Moving down the body, the sixth chakra sits in the forehead just between your eyes and is identified with the pineal gland. This chakra is associated with psychic and intuitive powers, the mind, and wisdom, and its color is deep indigo or purple, sometimes combined with silver. This chakra is commonly referred to as the "third eye."

The fifth chakra is located in the throat and is associated with all matters of communication and self-expression. Its color is sky blue.

The fourth chakra is the heart chakra, and is associated with love, benevolence, selfless giving, and forgiveness. Its color is sometimes described as green, at other times as pink with gold.

The third chakra is centered in the solar plexus, and is associated with power, will, and the energy to do and accomplish. It is the seat of your personality, ego, and self-esteem. Its color is yellow.

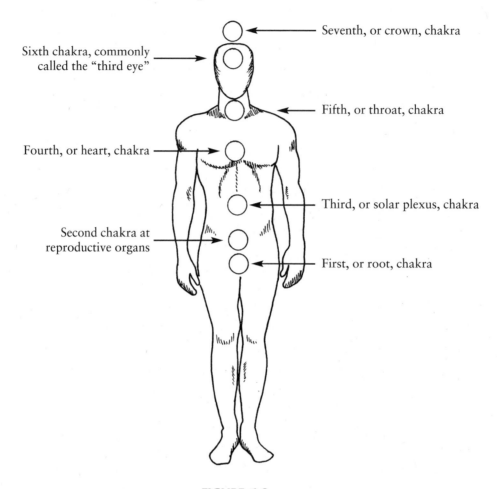

Sixth chakra, commonly
called the "third eye"

Fourth, or heart, chakra

Second chakra at
reproductive organs

Seventh, or crown, chakra

Fifth, or throat, chakra

Third, or solar plexus, chakra

First, or root, chakra

**FIGURE 6.2**
The chakra system.

The second chakra is located near the reproductive organs and is associated with sexuality, desires, and reproduction. Its color is orange.

The first chakra sits at the base of the spine, and connects you to your body and the material world in general. Its vibration or frequency is considered to be slow and dense, which corresponds to the denseness of physical matter. The color of this chakra is deep red.

If you are working with sexual issues or the health of reproductive organs, for example, you may wish to center yourself in the energies of the second chakra for your magickal working. If you are doing work involving psychic and intuitive skills—like divination, for example—you may wish to center yourself in the energies of the third eye. Most Pagan magickal work, especially work done publicly or in larger groups, tends to be centered in the heart chakra in order to help keep the emotions clear and ethics true.

The concept of Centering is found in several Eastern traditions, and is not unknown in Western traditions, such as Christianity. In her twenties, Joyce lived in a convent for a year, and while there she was taught the practice of "centering prayer." The essence of this prayer involved becoming quiet and focusing on the center of her being, and in that center discovering the divine, however it manifested itself. Often, it took the form of an energy, such as love, strength, power, healing, peace, forgiveness, beingness, or creativity. Joyce was encouraged to think on that energy if her mind began to wander so that she would become recentered in it.

The intuitive healer Caroline Myss suggests that the seven chakras correlate with the seven Christian sacraments.[2] This is an interesting blending of concepts for those who come from a Christian background. According to Myss, the chakras and the sacraments combine to express archetypal forces that empower our physical and energetic systems. For example, according to Myss, the first chakra correlates to the sacrament of baptism, which is symbolic of new life on both the physical and spiritual planes. The second chakra corresponds to the sacrament of communion and the act of honoring each other in our relationships. The seventh and last chakra, located above the top of the head, corresponds to the sacrament of extreme unction (commonly called "last rites"), and represents our connection to spirit.

Pagans frequently choose to focus on or center themselves in various energies at various times, depending on their purpose. Exactly what these energies are will be interpreted by each Pagan according to his or her belief system. Pagans may see these energies as natural occurrences, as spiritual connection points, or as aspects of the Divine.

Grounding and Centering is a technique that helps many Pagans enter a receptive state before performing magick. Other techniques, such as meditation or simply becoming quiet, can work just as well. Try a couple of different methods and see what works for you.

## Forming an Intention

Why are you doing a magickal working? Obviously, something has motivated you to interact consciously with the universe. Take the time before you begin to frame your intention carefully. Probably the most important thing you can keep in mind here is the saying, "Be careful what you ask you for; you just may get it."

Joyce's father told the story of a man who worked diligently on his church's picnic. As the time for the picnic grew closer, this fellow began to pray hard that it not rain. He prayed every morning, he prayed every lunch hour, and he prayed every night. This went on for days. Finally, the morning of the picnic dawned bright and sunny. The fellow got up and was very pleased until he looked out the window and saw three inches of snow on the ground.

As you design your intention, keep your ethics uppermost in your mind, consider the situation, weigh the possible consequences, and then form your intention. Do the best you can and trust in the rest. Focus on the outcome, not the means of getting there. The universe seems to have a sense of humor, but it is trustworthy. If you think you may overlook something, ask the universe to get back to you if it is not sure how to proceed.

When you are forming an intention for someone else, such as for a healing, keep in mind that you may not fully understand what the other person needs or wants. You may not know what is best in a given situation. At such times it might be better to ask for whatever is most needed and leave it at that. If energy is being sent, let the receiver decide what to do with it. This is not watered-down magick, it is simply respect for the free will of others.

Since we are not "command mode" magicians, we believe it's not possible to force an unwanted result on others anyway. A number of Pagans would disagree with us on this point, especially those who believe in curses and other forms of negative magick. We hold a different view, and believe in the cooperative nature of the universe.

## Projecting into the Universe

The third step in magick is projecting your intention into the universe. This can be done any number of ways. You can visualize your intention being delivered as a letter or e-mail to different levels of reality. You can imagine your intention being flashed onto the screen of the Cosmic TV, carried back through the signal to the station and network, and from there to the creators and writers who can help. You can see your desire being wrapped with a big bow and carried away by fairies or angels. If you have a strong belief in a God or Goddess, you can present your intention to him or her and leave it to be acted upon. You can write your intention on a piece of paper and burn it, visualizing the flames taking it where it needs to go. You can trace your intention or a symbol for it into salt or flour, and then send it to the universe by blowing the salt or flour into the wind or dissolving it in water and pouring it on the ground. You can stand up and speak your intention aloud as though you're having a conversation with a friend. You can write your desire or a symbol for it onto a stick, and then drop the stick into a river to be carried away.

These are just a few examples of the many ways an intention can be projected into the universe. There is no right or wrong method. Again, however, other Pagans, particularly those who practice ceremonial magic, may disagree since ceremonial magicians place a great deal of emphasis on the precise techniques of their rituals.

Emotional intensity plays a big part in successful projection. Intensity can improve how effectively your intentions are conveyed to the universe. Remember, you are enlisting the aid of other consciousnesses, or, depending on your beliefs, the aid of your Deities to help you achieve your purpose. Open yourself up and let the universe hear what you have to say. In return, be open to what the universe has to say through impressions, messages, or ideas that come to you in dreams, daydreams, or meditation. Give your intention some of your time and energy. If it's important enough to do magick about, it's worthy of some effort on your part. Spend a few days or weeks forming and empowering your intention. Think about it, meditate about it, or visualize it. Not only will your efforts assist the magickal working, they will help you become more clear about what it is you truly want and how important it really is to you.

## Letting It Go

After you've done the preparatory work, you need to let your intention go so that it can do its own work. This doesn't mean you must forget about it. This doesn't mean you can't continue to meditate on your intention and reproject it from time to time, especially if the matter is an urgent one. Yet at some point you need to let go of controlling what your intention does and how it does it. Your desire has just gone up on a cosmic webpage, and people, opportunities, developments, and results can pop up that never occurred to you. The creativity of the universe is limitless, so let it line things up for you in its own way.

Imposing some limits on what is acceptable will be necessary, but you don't want to shackle the universe to the point it can't perform. Let's say, for example, that your intention is to have a large sum of money over the next five years. It is a good idea to limit the universe in your intention so that it does not provide you the money from the lawsuit you win by being paralyzed in an accident. It is not a good idea, however, to insist that the money come only from winning the lottery, since other opportunities might come along, such as a promotion.

After you let go of your intention and allow it to start its work, then you must begin *your* work. The universe is not your personal servant. You don't really expect it to pull together hundreds of thousands of synchronicities while you munch bonbons? Magick is a team effort. You've got to pull your weight and do your share, and we don't just mean magickally. You have to do things in the physical world that support your desired outcome. Make a list of all the things you can reasonably do to help your intention come about, and then go do them.

## THE ICEBERG

A couple years ago we had a conversation with a Christian fundamentalist in which we discussed magick, divination, and tarot cards in particular. He asked us questions, and we did our best to explain our perspective on how tarot readings are done and for what purposes. The more we explained, the more bewildered he became. Finally, he interrupted us and said, "Yes, but what do you think you're contacting when you do this stuff? When you ask for a spirit to tell you things, what kind of spirit do you think you're getting? God doesn't work this way. You're working with the devil."

Occasionally, Joyce and I have moments when we realize we've been involved in Paganism so long that we've forgotten how the general culture looks at things.

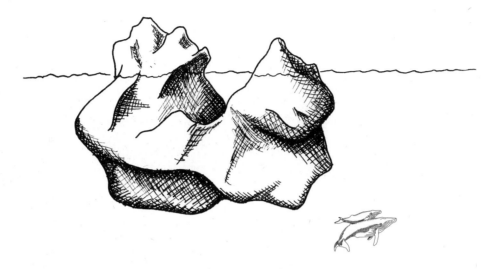

**FIGURE 6.3**
The iceberg model.

This was one of those moments. His comment contains several assumptions, beginning with the one that divination relies on spirits. His other assumptions relate to the nature of God and the reality of Satan, but we'll leave those alone for now since we've already covered them in chapters 3 and 4.

I responded by asking him why he assumed magick is performed by consulting spirits, good or evil. Apparently he had never considered this question. For our Paganism classes, Joyce and I created a model of how magick works called the "iceberg." It seemed appropriate to share the iceberg model, and so I drew it for him. The iceberg model pulls together the Pagan concepts of profound interconnectedness, levels of reality, and communication among parts of the whole. We realize it's a somewhat simplistic model, but it's still helpful in illustrating the principles of magick and interaction with the living universe (Figure 6.3).

The part of the iceberg that sticks above the water represents physical reality. From the perspective of the iceberg's top, the physical world appears to be made of pieces that are separate and distinct from each other (Figure 6.4).

However, when you mentally shift your attention below the water—that is, below the surface of things—what do you see? What is the main thing we all

**FIGURE 6.4**
Physical reality as represented by the iceberg model.

learned about icebergs as kids? That there is much more of the iceberg below the surface than above the surface. We propose that this is also true for the nature of reality and of our selves. When you quiet yourself and allow your attention to drop below the surface of things by becoming receptive, then you can begin to see a new landscape. Below the surface you see that the iceberg is gigantic. In an ice field, some of the icebergs may touch or are joined. Although each of us seems to be separate and individual above the surface, below the surface we see that what "I" am is a lot more than what we thought "I" was. And what "I" am is in contact with what "you" are. Like the icebergs, our deeper natures are interconnected. As magick and divination occur, we drop below the surface of things and connect with each other to exchange information and cooperate for common goals.

I told the fundamentalist that if I were to read his tarot cards, for example, I would mentally drop below the surface, find where my iceberg touches his iceberg, and then ask his inner, spiritual self what it most needed to know right now. I would get some impressions that I would then try to express in words. "So," I said, "this is what divination is about from the Pagan perspective. It is one expression of the profound interconnectedness of life and our ability to work together and communicate because of it. What do evil spirits have to do with any of that?" He stared at the iceberg drawing for several seconds, then looked up at me. His expression was a mixture of surprise, acceptance, disbelief, and fear all at once. In that moment I knew that he got what I was saying. I could also see that he wasn't ready to accept that he got it, and our discussion came to an end.

**my journal**

**MAGICKAL BELIEFS**

- Five things I believe about magick are . . .
- The ways in which my beliefs about magick have changed over the past few years are . . .
- The things I want to learn about magick right now are . . .
- The things I most want to do magickally right now are . . .
- Is there anything about magick I fear? Where did I learn these fears? What useful purposes might my fears serve? How do they limit me?
- What would my friends and family think of my interest in magick?
- What would my religion of origin think?
- Five ways in which my religion of origin practices magick are . . .

**questions to discuss**

**UNDERSTANDING MAGICK**

1. Has there been anything you've learned about magick that has surprised you? Is there anything you've learned that doesn't make sense, doesn't seem right, or that makes you uncomfortable?

2. Have you had any experiences with magick? What were they, and what happened?

3. Do you think the general culture and other religions misunderstand what Pagans mean by magick? If so, how?

**visualization**                          **EXPLORING THE ICEBERG**

*Remember to pause at the dots (. . .) to give people time to visualize. You may wish to bring blankets, warm drinks, and a snack to share following the visualization, in case anyone seems to need a boost in getting reoriented.*

Get in a comfortable position. If you are sitting, put your feet flat on the floor. If you are lying down, put your arms down beside you and your legs out straight.

Close your eyes. I am going to lead your breathing for a few minutes, so breathe with me.

Breathe in through your nose: 1, 2, 3, hold, 1, 2, 3, hold; and out through your mouth: 1, 2, 3. In through your nose: 1, 2, 3, hold, 1, 2, 3, hold; and out through your mouth: 1, 2, 3. [*Repeat for five or six breaths. Time your words and numbering so that the breathing in, holding, and breathing out occur at equal intervals.*] Now relax and breathe normally. . . . Feel yourself breathing in and out. [*longer pause*]

Starting with your feet, you will notice that you are being filled with the color of relaxation. . . . Pick a color that relaxation is for you. . . . This color begins to fill your feet, and they relax. . . . The color moves on up your legs. . . . As your legs fill with the color, they get heavy and relaxed. . . . The color moves on up into your back. . . . It moves on up your spine. . . . You can feel all the tension in your back relaxing. . . . The color fills your chest and neck. . . . It flows into your shoulders and down your arms. . . . The color begins to fill your head. . . . You can feel the little muscles at the back of your neck relaxing . . . and then the muscles around your eyes. . . .

Your color of relaxation completely fills you now and surrounds you like a cocoon. . . . In this cocoon, you are perfectly safe and comfortable. . . . In this cocoon you can travel anywhere and return whenever you like. . . . Now, wrapped in your cocoon you imagine yourself beginning to float up. . . . You begin to fly toward the ocean. . . . Below you the land begins to give way to the coast. . . . You are getting closer. . . .

You can smell the ocean now. . . . Then you can see it—the water stretching out before you. . . . Dotted through the water you can see icebergs floating. . . . You begin to fly toward one of the icebergs. . . . As you approach, you see that near the top of the iceberg is a small shelf or plateau that is wide enough for you to land on. . . . Your cocoon comes to rest on this shelf, and you sit on the iceberg. . . . You notice that you are so comfortable in your cocoon that you do not feel the coldness of the ice at all. . . . You are perfectly comfortable. . . .

You can see that you are fairly high in the air. . . . From here you can see a vast expanse of ocean. . . . This ocean has many icebergs in it. . . . You are surrounded by a field of ice. . . . Some of the icebergs you can see are large, and others are barely sticking out of the water. . . . You notice how they all appear separate and distinct from each other. [*longer pause*]

Now you notice that next to you is a set of stairs carved into the ice. . . . These stairs are going down toward the surface of the water. . . . Let yourself glide toward this stairway. . . . Let yourself begin to glide down them. . . . You don't have to worry about falling; you can simply float down them with no effort at all. [*longer pause*] The stairs bring you to the edge of the water . . . and you can see that the stairs continue on down into the water. . . . You notice that your cocoon makes a perfectly good diving suit. . . . You are completely enclosed, perfectly warm, and have plenty of air. . . .

Now let yourself continue to glide down the stairs and into the water. . . . The water comes to your knees, your waist, your shoulders, and then over your head. . . . You don't have to worry at all about being underwater. . . . You can breathe just fine. . . . Above, you see the surface of the water. . . . Anytime you need to, you can leave by just going back up the stairs. . . . Take a moment and look around you. [*longer pause*] [*If anyone appears to be struggling with breathing, give the suggestion to relax and breathe—to take a big breath and let it out—several times until the problem ends. If the problem persists, approach the person and whisper in their ear that they can come up out of the water and end the visualization.*]

Continue to glide down the stairs until you come to a big deck made of ice. . . . You see the words "Alpha Deck" written on the ice. . . . As you look around, you can see all the icebergs from below. . . . They are very big. . . . They stretch in all directions. . . . In some places they are so thick that they touch. . . . You have no trouble seeing through the water; it is very clear. [*longer pause*]

You begin to swim away from the Alpha Deck, but you don't go any deeper. . . . Several feet above you, you can still see the top of the water. . . . Begin to swim around your iceberg. [*longer pause*] This is the vaster, deeper part of you; . . . the part of you that is in contact with other levels of reality. . . . You are much bigger than you thought you were. [*longer pause*] Keep swimming around your iceberg. . . . Go up to it and lay your hands against it. . . . How does it feel? . . . What emotions are there? . . . Open yourself to the larger, deeper you. [*long pause—up to a minute*]

Now you can finish swimming around your iceberg, and head back toward the Alpha Deck. . . . Across from you are other icebergs. . . . Begin to swim toward them. . . . How do they appear to you? . . .

You recognize one of the icebergs as belonging to a friend of yours, or someone who is very dear to you. . . . Swim toward this iceberg. . . . How does it look? . . . Is it different from yours? [*longer pause*] Swim close enough you can put your hands on the iceberg. . . . What do you feel? . . . Does your friend communicate anything to you? [*long pause—up to a minute*] Give your friend a greeting, tell him or her it is you by name, and that you'll see him or her later. . . .

Begin to swim back to the Alpha Deck. . . . Know that you can return any time you wish. . . . Move toward the stairs . . . and begin to glide up them. [*longer pause*] Soon you break through the surface of the water. . . . Keep gliding back to the top of the iceberg, to the shelf where you began. . . . Notice how different everything appears from on top than from below. [*longer pause*]

You now begin to fly back to the place where you began. . . . You leave the ocean behind. . . . Ahead you see yourself in this room, sitting in your chair (lying on the floor). . . . You feel your cocoon begin to dissolve away and flow out through your feet. [*longer pause*] It leaves you feeling relaxed and invigorated. . . . Wiggle your fingers and toes . . . and when you are ready, open your eyes.

*Invite comments from everyone. How was the visualization for them? What did they experience? Share the warm drinks, snacks, and blankets with anyone who feels the need for them.*

# THE APPLICATIONS OF MAGICK

The most common uses for magick are energy work, divination, conscious creation, and spiritual growth.

We've already identified some energies in our discussion of Grounding and Centering. An energy can be described in a number of ways, such as a feeling, a current, a force, or a point of mental focus. *Energy work,* then, means magickal work that is done with specific types of energies.

Some of the more commonly used magickal energies are healing, love and comfort, justice, creativity, forgiveness, letting go, and self-empowerment. Someone helping with a healing will ask that healing energy be sent to the person requesting it, and may "plug" themselves into this healing current to help the process along. Those who work frequently with healing energies will tell you that these energies are a current or force, a state of mind, a mental space, or an aspect of God, that feels different from any other kind. They know when they are plugged into it successfully and when they're not. The more you work with one energy, the more you feel at home in it.

Energies of love and comfort are often sent in times of pain, stress, grief, and loss. These energies are supportive. Some magick users work with the energies of justice in order to help criminals be caught, right wrongs, and help people find peace and personal growth in difficult or unfair situations. The energies of forgiveness and letting go are sent to those ending relationships, going through difficult transitions, or struggling with how to handle hateful feelings and the urge for revenge. Energies of self-empowerment help you plug into your personal center, call up your vitality, willpower, and courage, and help you move forward into action.

Energy work focuses on sending the energy where it needs to go and is not as concerned with the result as are other types of magick. Although the energy worker may hope for a specific outcome, the energy is frequently left to do its work in its own way, to be accepted or rejected as the receiver chooses. Some years ago Joyce and I belonged to a metaphysics study group. One of my first and most powerful experiences with magick—a healing ritual—occurred with this group. A member of the group—whom I'll call Terry—had an injured back and was in quite a bit of pain. The day before the healing ritual she went to see a chiropractor to try and get some relief.

The ritual itself was fairly simple. All of us got grounded and centered and then stood in a circle around Terry. We then created a sacred space with a brief intoning of sound. Next, we followed the instructions of our leader—whom I'll call Cheryl—in breathing together and raising energy for the healing. As we raised energy, Terry concentrated on putting herself into a receptive state for receiving healing energies. As the intensity of the energy grew, we directed it to Cheryl, and she directed it to Terry. She used a tool for this purpose—a large quartz crystal—which she placed on or near the injured spots on Terry's back. For several minutes we continued to raise and flow the energy to Cheryl, and through the crystal to Terry. After about ten minutes Cheryl gave a signal and we let the energy go and grounded ourselves. Terry felt somewhat fatigued and light-headed, and though she thought she felt better, she was too worn out to be sure. I felt tingly and energized from the experience.

The next day Terry had another appointment with her chiropractor. By the time of the appointment she was feeling a lot better. The chiropractor examined her, became perplexed, and asked her if anything unusual had happened to her since the last visit. She said the only incident of note was the healing ritual, and she described it briefly. He then remarked that he had never seen someone so energetically out of balance as she had been two days before be so perfectly in balance and healthy now. It truly amazed him and he observed to Terry that whatever her friends had done, it worked! The observations of the chiropractor, who did not know of our work and did not particularly believe in our methods, were very significant and meaningful to me, and gave me a great deal of confidence in the magickal universe.

When you use magick to draw circumstances and people to you to help you build your reality, you are engaging in *conscious creation*.[3] Your thoughts, needs, and desires constantly radiate out from you, whether you do deliberate acts of magick or not. By the same token, the thoughts, needs, and desires of others constantly radiate to you. Your deeper self receives all this input and sorts through it. As you do the work of conscious creation, you attract to you the people, objects, and situations that want to assist you for their own reasons. You in turn assist others in their conscious creation.

You consciously create all the time. You design your reality anew many times every second as you "blink" back on in this universe. But you don't do this conscious creating in a vacuum. The needs and desires of all of consciousness are striving together in this endeavor, sometimes clashing and sometimes blending.

Conscious creation is probably the most familiar aspect of magick, and the one most people are likely thinking of when they talk about performing magick.

*Divination* is a form of magick whose primary focus is on receiving information. The purpose might be to help someone with a personal problem, to assist in spiritual growth, or even to ferret out information to catch a criminal, solve a mystery, or evaluate character. Psychic and intuitive work, then, are forms of divination.

The iceberg model helps explain how divination works. The diviner becomes receptive and then mentally drops down below the surface of things. From this deeper level, he or she can hop from iceberg to iceberg, if necessary, and ask for the required information. The information may come to the diviner in the form of words that are "heard" or "seen," as feelings, smells, or physical reactions, pictures, or as direct knowledge.

What about predicting the future? Diviners cannot predict the future. However, since we are all engaging in conscious creation, we imagine and plan events and situations in the implicate and super-implicate orders, just as a house takes shape in the mind of an architect long before any actual building begins. Events and situations "exist" in other levels of reality, then, in the same way the house exists in the architect's thoughts. Many consciousnesses may be required to create an event or situation; many synchronicities may have to be arranged to pull people, places, and resources together. While this is occurring, the events or situations hover as probabilities in the implicate or super-implicate levels of reality. They will not become actualities unless and until they unfold into physical reality. A good diviner can sense the probabilities that are building up and describe them. A good diviner also knows that a probability might never unfold into physical reality, that the person building a probability may change his or her mind about it at any time, and that the details of it can shift rapidly. Reading probabilities and expressing them in accurate and appropriate ways is an art in itself.

Many Pagans doing divination use runes, tarot cards, or other tools to help them. Although the symbols on the tools may impart information on their own, the information shared by the diviner *is not coming from the tool*. It is coming from within the reader as he or she steps into a deeper reality where all of the universe is interconnected and all information is accessible. The tools are no more than that, and are, in the final analysis, not a necessity.

The fourth way in which magick is used is for *spiritual growth*. Practitioners of magick may go into a receptive state and sink down into deeper levels for no other reason than to commune, contemplate, find bliss, touch their concept of God, or feel their oneness with all things. Learning can also occur here, as can mystical experience and insight.

Used in this way, a Pagan's magickal practice is a practice of prayer. In fact, to many Pagans, the words *magick* and *prayer* are synonymous, their only difference being the belief systems in which they are wrapped. Magick used for spiritual growth is equivalent, to most Pagans, to what others call "contemplative," "mystical," or "centering" prayer. What others call "petitionary" or "intercessory" prayer, or prayer that asks for something, Pagans call energy work or conscious creation.

## visualization                                    THE HIGHWAY

*Remember to pause where marked by dots (. . .) to give those participating time to visualize. This visualization offers another way of connecting into the universal flow. Some students will respond better to the iceberg model and others to the model of a highway. After both have been tried, discuss their experiences and preferences with them.*

Get in a comfortable position. If you are sitting, put your feet flat on the floor. If you are lying down, put your arms down beside you and your legs out straight.

Close your eyes. I am going to lead your breathing for a few minutes, so breathe with me.

Breathe in through your nose: 1, 2, 3, hold, 1, 2, 3, hold; and out through your mouth; 1, 2, 3. In through your nose: 1, 2, 3, hold, 1, 2, 3, hold; and out through your mouth, 1, 2, 3. [*Repeat for five or six breaths.*

*Time your words and numbering so that the breathing in, holding, and breathing out occur at equal intervals.*] Now relax into normal breathing and listen to yourself breathing in and out. [*longer pause*]

You begin to feel yourself relaxing. . . . Let go of your day, of everything that happened, and of all the things that concern you. . . . Feel the relaxation begin in your feet and flow up your body. . . . Your legs relax . . . and now your lower back. . . . Feel the relaxation move up your spine . . . into your shoulders . . . then down your arms. . . . Let all those muscles in your neck and face relax. . . . Relax the muscles around your eyes. . . . Enjoy the feeling of your body being completely relaxed. [*longer pause*]

See yourself climbing into a car. It's a little car, only big enough for you to fit in it. . . . Somewhere nearby is a highway; perhaps a highway you drive on every day. Picture this highway. . . . Begin to drive your car toward the highway. . . . You are drawing near the intersection or entrance ramp of this highway. . . . Don't get on the highway yet, but pull over to the side. [*longer pause*]

Take a moment to really see and become aware of the highway you are parked next to. . . . See the road stretching far into the distance on either side of you. . . . Notice the cars on this highway. . . . They look just like yours. . . . Hear the cars whizzing past you. . . . See them entering and leaving the highway at your exit. [*longer pause*]

From where you have pulled over, you can see back down the road you drove to get here. . . . It leads back to where you started this visualization. . . . In another direction stretches the highway we will soon get on. . . . It disappears into the distance. . . . Just like a real highway, this one connects you to all parts of your town or city. . . . It connects you to all neighboring cities . . . and from there it connects you to all the cities in your state . . . and to every state in the country. . . . There is no road or highway you can travel on that isn't ultimately connected to every other road everywhere. [*longer pause*] Where you are right now, you are connected to every other place. . . .

Now pull your car onto the highway. . . . You don't have to steer it, just lean back and will the car to move forward. . . . Let it move. [*longer pause*]

Inside your car you see a button for a radio. Turn the radio on. . . . On this radio you can hear the people in all the other cars talking to each other.

[*longer pause*] They are telling each other what they have seen and encountered on other parts of the highway. . . . They're talking about where they're going and what they want to do when they get there. . . . . Some of the cars agree to go together. . . . Others decide to go assist at a situation happening on a nearby highway. . . . You don't have to react to these conversations, just listen. [*long pause*]

Your car keeps traveling down the road. . . . In the distance you see an exit ramp. . . . As you get near it, take the exit ramp and turn around. . . . Head back in the direction you just came from. [*longer pause*] Just lean back and relax, tell your car to take you back to where you began, and keep listening to your radio. [*long pause*] You know that even though you're just listening for now, you could speak and be heard on the radio too if you wanted. . . .

Up ahead you see the intersection where you got onto the highway. . . . Exit. . . . Drive your car to approximately the place where you got into it. . . . Stop the car and get out. [*longer pause*] Begin to walk away from the car and back toward yourself in this room. . . . Feel your body. . . . Feel yourself sitting in your chair (or lying on the floor). . . . Become aware again of your breathing. . . . Flex your arms and legs. . . . When you're ready, open your eyes.

*Remember to get a comment from everyone. Ask which visualization worked better for them, the iceberg or the highway, and why. If one method works really well for them, they can use it to continue to build their feeling of connection with the universe.*

## THE LIMITATIONS OF MAGICK

No one knows exactly what the limits of magick are. As our understanding of the physical universe, human consciousness, the mind-body connection, and psychic and intuitive abilities expand, so does our understanding of what is magickally possible.

A few commonsense limitations, however, are good to keep in mind. First, *your intentions are not the only ones in the universe.* The results of your magick may be partially constrained by the conflicting desires of other consciousnesses in the universe. You don't live in isolation, you are part of a web; approach magick accordingly.

Second, *don't plan on violating the laws of physics.* Go collect all your Hollywood movies that show witches flying about their living rooms and turning neighbors into toads, and throw them into your mental trash can. The physical universe operates according to certain rules in order to allow you to function, to work with, and experience matter in a stable way. You are not going to be able to defy the law of gravity and fly around your living room in this order of reality. Within the implicate and super-implicate orders of reality, however, you can fly anywhere you want, because these deeper levels are outside of space-time. While in these levels you can arrange things so that when you "blink" back on in physical reality, you begin to set up a different environment for yourself. If the scientists who believe we blink in and out of these deeper levels billions and billions of times a second are correct, then your opportunities to re-create your world are almost limitless. Potentially, you can move from health to disease, or disease to health, from negative situations to positive ones, or positive to negative ones. Sometimes this change seems to happen effortlessly, and at other times it seems to take a lot of time, effort, and cooperation. Some of these reality shifts look miraculous when they finally unfold into the explicate order, or physical world, but they are using the blinking on and off of physical reality to accomplish the act of conscious creation. This is not a violation of physical laws, it appears *to be* the process that underlies physical laws.

Another limitation of magick is your *ethics,* which we explore further in the next chapter. Why spend your time and energy cooking up mischief and trying to hurt others? Why do you think you can succeed in hurting others magickally anyway? There's an interesting belief to think about. If the universe is truly cooperative, you may run into difficulties if your target isn't willing to be injured. Think instead of all the positive things you could be doing for your self and your world in the time it would take you to focus negatively on someone else.

One final limitation to magick is the *time, energy, and effort* you have to give to it in your life. Monks and nuns have a lifestyle that gives them maximum time to devote to spiritual practice, contemplation, and prayer. Most of you aren't able to live that kind of lifestyle, or create that kind of space for your spiritual, magickal prayer lives, so you have to do what you can with the time you have.

Making time for magick—whether for spiritual growth, divination, energy work, or conscious creation—is always a challenge. All the more reason, then, not to waste your precious time on harmful or unproductive intentions.

## exercise          IMPROVING ON YOUR SUCCESSES

Take out the inventory of your successes that you made in chapter 2 in the "Appreciating Your Successes" exercise. Take a brief moment and review what you wrote. Add any accomplishments you may have overlooked then.

Pick a couple of the successes that you specifically want to continue to work on or improve. Perhaps it's a work in progress, an ongoing project, or a skill you want to continue to refine. Note these on a separate sheet of paper. Taking them one at a time, ask yourself what has changed in your progress on this skill or endeavor, if anything, since you first made note of it in chapter 2. Think back on how it all began for you. How did you first make contact with the opportunity? When did you first begin to experience some success with it? How did that come about and what happened? Think about the various people, resources, and timing that have come together to get you where you are now. Did you just happen to meet certain people who could help you, or be in the right place at the right time? Did you coincidentally see an article or read a book that started things going? Think of all the influences, coincidences, and synchronicities that relate to your accomplishment, and write them down. What was your reaction at the time? How does it look now from your current perspective? Note what actions you took in response to each of these influences.

Compare the notes you made throughout chapter 2 concerning your beliefs, thoughts, and emotions with the influences you just identified. Do you see any important connections? Are there any patterns? How have all of these elements worked together to assist you in your conscious creation?

Now imagine yourself and this success out into the future. Pretend that you are writing a brief article about yourself five years from now. What has happened? Where does your accomplishment take you? Write down a paragraph or two. You can be playful and imaginative, but be sure to include aspects that you really believe could happen. Then take your "article" out from time to time and see how you are doing in its conscious creation.

## questions to discuss                    **EXPERIENCES WITH MAGICK**

1. What is your definition of magick and how do you think it works? What magickal techniques do you use that work well for you?

2. Have you had any experience with divination? What happened? Have you done any energy work or conscious creation? What was the purpose of the work and what happened?

3. What magickal experiences have you had using prayer? Have you ever witnessed a miracle? How would you explain these experiences if you were a Christian? If you were a Buddhist? A Hindu? How would you explain these experiences from a Pagan perspective? Does the nature of the experience seem to change based on what belief system you use to describe it?

4. What do you think limits your magick, if anything? What are your magickal ethics? What is your opinion of harmful magick, and would you ever engage in it?

5. What advice would you give someone just starting out in magickal practice?

## YOUR MAGICKAL PAGER

One day you're driving down the road on an errand to the post office. As you drive, you're thinking about your current job. You're unhappy with it, you know you need to move on, but you're uncertain what to do next. You've meditated about your situation, you've made a list of the things you want in a job, put the list on your altar or refrigerator, and occasionally projected it into the universe. You wonder how it's all going to turn out and if this magick stuff is going to make any difference.

Out of the blue you have the urge to turn into the parking lot of a grocery store you are just going by. "I don't want to go there," you tell yourself, "I'm going to the post office," and so you pass up the store. Again you have the urge to stop, but by now you've gone past the store and you'd have to turn the car around and go back. The thought of this annoys you, not to mention that the urge makes no sense to you at all.

However, on a whim you turn around and go back to the store lot, all the while telling yourself this is ridiculous. You get there and pull into a parking space wondering what to do now. Leave, go in, what? You feel stupid. While you're pondering your next move, a woman walks in front of you headed for her car. She's carrying two overstuffed bags and trying to convince a toddler not to have a tantrum in the parking lot.

As you watch, the child breaks away from her and makes a dash for the street. The woman moves suddenly after the child, and one of her bags goes flying, its contents spilling everywhere. Without thinking, you leap from your car and begin to pick up the spilled food and put it back in the bag. The woman gets the child in her car and quieted down. She gives you a smile, and, looking harried, says, "Thanks. I appreciate the help. What a day this has been. Hope I didn't interrupt your shopping."

"No," you say, "that's the odd thing. I didn't come here to shop. I was driving by thinking about needing a new job and then had the urge to pull in here." Rather than laugh at you, the woman looks at you intently and says, "What kind of job are you looking for?" You tell her and she says, "My husband runs a small company and is looking for help in that area, but hasn't had any time to interview people. Let me give you his card." She does, and two weeks later you find yourself in a new job that promises to be very satisfying for you.

What happened here? From the Pagan perspective, magick happened. You let your intentions be known to the universe, and it answered you. It set up a synchronicity in the store parking lot that helped both your needs and an employer's needs be met. The universe alerted you by giving you a *magickal page,* that is, an impulse or urge to do something unexpected.

We get magickal pages all the time. The problem is we aren't listening, or we don't trust ourselves that we're hearing pages properly, or maybe we want something grand to happen rather than get urges to turn into parking lots. Half of good magick is in the doing, the other half is in the listening. Turn on your inner beeper and start listening for those magickal pages. When you do, the universe will open up in amazing ways.[4]

## exercise

## WORKING WITH YOUR MAGICKAL PAGER

For the next two weeks, carry a small notepad with you everywhere and note each time you believe you receive a page from the universe. It may come by means of an unexpected impulse, urge, or impression. You might write "Had the feeling I should check the house at lunch today," or "Felt I shouldn't go to the game this weekend." Then write down your action. Did you check the house? Did you give away the tickets to the game? Note what you did and why, and what the consequences were.

Before you decide whether or not to follow through on a magickal page, ask yourself the following questions. Write the questions down on the first page of your notepad so you will always have them on hand:

> If I answer this magickal page, will I be doing something . . .
>
> 1) that is obviously harmful to myself or others, that disregards safety, that is offensive to me, or is unethical?
>
> 2) that will cause me to fail to perform a responsibility or job duty, cause me to break a promise, to be late, or unable to make an obligation?
>
> 3) that is illegal?

If you answer yes to any of these questions, don't answer the page. Make a note of it and study it later. Authentic magickal pages won't require you to behave dangerously, offensively, unethically, or criminally. Answering a page is not an excuse to blow off your boss, your parents, or your friends, or to behave irresponsibly.

You may also find it helpful to begin each morning with a brief visualization to remind you to be open to pages during the day, and to encourage the universe to send them to you. Begin this visualization by taking ten slow, deep breaths. Then see yourself either going beneath the surface of the ocean or sitting next to the highway intersection, whichever works better for you, and feel yourself moving into the flow of the universe. Once there, turn on your car radio and leave it on, or pick another image of receptivity that works for you, such as putting an antennae on your head. Then say the following or similar words: "I am open to the flow of the universe. I am a part of the web. I am open to receiving and hearing the pages the universe sends me today."

At the end of the two weeks, study your notes for any patterns. How many pages did you receive? What decisions did you make regarding answering the pages and why? Did the pages tend to come at certain times of the day or on certain days of the week? While you were doing a specific activity? Were you surprised by any of the results?

## keys to success    BECOMING A MAGICKAL PERSON

You may find the following steps helpful as you begin to move toward the goal of becoming a more magickal person:

**Embrace a magickal mindset.** Open yourself to the idea that as a part of the profound interconnectedness of the universe, you are a cocreator of this reality. Your thoughts, will, and intentions are heard by all the intelligences and consciousnesses surrounding you, just as you hear all of them. The exercise at the end of this chapter can help you get started in using this channel of communication. Take out your old beliefs about magick and really give them a looking over. Be open to trying on new ideas and seeing if they work for you.

**Develop spiritual relationships.** What is your idea of the Divine, and what is your relationship with him, her, or it? If you want to work with specific energies such as healing, how do these energies feel or appear to you? What is your relationship with them? If you are drawn to the four elements of physical life—earth, air, fire, and water—how do you relate to them? Spend some meditation time with the Deities or energies that are meaningful to you. You don't have to do or say anything brilliant while you're communing, just be present and open to making a connection. In time you will feel at home with the energies or Deities you work with. You will know where to look for them and how they feel when you find them, and it will become easier to work with them magickally because of your close relationship.

**Put off labeling your magickal experiences.** As we suggested in chapter 2, resist the urge to immediately start pigeonholing and labeling your experiences. Simply allow yourself to be open to phenomena as it happens and resist deciding what to call it for now. Your past beliefs may be inadequate to cover what is happening to you as you develop magickally. These old beliefs are more likely to act as restrictive filters than helpful descriptions. Over time you will have many magickal experiences and will begin to gravitate toward beliefs that describe your current understanding.

**Let magick be wherever you find it.** For some people it is disappointing to discover that magick can be no more than an urge to turn into a parking lot. They want fanfare, a choir of angels, or the sweepstakes van outside their house. There is nothing so humbling as finding the extraordinary hidden in the ordinary. As you work with it, magick will adjust your expectations and help you move from Hollywood special effects to something more mature and lasting. Look for magick in the ordinary things in life, in the ordinary moments, and you will find it without fail.

Also, and this is a hard one for many Pagans, let magick be wherever you find it, particularly if you find it somewhere non-Pagan. Have problems appreciating the magick of a bah mitzvah, monks singing Gregorian chant, a healing through the laying-on of hands, the celebration of Ramadan, or a Seder meal? If so, the problem is not with the magick. Whip off your filters and your prejudices and see magick for what it is, wherever it is.

**Slow and steady wins the race.** Work magickal practices into your daily life in a way that is sensible and sustainable. Be steady and consistent in your efforts. A half hour with magick twice a week is better than a day-long marathon once a year. Let magick become an ordinary part of your day, and keep your life in balance as you do.

**Keep your ethics strong.** The ability to form and then live by your ethics is a direct function of your spiritual growth and overall maturity. Read the next chapter carefully and take the time to develop your ethics. There is never any reason to act against your ethics when practicing magick. Your ethics and your spiritual practice should never be in conflict. Avoid working magick with any person or group that tells you otherwise.

**Trust yourself.** It's easy to dismiss intuitive urgings, to write them off as imagination and daydreams, to put down your abilities because they're just so, well, ordinary. Joyce and I both struggled with these feelings when we first began working magickally, and we see it in almost all of our students at one time or another. It is a natural part of getting started and being unsure of yourself. Just hang in there.

It's also easy to dismiss or distrust intuitive urgings if you were raised to believe that all inner urges are sinful, or that information coming from your subconscious is coming from the devil. As we mentioned at the beginning of the book and explore more fully in the next chapter, one of the most important ideas Paganism promotes is that *there is nothing wrong with you.* There is nothing wrong with how you are made, and there is nothing wrong with your nature. You don't have to fear your subconscious, your intuitive urgings, or the magickal pages you receive. This distrust is so ingrained in many of us due to our upbringing, however, that it can take a lot of time and patience to overcome it.

**Trust the universe.** In addition to being taught to distrust yourself, you may also have been raised to fear the universe, believing that at any moment you will become a victim of the battle that rages between the forces of good and evil. Cosmic boogeymen lurk everywhere and constantly seek for ways to harm and deceive you. This is part of the control through fear we discussed in chapter 4. Paganism does not teach fear, nor does it try to control its members through fear. Paganism takes the position that just as there is nothing wrong with you, there is nothing wrong with the universe. Because most Pagans believe in the profound interconnectedness of all things at every level of reality, Pagans see the universe as supportive and trustworthy. Paganism encourages you to go test this idea for yourself. Again, time, patience, and experience will help put your old fears to rest.

exercise

## A MAGICKAL WORKING

For this magickal working you will need to acquire beads, described below, and a length of necklace cording. You should be able to find the materials you need in either a crafts store or bead shop. The advantage of a bead shop is that you can usually buy beads individually. Pick whatever size, shape, and material of beads that speak to you. Gemstones, wood, metals, and plastics are all fine. Colors are suggested below, but if a bead of a different color gets your attention for that association, then go with it instead. If you are familiar with modeling clay, or work with resins, ceramics, or wood, you can make your own beads. Be sure that the hole of the bead is large enough for the necklace cording to go through. The cording should be long enough for a necklace, plus fifteen knots or so. You can always cut some length off after the working if the necklace is too long. String and yarn can also work for the cording, but be sure that the material you use will make a knot big enough to hold the beads in place. For the working you will also need a candle, incense, small cup of water, and a small container of salt or a salt shaker.

You will need the following beads:

- One yellow bead to represent the east, air, and the powers of the mind and intellect.

- One red bead to represent the south, fire, and the powers of the will, creativity, fertility, and sexuality.

- One blue bead to represent the west, water, and the powers of emotion, wisdom, intuition, and the subconscious.

- One black or brown bead to represent the north, earth, and the powers of faith, renewal, endurance, and the physical realm.

- One white, clear, silver, or purple bead to represent spirit and spiritual matters.

- One bead to represent your interconnectedness with the universe. Choose any shape or color, though one with many lines, colors, or a busy design is desirable. The bead's movement in color and design should evoke the constant movement, communication, and exchange that comprise our connection to everything.

- One larger bead for the center, which represents your openness to magick and becoming a more magickal person, willing to accept your place as a responsible and interactive participant in the universe.

Before beginning this working, read through the rest of it so you will know what to expect. Then create an altar space. You can use a table or even the floor in front of where you are sitting. You'll need to be able to reach the surface of the altar easily during the working. Cover your altar with a cloth if you wish, and light a candle and some incense. Set out the containers of salt and of water. Put your beads and necklace cording on the altar too. Put on some soothing, meditative music if you like. Turn the lights down. Make sure you have about a half hour in which you won't be disturbed.

Once your altar is set, the music is on, and the lights are turned down, sit quietly for a few moments. Take five minutes to breathe deeply and relax. Clear your mind.

Now lay out the beads in the following pattern:

| earth | fire | spirit | open to magick | interconnected-ness | water | air |
|-------|------|--------|----------------|---------------------|-------|-----|
| 1 | 3 | 5 | 7 | 6 | 4 | 2 |

You will be working with the beads in the order they are numbered, beginning with the outermost bead on the left (#1), then the right (#2), then the next bead in on the left (#3), then the right (#4), and so forth.

Starting with the earth bead, take each bead in order and cleanse it with the elemental symbols on your altar. To do this, sprinkle the bead with salt and say, "I cleanse you with earth," then put the bead in the smoke of the incense and say, "I cleanse you with air," then pass the bead through the candle flame swiftly—don't singe your fingers and watch out for long sleeves—and say, "I cleanse you with fire," and finally dip the bead in the cup of water and say, "I cleanse you with water." Do this for each of the beads, working your way to the center bead by alternating left to right. When you are finished, pause again for a few moments and breathe deeply.

Pick up your necklace cording and find the middle. Keep your finger there while you slide the large center bead to the middle and say, "I open myself to the magick that surrounds me." Tie a knot on either side of the bead, making sure the knots are large enough to hold the bead in place. Tie more than one knot if necessary. As you tie each knot say, "I am the magick."

Working backward, go next to the bead of interconnection and say, "I am the web, I am the flow, I accept my interconnectedness with all things." Again, tie a knot on either side of the bead and upon making each knot say, "I am the magick."

Add the spirit bead to the necklace next and say, "I open up all that is spirit and spiritual in me to the magick of the universe." Tie the knots while saying, "I am the magick."

Next add the water bead and say, "I open up my emotions, wisdom, and intuition to the magick of the universe." Tie the knots while saying, "I am the magick."

Add the fire bead and say, "I open up my fire, my drive, my sexuality, passion, and creativity to the magick of the universe." Tie the knots while saying, "I am the magick."

Add the air bead and say, "I open up my mind, my thoughts, and intellect to the magick of the universe." Tie the knots while saying, "I am the magick."

Add the earth bead and say, "I open up my body, my senses, my health, and my physical world to the magick of the universe." Tie the knots while saying, "I am the magick."

Now tie the necklace together at the ends and put it on. Sit quietly for several moments more, and when you're ready, extinguish the candle and dismantle the altar.

The necklace will remind you of your profound interconnectedness with the universe, and the work you are doing to be open to magick and participate in it. At least once a week, when you have a quiet moment, take the necklace off and meditate briefly on each bead. As you go through the element beads, see your mind, body, heart, and will engaged and participating in the cocreation we call reality. Feel your connection with this physical world.

As you meditate on the spirit bead, feel yourself as a spiritual being, free from the bonds of time and space, and link with what is most meaningful to you in your spiritual core. For the bead of interconnection, ponder what helps you feel connected and what you can do to foster this feeling. Visualize your connection in terms of the four elements—how does interconnectedness exhibit itself in your mind, emotions, body, and creativity? See it all coming together for you as you meditate on the center bead. Reaffirm your openness to participating in this creative, cooperative universe. Remind yourself that you are the magick.

# ETHICS AND
# PERSONAL RESPONSIBILITY

At the beginning of this book we identified what we believe to be the two most important and central themes of Paganism. One is a belief in the profound interconnectedness of all things in the universe. The other is the belief in blessedness—that there is nothing wrong with you or any part of the universe. In this chapter we take a look at the latter concept: what it means to Pagans, its effect on Pagan expectations regarding human behavior, and its effect on the formation of Pagan ethics. We also explore two ethical systems adopted by many Pagans.

## WHO ARE YOU?

No discussion of ethics, especially in a religious context, can go very far without acknowledging the assumptions you make about who you are and what sort of nature you have. These assumptions shape your beliefs regarding what you expect of yourself and why. If you live in the Western world, you are likely to be most aware of and influenced by Western religion (specifically Judaism, Christianity, and in many cases Islam as well) and its associated culture.

The Western religious perspective states that human beings are composed of one "self," which is finite. Because of the Fall of Adam and Eve in the Garden of

Eden, human beings are flawed. This flaw is not a matter of behavior, but of nature. In other words, even if you behave perfectly throughout your life, you are still flawed because your nature is marked by the sin of Adam and Eve. Most of the Western religions teach that human beings have a soul that survives death. After death, this soul faces judgment by God. This judgment can have only one outcome due to the flawed nature of human beings—punishment and annihilation. This punishment can only be averted by the acceptance of certain religious beliefs and practices, which vary depending on the religious tradition, but are often referred to as a means of "salvation." What you are being saved from, of course, is the eternal punishment or annihilation brought on not by your merits, but by the flawed nature of your being.

In summary, Western religion might state its view on the nature of the self as, "There is something wrong with you and you need our beliefs and practices to fix it." To be fair, this view is not limited to the West. Indeed, many of the world's religions promote some form of this belief. The "thing" that is wrong with you may be called ego, sin, karma, desires, the capacity to make choices, original sin, engrams, debt from past lives, or ignorance, but whatever it's called, it is considered a flaw within your nature from which you need to be saved or freed through a religious practice.

Although Pagans may adopt the Western belief about the self if they choose, Paganism offers an alternative view of the self that is multidimensional and unflawed, a self that expresses itself in many ways simultaneously, and is unlimited by space and time. We'll cover this more below. To a Pagan, the story of the Fall is a mythological story similar to those from a variety of cultures that attempt to explain the origins of humanity. Most Pagans give the same weight to the stories of Mount Olympus, for example, as they give to the story of the Garden of Eden.

Pagans, therefore, have no theological basis for accepting the belief that human nature is flawed. They also reject the idea that people need religion in order to be saved from this supposed flaw in themselves, and embrace the concept that people are born with all the potential skills they need to make moral and ethical judgments. Pagans appreciate, however, the role that organized religion plays as a social institution that acts as a repository of wisdom, a source of ethical guidance, and provides fellowship and a means for like-minded people to support each other. As we saw in the first chapter, about half of all Pagans prefer solitary practice, while the other half belong to churches or similar groups.

Many of the difficulties experienced by Pagans and non-Pagans while discussing their beliefs arise from this fundamental difference in opinion about human nature. The belief structure that results from the premise that humans are flawed is very different from one built around the premise that humans are not flawed. Discussions may end up not being particularly fruitful or enlightening unless the parties realize that they are beginning from very different assumptions.

## THE MULTIDIMENSIONAL SELF

The alternative view of the self that Paganism offers flows naturally from the idea of the universe as alive, conscious, and cooperative, and operating not only at levels that are physically grounded in time and space, but also in levels outside of time and space.

If the universe enfolds and unfolds itself from more subtle levels, or "blinks" off and on rapidly from those levels, then what might the self as it exists in those other levels be like? Answering this question is difficult since each of us is so focused on our physical self as we exist in this point of time and space that we cannot picture ourselves outside this reality. To help us break loose of this perspective, let's imagine that we meet a "plate person." This person lives in a purely two-dimensional world, such as on the surface of a plate. He or she can move forward, backward, and from side to side, but not up and down. The person does not even have words for up and down, or concepts to explain what it is. How would you convey to such people the idea of a third dimension, that of height and depth? To do it, you cannot take them off the surface of the plate. In essence, you are asking them to imagine a condition that, while perfectly understandable to you, is outside their experience completely.

Each of us experiences a similar difficulty to that of the "plate people" when it comes to imagining ourselves outside physical reality. We tend to project our two dimensionality, so to speak, on to what may be a three- (or more) dimensional realm. When we blink off into these other realms, what happens there is perfectly understandable in that level, but when we blink back on in this reality, we find that translating the experience is nearly impossible.

Your everyday consciousness exists in a dimensional world of space and time. Imagining the form that your consciousness, or self, would take in Bohm's implicate order, for example—which has no dimensions, space, or time—is very difficult, but try to picture yourself there for a moment. In the implicate order you have no body, so your consciousness will not be limited to a defined space. Because of this freedom, your consciousness might seem more expansive to you than what you experience in your physical self. Without the restrictions of a physical body, your consciousness may be able to expand throughout the entire region of the implicate order. Of course, there's no time in the implicate order either, so your consciousness could be arranging experiences without regard for the linear passage of time as you experience it. In other words, in the implicate order your past and future are happening simultaneously. If you "drop down" into the implicate order by means of meditation, magickal practice, or prayer, you might be able to access your potential past and future selves, and the wisdom, skills, and advice they possess.

If the universe is multidimensional, then there may be levels deeper than the implicate. Bohm calls the next level the super-implicate order. The super-implicate order is one step closer to the Ground of all things, if such a Ground exists, and therefore one step further removed from the physical. It is more "subtle," according to Bohm, than the implicate, which directly interfaces with the physical realm. Therefore, the nature of your consciousness at this level may be even harder for you to imagine. Bohm theorizes the super-implicate order as a director or overseer of the implicate order, much as a TV studio creates the information going to the Cosmic TV from the transmitter. Consciousness may be more expansive and diffuse at this level than at the implicate order, and able to access even deeper regions of mind, intention, and purpose. These purposes create the probabilities and potentialities that are organized in the implicate.

There is no reason to assume that this more expansive self limits itself to creating the "you" that you know. That is, consciousness at this level may project itself into the implicate, and thereafter the explicate, at multiple points that become multiple "selves" or objects. This may account for the phenomenon or belief in past lives and reincarnation. In other words, from your view here on the plate, the multiple creative expressions of your expanded self are interpreted by you as reincarnational or past lives, or just as likely, as future lives. Remember that time means nothing at these deeper levels, and it is possible that all these expressions, or selves, of consciousness—past, present, and future—exist simultaneously. If you could "drop down" into these deeper levels of yourself in dreams, prayer, or meditation, you might be able to access all of your "simultaneous selves" and their experiences, wisdom, skills, and advice coming from the super-implicate order.

There is also no reason to assume that the expansive self of the super-implicate order only expresses itself in human form, or only as animate objects, or only in terms of this universe, or even this dimension of reality. It may not be possible to fathom the infinite ways in which consciousness expresses itself from this level.

At even deeper levels, such as the super-super-implicate order, you may find that the distinctions between various selves begin to blur, and that these vast expressions of consciousness directly access and experience each other. If you were able to "drop down" into this region through meditation, magick, or mystical experience, you could potentially access the knowledge and wisdom of the entire sea of consciousness. At even deeper levels, these vast groupings of consciousness may blend into the Ground of all things, however you conceive of it.

Bohm suggests that the levels you "blink" through and that consciousness occupies may go on infinitely, but this is about as far as most of us can go conceptually before it gets too mind-boggling. As it is, we have moved a long way from the Western view of the self as one finite entity contained in this body until death.

## THE AFTERLIFE

Many Pagans do share the Western belief, however, that consciousness survives death, as stated in principle 7. Some Pagans view physical existence as an intrusion, or "blinking on" of consciousness into the explicate, or physical, world. Death, then, is seen by these Pagans as the withdrawing of consciousness back into the deeper realms from which it came. Consciousness continues to exist despite this withdrawal.

There is no requirement that a Pagan believe in an afterlife, however, and not all do. Some Pagans believe that the human spirit or consciousness is reabsorbed by the universe, or the divine Ground. In some cases these Pagans may believe that the spirit retains its individuality, and in other cases not. We know Pagans who doubt consciousness survives death at all, and without evidence to the contrary, choose to believe that death annihilates the individual. In our experience, however, most Pagans believe in some form of afterlife, depending upon their tradition. The Asatru, for example, call their afterlife "Valhalla" and Wiccans call theirs the "Summerland." Christopagans may retain their belief in a form of heaven and hell. Some Pagan euphemisms for death include "crossing the Veil," being "enfolded by the Goddess," going "home to the Lord and Lady," and "joining our ancestors." Some, but not all, Pagans believe in reincarnation.

## THINKING ABOUT HUMAN NATURE

- Who do I believe that I am? How was I made, how did I get here, and why am I here? What is the purpose of this life? What is the nature of my self? Am I finite or something else?

- I was raised to believe that the sort of nature humans have is . . .

- Three ways I agree with this view of human nature are . . .

- Three ways I disagree with this view of human nature are . . .

- Does what I believe about the nature of myself or human nature make any difference in terms of the sort of person I am or how I will choose to act? Why or why not?

- What would your friends and family think of Paganism's view of the self and human nature? What would your religion of origin think?

- List three objections they would have to these views and why . . .

- I currently believe the following about death and the afterlife . . .

- The origin of my beliefs about death and the afterlife are . . .

- Does what I believe about death and the afterlife make any difference in terms of the sort of person I am or how I will choose to act in this life? Why or why not?

## visualization                    **FINDING THE DEEPER YOU**

*Before beginning this visualization, you may wish to be prepared with warm drinks, blankets, and snacks to help reorient participants when the visualization is finished.*

Get in a comfortable position. If you are sitting, put your feet flat on the floor. If you are lying down, put your arms down beside you and your legs out straight.

Close your eyes and let yourself relax. . . . Breathe slowly in and out and feel your heart beating throughout your body. [*longer pause*] I am going to lead your breathing for a few minutes, so breathe with me.

Breathe in through your nose: 1, 2, 3, hold, 1, 2, 3, hold; and out through your mouth: 1, 2, 3. In through your nose: 1, 2, 3, hold, 1, 2, 3, hold; and out through your mouth: 1, 2, 3. [*Repeat for five or six breaths. Time your words and numbering so that the breathing in, holding, and breathing out occur at equal intervals.*] Now relax and breath normally. . . . Feel yourself breathing in and out. [*longer pause*]

Starting with your feet, you will notice that you are being filled with whatever color relaxation is for you. . . . This color begins to fill your feet, and they relax. . . . The color moves on up your legs, and as your legs fill with the color, they get heavy and relaxed. . . . The color moves on up into your back. . . . It moves on up your spine. . . .You can feel all the tension in your back relaxing. . . . The color fills your chest and neck. . . . It flows into your shoulders and down your arms. . . . The color begins to fill your head. . . . You can feel the little muscles at the back of your neck relaxing . . . and then the muscles around your eyes. . . .

Your color of relaxation completely fills you now and surrounds you like a cocoon. . . . In this cocoon you are perfectly safe and comfortable. . . . In this cocoon you can travel anywhere and return whenever you like. . . . You see a flying carpet approach your cocoon. . . . You step onto this carpet and it begins to carry you away. . . . See yourself flying up and away on this carpet. . . . You see yourself flying over this building, and over the houses of the city (or countryside) where you live. [*longer pause*]

Your carpet is going to take you to the place that you consider the most powerful place in the world. . . . This place may be somewhere in nature, like a mountaintop, a meadow, a canyon, or a seashore. . . . It may be a place from your childhood . . . or from your dreams. . . . Picture this place in your mind now. [*pause one minute*] The magic carpet flies you closer and closer to this powerful place. . . .

You have arrived, and the carpet stops. . . . You get off the carpet and stand up. . . . Look around at your power place. . . . Let the power of this spot fill your being. [*pause one minute*] Imagine that the power of this place emanates from the heart of the universe. . . . In this place you can touch the vitality and creativity of the universe itself. . . . Feel yourself begin to expand, and swell as you absorb this creative power. [*pause up to a minute*]

You see a figure coming toward you from a distance. . . . As it comes closer you realize that this figure is yourself, as you would be if you were able to absorb even more of the universe's power than you can now. . . . The you that is approaching is an expanded, richer, fuller, more powerful you. . . . Let it take whatever shape or form you wish.

This expanded part of you is not confined or limited to your present body. . . . This you exists outside of time and space. . . . It is free to move anywhere it wishes. . . . It sees purposes and designs you do not. . . . It holds all of your potentials within it. . . . You and your expanded self are now fairly close; you can see it quite clearly. [*pause one to two minutes*] You can begin to feel coming from it the great and unconditional love it has for you . . . and a tremendous acceptance and feeling of support. . . . It wishes nothing but good for you. . . . Let these feelings flow over you. [*pause one to two minutes*] Is there anything it wants to tell you? [*Pause one minute. Watch the students here and go longer if they are absorbed.*]

Behind the appearance of your expanded self that you are seeing now, you sense the even greater and more unlimited power of the universe. . . . It is as if your expanded self stands in front of an open door, long hallway, or wide vista that stretches out behind it and leads to even greater depths . . . or that it stands poised at the tip of a vortex of power that flows out beyond it and that it cannot contain. . . . Sense the even greater expansiveness that lies behind or around your greater you. [*pause one minute*]

Now approach your expanded self and ask to step into it so that you can experience the more expansive and powerful you. [*longer pause*] Your expanded self is somewhat transparent since it doesn't really have a body, and you can step right into it and embrace it. . . . See yourself doing this now. [*longer pause*] Let yourself expand with it as much as you are able. . . . Feel the power and energy of the universe into which it is tapped pour through you. [*longer pause*] What do you feel? . . . What do you see? . . . What do you hear? . . . Take as much as you can stand. If it becomes too much, ask it to back off a little. [*pause two minutes or so; watch the group*]

Now step back and out of the image of your expanded self. . . . Say thank you and goodbye. [*longer pause*] If there is anything else your expanded self wishes to say to you, it does so now. [*pause up to one minute*]

Say thank you and farewell to your place of power . . . and know that you can return to this place anytime you wish. . . . Climb back onto your magic carpet and begin flying back to where you began. . . . You can see the building where you are sitting. . . . You fly back into this room and your body. . . . The carpet disappears and leaves you resting comfortably in your cocoon in this room. . . . Now feel the cocoon begin to dissipate and let the color that filled it flow out through your feet and into the floor. . . . You are filled with a sense of peace, love, and power that will stay with you for several days. . . .

Now wiggle your fingers and toes, and feel yourself fully in your body. . . . When you are ready, open your eyes.

*Get feedback from everyone, and be sure the group grounds any excess energy. Share the drinks, snacks, and blankets as necessary.*

**questions to discuss**                    **SHARING THE DEEPER YOU**

1. What did you experience in the visualization? Did your expanded self have anything to say to you? If so, what? What is the strongest feeling or impression you received in the visualization?

2. What effect, if any, will your emerging view of the self have on your spirituality? On your practice of magick? On how you live your life?

3. Identify one thing you feel the urge to do or explore since the visualization. Why do you think you have this desire now, and what will you do with it?

# ETHICS: WHAT ARE THEY?

Most of you want to do more than just live your lives without thought, care, or purpose. You want to have goals that feel worthwhile and you want to know if your conduct toward others is fair and just. In other words, you reflect upon your choices, your actions, and your lives as you live them, and you tend to measure yourselves and your conduct against a chosen ideal. Ethics is the study of what is right (that is, which actions are correct) and what is good (that is, which goals should be pursued). Ethics explores ways in which concepts about the right and the good are applied to everyday life. Ethics, then, is the study of values.

While some of your values may arise from genetic predisposition and social pressure, for the most part they are freely chosen beliefs. How do you know that what you choose as value beliefs are true? The ethical scholar Hunter Lewis identifies six ways in which people tend to come to believe or "know" anything, including values.[1] Since these six ways underlie, in one combination or another, every ethical system we could discover, we include them here. The six ways of knowing and of choosing values are:

**Authority.** You take someone else's word that something is true because you believe the external source to be an authority in that area.

**Logic.** You subject beliefs to logical tests to determine their validity. For example, since A is true and B follows from A, then B must also be true.

**Direct experience.** You believe something is true because you've seen it, heard it, done it, or touched it for yourself.

**Emotion.** You feel that something is right and true, and judge actions by your emotional reaction to them.

**Intuition.** You rely on gut reactions and your subconscious, intuitional insights in order to form judgments.

**Science.** This is a form of direct experience. You decide something is true because you can test it empirically. That is, you form a hypothesis, test it in experiments, and then determine it to be true.

Ethical systems tend to utilize these six ways of knowing in one fashion or another. Some systems focus on the thoughts and emotions of the actor in determining whether an act is correct (intentionalism). Others focus on the consequences of an act, the likelihood of which can often be reasoned out logically (teleologism). Other ethical systems ignore both the actor's intentions and the act's consequences, and focus on the inherent qualities of the act itself (formalism and objectivism), which are then judged either by emotion, intuition, or the commands of an authority. Actions can also be judged by their usefulness (Aristotelianism), the amount of pleasure they bring (hedonism), whether such behavior is found in nature (naturalism and social Darwinism), whether everyone can be encouraged to engage in this action (Kant's categorical imperative and deontologism), whether it will help develop personal potentials (self-realization), or whether or not it is willed by God (Western religious ethic).

Since most of you encounter the Western religious ethic on a regular basis, we think that Pagans should have a basic understanding of how and why it works. Also, Pagans occasionally find themselves accused of having no ethics because they have not adopted the Western religious ethic specifically, and should have some means of responding to this criticism. Let's take a closer look at this ethical system.

## THE WESTERN RELIGIOUS ETHIC

According to Burton Porter, an ethical scholar, the Western religious ethic tells us that a good life is one in which people believe in God, accept his word as authoritative, and live so as to fulfill God's design for humanity.[2] Humanity is called upon to perform certain actions because those actions have been willed by God. Not performing these actions is called sin. In the Western traditions, the Bible is considered the source of knowledge concerning what God requires, and to many Jews and Christians, the scriptures are considered infallible. Scripture, together with theological interpretation, essentially comprises the religious ethic of the West.[3] Some Muslims may view the Koran in a similar light. This type of ethic is based in Lewis's first way of knowing, or authority. It is also called a formalistic, objectivistic, or deontological approach.

Since this ethic focuses on performing actions because they are willed by God, some ethicists pose the following question to followers of the Western religious ethic: Does an act become right because God wills it, or does God will actions because they are right?

If you take the approach of the first part of the question—that an act is right because God wills it—then what happens if God wills something immoral, cruel, or unjust? Can God's willing an act make right something that is wrong? If God were to say, for example, that torture is okay, does that make it okay? If God were to say that caring for the sick and elderly is bad, does that make it bad? If you say yes, then there are potentially no limits to behavior. History shows that adopting this approach to the religious ethic has in fact resulted in immoral, cruel, and unjust behavior on occasion. Many followers of Western religions resist this result and answer no to this part of the ethicists' question, not only because saying yes would destroy any claim that their ethical system is actually ethical, but also because saying yes offends their own moral sensibilities.

Most members of Western religions today probably agree with the second part of the ethical question—that God wills actions because they are right; or put another way, God only wills actions you believe to be right. If this is so, then what part is God actually playing in the deciding of your values? Hasn't God's approval of an action become secondary to your own? From this perspective, what you call God's decrees is really a reflection of your own ethical standards. If God "tells" you to do something against those standards, you will decide the message isn't from God and will not act on it.

As an example, a parishioner goes to his minister and says that God is telling him to murder his family as a sacrifice. Should the minister tell the man to go ahead and murder them since God is telling him to do it? Take the time to stop and answer this question.

Might the minister instead say that murdering one's family is wrong, and the message isn't coming from God? Should the minister try to do something to stop this man? In the United States the minister may be under a legal duty to report this incident to the police if it appears the family is in real danger. Let us say that the minister does not encourage the parishioner to follow God's command in this instance. In fact, the minister decides that because the command encourages an unethical act, it is not even from God. He also believes the family is in danger and so he reports the parishioner to the police. The minister takes these actions on Saturday. On Sunday morning he goes to church and prepares to preach his sermon. The topic? The story of Abraham preparing to murder his son at God's command. The minister delivers a sermon praising Abraham's faith in God and his willingness to follow God's commands even to the sacrificing of one of his own. In his sermon he praises an action that in his personal life he has condemned. Should we not leave church a little confused?

Perhaps we want to straddle both sides of this ethical dilemma. We want to follow the decrees of whatever Deities we believe in, but we also want and expect our Deities to decree only reasonable and ethical things. We want to be able to form our own ethical judgments, but are afraid to trust ourselves and take complete responsibility for the ethical judgments we make. If we were raised in a Western religious tradition and taught that our natures are flawed, then we may feel that we are incapable of being ethical. Part of us feels that it's wrong for a man to murder his family if God tells him to, but the other part is so unsure of our innate moral sentiments that we don't know what to think when we read that God tells Abraham to do it.

Since many Pagans were raised in Western traditions, dealing with this confusion is not uncommon. Remember that Paganism has no theological basis to support the view that humans are flawed. Therefore, Pagans tend to believe that people are capable of making ethical judgments for themselves under normal circumstances. This doesn't mean that Pagans shouldn't look to outside sources for input and guidance when choosing values and making ethical judgments. Indeed, Pagans are encouraged to explore all sources. However, the final decision about which ethics and values you choose and how you act on them is up to you.

# ETHICS: THE PAGAN APPROACH

Paganism begins with the concept that ethics and values are *freely chosen beliefs*. Paganism's first two principles state that you are responsible for the beliefs you choose to adopt, and are responsible for your actions. With the freedom to choose comes the responsibility for the choices you make. You are responsible for your ethics, your actions, and the consequences of your actions. You are responsible for the kind of reality you help build based on the choices you make.

Of course there is always the possibility that people will make poor choices and try to avoid their responsibilities. Some belief systems have decided that the fact that humans might choose poorly is proof that human nature is bad. Since you are inherently bad, they say, you cannot trust yourselves to make good choices at all. As one of Joyce's relatives, a Christian fundamentalist, put it, "If it weren't for the threat of hell, no one would ever do anything good."

Paganism asserts that giving up on your ability to make good choices will only assure that you never make any. Handing your power and responsibility over to others only makes your ethical muscles weak. If you want to grow and become ethically strong, then you must use your muscles frequently and accept the risk that comes with doing so. Handing your power over to others—such as a cultural or religious authority—is no guarantee of good results in any case. History is full of examples of such authorities supposedly adhering to very strict religious or cultural principles who nevertheless did horrible things. The threat of hell or any other punishment by a Deity is no guarantee of either good ethics or good choices. This is because ethics are freely chosen beliefs, and how you act on them is a personal decision made fresh every day, despite religious or cultural rhetoric to the contrary.

After beginning with the proposition that ethics and values are freely chosen beliefs, Paganism then goes on to say that *there is nothing wrong with you*. There is nothing wrong with your nature and you are not flawed because you are human. There is nothing lacking, damnable, or worthy of punishment in your spiritual essence. You are born with all the potential skills you need to make sound moral and ethical judgments. You can evaluate the merits of ethical systems for yourself and design a personal ethic that expresses where you are in your spiritual growth at this time and challenges you to grow to even greater levels. You can decide for yourself what your ideals are and measure yourself against them. You do not necessarily need religion to be a moral person, but you may find religion helpful as a source of inspiration and as a place to meet and mingle with people of like mind.

Paganism is not the only ancient or modern religion to state that there is nothing wrong with you, but it is currently in the minority. Abandoning the idea of being flawed is extremely threatening to some people. They fear that if this belief is removed, the world will come tumbling down and humanity will be only one step away from chaos and anarchy. Once again, Joyce's relative summed up this fear: "If you think people can make moral decisions for themselves, then you are no better than Hitler." Are people so thoroughly rotten that civilization will collapse if Paganism's ideas about human nature become the norm? Are Pagans living in a fantasy world to think that people are born with the potential skills needed to form adequate moral judgments? Is it only the fear of an ultimate punishment that keeps us all from turning into criminals or worse?

If it is human nature and instinct to be wicked, then the rules of society and even religion seem awfully fragile against the force of such basic instincts. Rather than focus on why some people become criminals, each of us might be better served to ask why more people are not criminals. Yet society is orderly most of the time. We take the peacefulness and predictability of human interactions for granted and plan our lives accordingly. The vast majority of us follow the rules, wait our turn in line, honor our promises, obey the law, help those in need, care for our children, cooperate with and respect the rights of others, and do our jobs even though the boss isn't watching.

Bombings, shootings, and other tragedies make the news because they are sensational, and they are sensational because they are unusual in the course of human interaction. Most of us find such events abhorrent. If human nature were corrupt, such incidents would be neither unusual nor abhorrent. We would be made happy by such things when they occur and we would tend to encourage them. Instead, when we hear of the occasional person who enjoys violence and suffering, we believe there is something seriously wrong with him or her, and we call that person sociopathic, fanatic, diseased, or brainwashed.

Social scientists have observed that a moral sentiment emerges in children even before the development of language skills. Before the age where reasoning begins, children exhibit a regard for the well-being of others and anxiety at failing to perform up to a standard.[4] All around the world, children younger than eighteen months routinely offer food and toys to those around them as a way of establishing friendly relations.[5] Between the ages of eighteen and thirty-six months, half of observed youngsters spontaneously offered to share with other children without urgings from adults.[6]

Humans are social animals. It is possible that human moral nature springs in whole or in part from its social nature. Speaking from the standpoint of evolution, cooperative behavior is adaptive. Biology prepares you to be sociable. Some social scientists believe people are intuitive moralists who regularly judge the actions and motives of others as worthy or unworthy, even from an early age.[7] Moral sentiments are surprisingly uniform among children regardless of culture. In test situations, there are some things children will always identify as wrong, such as breaking promises, destroying property, stealing, and hurting animals, whether they live in the United States, India, Korea, Nigeria, or Indonesia.[8] The existence of a moral sense seems to be universal, and the development of a conscience seems to be tied to success in connecting socially with others from a young age. As the ethicist James Q. Wilson, said, "Conscience, like sympathy, fairness and self-control arises not out of repressed lust and rage, but out of our innate desire for attachment. . . . People with the strongest conscience will not be those with the most powerfully repressed aggressiveness but those with the most powerfully developed affiliation."[9]

However, conscience is not imposed on you. Wilson suggests that it is something you impose on yourself as you reflect on what it means to be human, and on what terms you can live with yourself.[10] The ethical sense does not guarantee ethical action, but it's interesting to note that when people do violate their moral sentiments they always give reasons and justifications for having done so—it was in the national interest, it was in self-defense, it was to make a profit for the shareholders, and so forth. Even when the reasons are sound or the action unavoidable, compromising ethics brings on discomfort. Yet when people follow their moral sentiments, they do not justify their behavior. Who ever heard of a Boy Scout feeling the need to justify himself for helping an old lady across the street?

It appears that nature has graced you with a basic ethical or moral sense and has prepared you to make judgments and distinctions. How this ethical sense develops will depend in part on your personality, the absence of disease and internal chemical imbalances, and what you learn from your family and society. The ideas that families and societies teach can either build on your innate senses or blunt and deform them. This is all the more reason for us as individuals and as a society to examine our beliefs carefully and choose those that will help us build an ethically strong reality.

If people have an innate moral instinct, then where does bad behavior come from? Each of us has other instincts and urges besides the moral one, and our ethical urges are in constant competition with these other desires. Poor behavior frequently springs from a conflict among our moral sentiments, our ethics, self-interest, and the demands of our society, which may encourage us for one reason or another to ignore our moral feelings. We often have to choose between competing emotions and obligations. If you must decide between telling the truth or protecting someone from harm, which will you choose? If you must decide between destructive behavior and doing your duty, which will you choose? If you must decide between keeping a commitment and meeting the needs of a friend, which will you choose? Our sociableness can be a two-edged sword. If you want to be liked and popular, are you willing to commit a crime to achieve it? If you want to be successful and admired, are you willing to do whatever you must to get to the top?

Right living requires you to strike a balance between your competing urges. Those who are able to strike this balance well are said to have character; that is, a set of personal traits people tend to admire, including ethical and moral integrity. As James Q. Wilson puts it, a good character is "not a life lived according to a rule, but a life lived in balance."[11]

**questions to discuss**      **EXPLORING VALUES**

1. Which of Lewis's six approaches to knowing and choosing values appeals the most to you? Which has the least appeal? Which one or two approaches do you think your current values are based in?

2. Do you have any personal experiences relating to the Western religious ethic? If you were raised in that tradition, what are your thoughts and feelings now regarding it? What parts of this ethic would you like to bring over into Paganism with you?

3. What is your reaction to Paganism's approach to ethics? Do you agree or disagree that humans seem to have a moral instinct? If Paganism's

perspective became the norm, what do you think would be the consequences to you personally and to the society?

4. Do you think people need religion in order to be ethical?

# PAGAN ETHICAL SYSTEMS

Since nearly half of all Pagans identify themselves as Wiccans, the Wiccan ethical system is the most common one practiced by Pagans. The Wiccan system is essentially twofold and consists of what is called the Rede and the Rule of Threes. Although it is a smaller tradition in Paganism, Asatru has also developed a fairly complex ethical system, and so we will look at both in some detail, beginning with Wicca.

## The Rede

The origins of the Wiccan Rede are not entirely clear. Gerald Gardner theorized it came from the legendary Good King Pausol, who is credited with saying, "Do what you like so long as you harm no one."[12] Isaac Bonewits proposes that Gerald Gardner created the Rede by modifying Aleister Crowley's Law of Thelema, which states, "Do what thou wilt shall be the whole of the Law. Love is the Law; Love under Will."[13] Although several versions of the Rede can be found, River and I learned it in the following form:

> Bide ye the Wiccan law ye must, in perfect love and perfect trust.
> Eight words the Wiccan Rede fulfill: 'An it harm none, do what ye will,
> Lest in self-defense it be. Ever mind the Rule of Three.
> Follow this with mind and heart, merry meet and merry part.

The most frequently quoted part of the Rede is the line, "'An it harm none, do what ye will." The word *an* comes from the Old English and means "if." Essentially, then, the ethic of the Rede states that you are free to do as you wish, as long as what you do doesn't harm others. Most Pagans interpret "others" to include animals, plants, people, and "inanimate" objects, as well as humans. This may seem like an overly simplistic ethic until you try to put it into practice. Living up to this ethic can be quite difficult and challenging. One of the central questions surrounding it, of course, is how to define harm.

Does harm mean intentional harm only, or does it include accidental harm? What about consequences? Are you responsible only for those consequences you can reasonably foresee, or are you responsible for all consequences regardless of whether they were foreseeable? For example, if you help an elderly woman board a train and stow her luggage, you may feel that you have done well and not caused any harm. The train later derails and the woman is killed. Were your actions harmful or not? In another example, several people are waiting for a parking space. Since you were there first, you take the spot. If one of the other people must park far away in an isolated section of the parking lot and is then mugged or slips on ice and breaks a leg as a result, are you at fault? If you did some magick or said a prayer before leaving home that you would find a good parking spot, is your spiritual practice also at fault? What if you don't know what will or won't bring harm in a certain situation? How should you define harm—as death, injury, mere inconvenience? Have you engaged in harm because you cut down a tree to build your house? Are you harming iron ore in order to smelt it into iron or aluminum to become a soda can? Have you engaged in harm because you harvested a head of lettuce for your dinner, or because you eat meat?

Some critics of the Rede as an ethic say it is too vague and too subject to personal interpretation to be useful. However, this is true of any system of ethics. Any ethical guideline is subject to vagueness and difficulty in interpretation. Take the Sixth Commandment from the Old Testament of the Bible, "Thou shalt not kill," for example. What could be clearer than this? You may read this ethical guideline and feel good about it; it makes sense to you, it seems obvious and reliable. Yet when it comes to interpreting and acting on it, you are in the same position with this Commandment as with the Rede.

If you cannot kill, does that mean you cannot defend yourself from an attacker? Can you defend your family? What if your country sends you to war and tells you to kill the enemy? What about killing animals for food? What about killing plants for food? If your farm has a sudden influx of grasshoppers, can you kill them to save the crops? What about that nest of hornets next to your children's sandbox? Can you get rid of the fleas on your dog? How about driving your car? What about all those insects that end up on your windshield, not to mention the potential for having accidents with other drivers?

The application of any ethic to a situation requires thoughtfulness and the sorting through of consequences. These are the ethical muscles we are talking about. All ethics require you to strike a delicate balance between competing interests.

From the Pagan perspective, the Wiccan Rede does not differ in principle from either the Golden Rule, which tells you to do unto others as you would have them do unto you, or Jesus' exhortation to love your neighbor as yourself. Even more significantly, Christian theologians preached a similar message from the very earliest years of Christianity. A notable example is St. Augustine, who prepared a treatise on the Gospel of 1 John and presented it at Easter in the year 407. In 1 John 3:23 we are commanded to "love one another." St. Augustine discourses on this theme at some length, and in Tractate 7 exhorts his listeners in language almost identical to the Rede. He says, "Once for all, therefore, a short precept is presented to you: Love and do what you will," and also, "Let the root of love be within; from this root only good can emerge."[14]

"Love and do what you will." This captures the heart of the Rede's ethical message, which is that you are free to pursue your life as long as you strive not to be an agent of harm, thereby treating yourself and the world with love and respect.

## The Rule of Threes

This Rule, mentioned in line four of the Rede, states that whatever you send out from yourself will come back to you threefold. Therefore, if you harm someone else, the harm will come back to you three times stronger. The same is true, however, of good intentions and deeds. Some Pagans believe this Rule operates immediately in this life, while others believe it may follow them to the afterlife, or, for those who believe in reincarnation, that it becomes a karmic debt to be repaid in future lives.

One criticism of this Rule is that experience shows it is not necessarily true, at least as experienced on this plane. Good people are not always rewarded with more good in their lives, while some really awful people become quite successful and seem to avoid illness, tragedy, or want of any kind.

The real strength of this Rule, in our opinion, is its emphasis on consequences. Think carefully about the consequences of your actions not because you fear punishment, but because what you do is powerful. What you do shapes your life, the world, and the culture. You are an important player in this drama of life. Looking at the Rule of Threes as a general principle concerning consequences, then, it is saying that you have to live with the results of whatever you do. This speaks to a truth River and I have seen time and again, which is that wherever you put your energy and focus determines to a large extent the reality you create around you. You are going to tend to surround yourself with the people and circumstances that support your beliefs and purposes. So if you are a mean, selfish person who will do anything to get ahead, for example, you shouldn't be too surprised to find yourself surrounded by people of similar character, or to find yourself in situations that reflect your mean values back to you. The consequence of having values is that you will frequently find yourself enmeshed in a reality of your own making that reflects what you hold dear. Therefore, choose your values and beliefs carefully, and act on them with a full appreciation of their creative power.

## The Virtues and Goals of Asatru

As you'll recall from chapter 1, Asatru is a tradition of Paganism that devotes itself to the northern Deities, customs, and culture, in particular the Norwegian, Scandinavian, Nordic, Germanic, and Teutonic. The Asatru writer Edred Thorsson identifies goals and virtues he believes have long been associated with Nordic and Teutonic culture. He sets these out in his *Book of Troth* to help Asatru and others develop their ethics and live a good life. The virtues Thorsson identifies, and which he calls the Nine Noble Virtues, are courage, truth, honor, fidelity, discipline, hospitality, industriousness, self-reliance, and perseverance.[15]

*Courage* is the bravery to do what you must and what you know to be right. *Truth* is the trait of being honest. *Honor* is nobleness of character and respect for this quality in yourself and others. *Fidelity* is loyalty to your country, family, and friends, and being faithful in your commitments to them. *Discipline* is focus and purpose, the willingness to make hard decisions, and put off short-term gain for a longer-term benefit. *Hospitality* is friendliness and the willingness to share and be generous with those who are in difficulty or far from home. *Industriousness* is an enjoyment of work, and the willingness to work hard and take pride in what you do. *Self-reliance* refers to your personal freedoms and independence, not only individually but as enjoyed by your family, clan, and nation. *Perseverance* is persistence, not giving up, and doing all you can to be as successful as possible under the circumstances.

Thorsson then goes on to identify goals that represent the aims and purposes in life toward which the Asatru, or anyone else, might strive, which he calls the Sixfold Goal. He considers these goals to be a divine gift and a reflection of divine qualities within you. The six goals are right, wisdom, might, harvest, peace (frith), and love.

*Right* is justice and the rule of law, and represents your rational faculties and desire to live in an orderly world. *Wisdom* is a deep, intuitive voice that brings you knowledge of the divine and your inner self. It is the source of your curiosity, sense of adventure, and desire to build your character. *Might* is strength, not only for defense but also to succeed in life's ventures. It encompasses your will to power, will to succeed, and your urges to defend and protect. *Harvesting* is a recognition of your reliance on the physical, organic aspect of life. It acknowledges not only the cycles of nature but also of economics. It speaks to your need to plant, reap, and then enjoy the fruits of your labors. *Peace,* called *frith* by the Asatru, is more than just a lack of war. It is a balanced, clear space that allows you to grow and move on to other levels. When you are in balance you are in a state of frith. *Love* is the feeling and high regard you have for others and yourself, and is also your passion for life. Love is erotic as well as fraternal, and through the gift of love you can appreciate physical pleasures, your sensuality, and the joy of being alive.

The Sixfold Goal and the Nine Noble Virtues combine together to create the ideals toward which the Asatru strive. They comprise an ethical system that identifies the good and the right, as discussed at the beginning of this chapter, and provide a standard against which any of us can compare our character and behavior.

## Blended Ethics

Pagans may use any source of inspiration they wish to help them form their ethics. Pagans may explore the scriptures and important writings of all faiths and cultures, the theology and precepts of any religion, the writings of philosophy, science, humanism, art, poetry, and nature. Because Pagans are free to do this, and in fact are encouraged to do so, they may devise an ethic that blends together what they consider the best of several cultures. Christopagans, for example, may combine the Wiccan Rede, the Ten Commandments, the Golden Rule, and Jesus' teaching regarding love for mankind into a unique ethic. Judeopagans may combine Jewish law and custom, rabbinical teachings, and the Kabbalistic system of mysticism into a unique Pagan ethic. Pagans interested in Eastern religions may adopt the Buddhist Eightfold Path, follow the Way of the Tao, or incorporate certain meditational disciplines into their Pagan spirituality.

Because Pagans may explore any source of inspiration and frequently study a wide range of religions and cultures, they can also develop viewpoints and lifestyles that differ from what is familiar in the West. Pagans do not usually share the bias against homosexuality, for example, and as a whole have no theological basis against same-sex marriages or in favor of only monogamous marriages.[16] Some Pagans are monogamous and some are polyamorous. Some marry or handfast only one person, some handfast into a group. If it's in keeping with their values, some Pagans form extended families that contain more than one couple or combinations of heterosexual and same-sex unions. Although we noted in chapter 1 that most Pagans in the United States are solidly in the middle class, not all Pagans choose to follow the capitalistic ideals of this country. Some Pagans embrace more agrarian or subsistence lifestyles that emphasize cottage industry and close family units. Some Pagans choose to join smaller communities that are self-supporting, rather than adopt a typical urban or suburban lifestyle. Some Pagans choose to avoid the mass market and consume only products that they feel support their philosophical and ecological beliefs. Such consumption choices aren't limited only to "things" such as food, clothing, housing, and cars, but may also include ways of consuming time and energy, such as watching TV or playing video games. Pagan lifestyle choices cannot be reduced to one description or another because they are so varied and diverse. For the most part, however, Pagans are extremely tolerant of various lifestyles and tend to support each other in the living of them.

## questions to discuss    ETHICAL SYSTEMS AND LIFESTYLES

1. What is your opinion of the Rede and Rule of Threes as an ethical system? Do you think it is sufficient? If you follow this ethic, have any issues come up for you while putting it into practice?

2. If a new Pagan asked you what system of ethics he or she should adopt, what would you say? If a new Pagan asked you how to tell a good ethic from a bad one, what would you say?

3. What is your opinion of the variety in Pagan lifestyles? How many different lifestyle choices have you personally come into contact with so far? Are there any that make you uncomfortable? If so, why? Would you ever want to be a friend to someone living that lifestyle?

## my journal    EXPLORING YOUR PERSONAL
## AND ETHICAL GOALS

- My goals for the next five years are . . .
- My goals for the next ten years are . . .
- My goals for the next twenty years are . . .
- I think the things that make life worth living are . . .
- When I die, I want people to be able to say the following things about me, my character, and values . . .
- The major components of a good character are . . .
- The ethics I live my life by right now are . . .
- The sources for my ethics are . . .
- The ways I wish my ethics were different are . . .
- Five things I don't believe I ever want to be a part of my ethics are . . .
- The ethic I wished everybody lived by is . . .

**A VIRTUOUS EXERCISE**

You become morally and ethically strong by exercising your ethical muscles. One of the ways you can tone your muscles is to develop a set of values and put them into practice. Values in action are more popularly known as virtues. One of the best ways, and perhaps the only way, to become virtuous and develop a good character is to practice.

The following exercise sets forth a year's program for the practice of certain virtues (Figure 7.1). The year is divided into six segments of two months each. These six segments represent the six goals of Asatru discussed earlier. For each goal, four virtues are identified that enhance or support living out the goal. These virtues include the nine Asatru virtues, to which have been added other related qualities and character traits. In the two months that are devoted to each goal, you may either practice all four virtues at once, or take them one at a time, spending two weeks on each.

Begin the exercise at the first of a month at any time of the year. On a calendar, write the goal for the month at the top. For example, on January and February you could write "Wisdom," and on March and April, "Right." Although we have assigned certain goals to certain months, feel free to rearrange them if you wish. Then for each month note the four virtues you will be practicing. If you decide to practice the virtues one at a time in two-week increments, then note the name of the virtue at the beginning of each week. This way, whenever you check your personal calendar, you'll be reminded of your virtuous exercise and where you are in it. If you have time, you might want to map out the entire year in advance.

If events in your life get you off track from this exercise, don't worry. Just pick up where you left off, or go on to the next virtue listed on your calendar. This exercise is intended as a lifelong practice, so any virtues you miss this time around you'll see again in the future.

A series of questions is provided to help you identify your beliefs about each virtue, determine how you can apply them in your life, note consequences and reactions, and finally gauge your success. If you keep a journal,

| Month | Goal | Virtues |
|---|---|---|
| January & February | Wisdom | Intuition<br>Good counsel<br>Devotion (to family, country, faith)<br>Ethics |
| March & April | Right | Truth & knowledge<br>Justice<br>Honor<br>Faithfulness |
| May & June | Love | Love for life<br>Generosity<br>Respect (for others & yourself)<br>Self-reliance |
| July & August | Might | Strength<br>Courage<br>Abundance<br>Discipline |
| September & October | Harvest | Industriousness & perseverance<br>Cooperation<br>Foresight & faith<br>Celebration |
| November & December | Peace | Hospitality<br>Loyalty<br>Patience<br>Balance |

**FIGURE 7.1**
A year of virtues.

you can write down your responses; otherwise, thinking through the questions from time to time can work as well. If you have a daily meditation practice, you might wish to remind yourself of your virtuous exercise at the beginning of each day, and at the end of the day review what happened and how well you applied your virtues.

## Questions to Consider

- What comes to mind when I think of this virtue or trait? What does it mean to me?

- How can this virtue or trait be applied in a productive way? How might it be misused? How can I apply it meaningfully in my own life?

- How did I successfully apply this virtue or trait in the last weeks/months? When did I fail to apply it? What happened to bring on this failure?

- What consequences and reactions resulted from both my successes and my failures? In what ways can I continue to improve on this virtue or trait in my character?

## keys to success    PUTTING YOUR ETHICS TO WORK

**Put your ethics to work.** All the ethical theory in the world means nothing if you never apply it. Start with small things and evaluate how your values are doing as you go along.

**Learn as much as you can about ethical systems.** This means all ethical systems—not just Pagan ones, not just modern ones, or just ancient ones. The more you can learn about human culture and how we choose our values, the better able you will be to keep your own in perspective. The more ethical systems you learn about, the more knowledgeable you will be, and the more ideas about morals and values you will have to ponder.

**Get to know yourself better.** How do you know what your values and priorities are if you don't take the time to find out? Listen to your inner voice, let it tell you about your goals and desires, your dreams, and what matters to you. Let your innate moral sense speak and pay attention to it. Have a little faith in yourself. Decide on your course of action only after you've checked with your own conscience.

**Keep your ethics and your religious practice in harmony.** Your spirituality should reflect your ethics, and you should never feel compelled to do something in your religious or magickal practice that violates your ethics and morals.

**Let your ethics grow as you grow.** You are not the same person now as you were when you were fifteen. Twenty years from now you'll be different yet. Your life experience gives you ever-changing perspectives. Hopefully, you will continue to grow and mature over the years. Let your ethics grow and adapt with you, and integrate your life experience into your moral character.

**Encourage others.** Encourage others in their quest for ethics, to form their values, and develop a strong character. Support them when they need it and don't be ashamed to offer your thoughts and opinions if you are asked for them. Let your own behavior be a model for others, not only in terms of what they can expect from you, but also what you expect from them. Since we all form moral judgments and opinions, it's okay to admit you have them too, and offer them where it's appropriate. You do not have to keep quiet when you observe an injustice or something that is morally offensive to you. Perhaps your point of view will help others see the situation in a way they haven't before, and might help them in ways you never anticipated.

# NOTES

## Chapter 1

1. Dawson, "Anti-modernism, Modernism, and Postmodernism," 131–56. Quoted in Jorgenson and Russell, "American NeoPaganism," 335.

2. 617 F. Supp. 592 (E. Dst. Va. 1985), affirmed on appeal, 799 F.2d 929.

3. Guiley, *Encyclopedia,* 241.

4. Bonewits, "Defining Paganism."

5. *Webster's New World Dictionary of the American Language,* 1984 paperback ed., s. v. "pagan" and "heathen."

6. Bonewits, "Defining Paganism."

7. Jorgenson and Russell, "American NeoPaganism," 333. Wiccans comprised 46.7 percent of Pagans responding.

8. RavenWolf, *To Ride a Silver Broomstick,* 12.

9. Farrar, Ferrar, and Bone, *The Pagan Path,* 28–31.

10. RavenWolf, *To Ride a Silver Broomstick,* 13.

11. Valiente, *The Rebirth of Witchcraft,* 10, 60.

12. Truzzi, "Occult Revival," 16–36.

13. Kelly, "Update," 140–41.

14. As reported by Survey.net at www.survey.net/info.htm at the beginning of 2002.

15. National Telecommunications and Information Administration, "A Nation Online."

16. Survey conducted by Hart and Teeter Research Companies, sponsored by NBC News and the Wall Street Journal, conducted October 25 through October 27, 1997, question ID number USNBCWSJ.970C25.R34B.

17. Survey conducted by Yankelovich Partners, Inc., sponsored by Time and Cable News Network, conducted between January 11 and January 12, 1995, question ID number USYANKP.95JA13.R34.

18. Jorgenson and Russell, "American NeoPaganism," 325–32.

19. Ibid., 332–33.

20. Russell, "Social Identities," 35.

21. The wording for principles four, five, and six is inspired by the writings of Jane Roberts, particularly Codicil #1 as excerpted from *Psychic Politics:* "All of creation is sacred and alive, each part connected to each other part, and each communicating in a creative cooperative commerce in which the smallest and the largest are equally involved."

# Chapter 2

1. The analogy of the mind as a camera and beliefs as lens filters was developed in the early 1990s by our teacher Moriah MacCleod, who tells us she was inspired by the writings of Jane Roberts.

2. The exercises in this chapter called "Intersecting Beliefs" and "Appreciating Your Successes," and the exercise in chapter 6 called "Improving on Your Successes" were inspired by Nancy Ashley in *Create Your Own Reality: A Seth Workbook.*

# Chapter 3

1. The facts surrounding Matthew Fox's story are contained in several dozen magazine and newspaper articles printed in the late 1980s and early 1990s, with the following sources providing a good overview: Tresniowski and Brailsford, "Making a Joyful Noise," 73; Wright, "The Sensual Christian," 78; and Brownstein, "The Taming of a New Age Prophet," 28.

2. Roberts, *The God of Jane,* 64. The brief summary of the demonization of outsiders contained here is explored in great detail in Pagels's work. We are also indebted to Pagels for inspiring our use of Satan in the mythological role of obstacle and opposition.

3. Ibid., 65.

# Chapter 4

1. Levenson, *Creation,* 44.

2. Pagels, *The Origins of Satan,* 40.

3. Ibid., 47.

4. Ibid., 142.

5. Origen, *Contra Celsus,* bk. 6, chap. 42. Cited in Pagels, *The Origins of Satan,* 143.

6. Pagels, *The Origins of Satan,* 142.

7. Origen, *Contra Celsus,* bk. 7, chap. 2. Cited in Pagels, *The Origins of Satan,* 143.

8. Irenaeus, *Contre Les Heresies,* preface to vol. 1. Cited in Pagels, *The Origins of Satan,* 155.

9. Tertullian, *Traite,* Prescription 6. Cited in Pagels, *The Origins of Satan,* 163.

10. Ibid., Prescription 7. Cited in Pagels, *The Origins of Satan,* 163.

11. Guiley, *Encyclopedia,* 341.

12. The entire text of this Bull can be found in Rosemary Ellen Guiley, *The Encyclopedia of Witches and Witchcraft,* 170–72, or in Heinrich Kramer and James Sprenger, *The Malleus Maleficarum,* xliii–xlv.

13. Ranke-Heinemann, *Eunuchs,* 185.

14. Aquinas, *The Summa Theologica,* part 2 of part 2, question 70, article 3.

15. Ranke-Heinemann, *Eunuchs,* 187.

16. Kramer and Sprenger, *The Malleus Maleficarum,* part 1, question 6.

17. Ibid.

18. Guiley, *Encyclopedia,* 341–43.

19. Ibid., 369. See also Gibbons, "Recent Developments," 2–16.

20. *New International Bible Dictionary,* s. v. "witch," "witchcraft."

21. Strong, *Concordance,* s. v. "qecem," "existemi."

22. Kramer and Sprenger, *The Malleus Maleficarum,* vii.

23. Campbell, *Hero,* 30.

24. Ibid., 35.

25. Ibid., 182.

26. Ibid., 352.

27. Jordan, *Encyclopedia of Gods,* 210, 295.

28. Ibid., 210.

29. Clark, *Zoroastrianism,* 1, 66–75.

30. Ibid., 89–92.

31. Ibid., 152–56.

32. Ibid., 77–83.

# Chapter 5

1. Grof, *The Holotropic Mind,* 5.

2. Friedman, *Bridging Science and Spirit,* 21.

3. Friedman, *The Hidden Domain,* 146.

4. Friedman, *Bridging Science and Spirit,* 56.

5. Ibid., 34.

6. Friedman, *The Hidden Domain*, 46.

7. Talbot, *The Holographic Universe*, 52.

8. Friedman, *The Hidden Domain*, 104–5.

9. Weber, "The Physicist and the Mystic," 197.

10. Inspired by Wolinsky, *Quantum Consciousness*, exercise 48.

11. Huxley, *The Perennial Philosophy*, 2.

12. Walsh, *Essential Spirituality*, 7. Professor Walsh states that the perennial philosophy contains four essential elements: (1) there are two realms of reality, (2) humans partake of both realms, (3) humans can recognize their divine spark and the divine ground that is its source, and (4) that realizing our spiritual nature is the highest and greatest good in human existence. See pages 7 and 8.

13. Harvey, *The Essential Mystics*, xi. We are indebted to Harvey for his description of the unique perspectives offered by the mystics of each religious tradition.

14. Transcribed by Dr. Henry Smith and first published in the *Seattle Sunday Star* on October 29, 1877.

15. This is a free rendering by Joyce Higginbotham of the *Tao Te Ching*, number 25.

16. This is a free rendering by Joyce Higginbotham of the *Svetasvatara Upanishad*, verses 16–20.

17. Harvey, *The Essential Mystics*, 88.

18. Prov. 8:1–4, 14, 22–30 King James Version.

19. This is a free rendering by Joyce Higginbotham of Rumi's Poem 280.

20. This is a free rendering by Joyce Higginbotham of Shabestari's *The Rosegarden of Mystery*.

21. This is a free rendering by Joyce Higginbotham of Hadewijch's *Poems in Stanzas* number 14, lines 55–75.

22. This is a free rendering by Joyce Higginbotham of Thomas Traherne's *Second Century*, sections 65–67.

23. Friedman, *The Hidden Domain*, 103.

# Chapter 6

1. Crowley, *Magick in Theory and Practice*, xii.

2. Myss, *Anatomy of the Spirit*, 80–89.

3. We were introduced to the concept of "conscious creation," and phrases similar to it, in the writings of Jane Roberts, and in George Winslow Plummer's *Consciously Cre-*

*ating Circumstances.* References to both can be found in the recommended reading list for this and other chapters.

4. For another perspective on this topic, we recommend chapter 3 of Jane Roberts's book *The God of Jane* in which she discusses her experiences and struggles with a similar phenomenon she labels "impulses."

# Chapter 7

1. Lewis, *A Question of Values,* 10–11. We are indebted to Lewis for inspiring the sentiments expressed in the preceding paragraph.

2. Porter, *The Good Life,* 231. We are indebted to Porter for his discussion of the Western religious ethic and the questions it raises.

3. Ibid.

4. Kagan, *The Second Year,* 122–26.

5. Eibl-Eibesfeldt, *Human Ethology,* 341.

6. Dunn, *The Beginnings of Social Understanding,* 177–182.

7. Wilson, *The Moral Sense,* 141. We are indebted to Wilson for inspiring our sentiments relating to humanity's innate moral sense, its reaction to destructive behavior, and a source of that behavior coming from competing urges.

8. Schweder, Mahaptra, and Miller, "Culture and Moral Development," 61. Cited in Kagan and Lamb, *Emergence.*

9. Wilson, *The Moral Sense,* 105.

10. Ibid., 115.

11. Ibid., 243.

12. Guiley, *Encyclopedia,* 363–64.

13. Ibid.

14. Augustine, *Tractates,* 6:223.

15. Thorsson, *A Book of Troth,* 114–19.

16. Some may find it interesting to note that only 17 percent of the world's cultures practice monogamy. See George P. Murdock and D. R. White, "Standard Cross-cultural Sample," 329–69.

# GLOSSARY

**Address anxiety**—The belief that a God or Deity can reside in only one "place" or "address" as determined by certain beliefs, and can therefore only be found within one particular belief system to the exclusion of all others

**Asatru Ethical System**—Based on the writings of Edred Thorsson, who identifies Nine Noble Virtues and the Sixfold Goal as an ethical system. The virtues are courage, honor, truth, fidelity, discipline, hospitality, industriousness, self-reliance, and perseverance. The goals are right, wisdom, might, harvest, peace (frith), and love.

**Beliefs**—Ideas that we have consciously or subconsciously accepted as true.

**Belief filters**—As a filter over the lens of a camera affects the qualities of the light that enters the camera, so do our beliefs act as filter of our experiences, "coloring" what we perceive, or even blocking input that does not match the expectations of our beliefs.

**Belief systems or structures**—Collections or groups of beliefs that build on and reinforce each other such that they fit together into a complex whole. Belief systems and structures are usually internally consistent in their logic.

**Earth-centered**—A religion whose liturgical, or sacred, year is based on the cycling of the seasons rather than the life or deeds of its founder, deities, or saints.

**Energies**—Feelings, currents, forces, or points of mental focus utilized in spiritual workings such as magick. Commonly used energies include healing, love, justice, forgiveness, self-empowerment, and creativity.

**Ethics**—The study of what constitutes the good and the right; that is, which actions are correct and which goals should be pursued.

**Four directions**—The four compass points of north, south, east, and west.

**Four elements**—The four forms that matter takes in the physical world—solid or "earth," liquid or "water," gas or "air," and plasma or "fire." Each of the elements is traditionally assigned to one of the four directions. Typically air is in the east, fire in the south, water in the west, and earth in the north.

**God Map**—A graphic representation of the range of ideas or beliefs about Deity, with the degree of transcendence to immanence running vertically and the degree of concreteness to abstractness running horizontally.

**Holidays**—The holy days most frequently observed by Pagans are the four solar holidays, or Quarter Points, which are the Summer Solstice (June 21), Winter Solstice (December 21), Spring Equinox (March 21), and Fall Equinox (September 21); and the agricultural holidays, or Cross-quarter Points, which are Imbolg (February 1), Beltane (May 1), Lammas (August 1), and Samhain (November 1).

**Holomovement**—A model of the universe proposed by David Bohm in which the universe rapidly enfolds and unfolds itself into and out of the physical realm (explicate order), and then into deeper levels outside of space-time (implicate and super-implicate orders). He proposes that this folding and unfolding, or "blinking on and off," occurs many millions of times a second.

**Interconnectedness**—The concept that all parts of the universe, whether small, large, "animate," or "inanimate" are connected at very deep levels that may extend beyond the boundaries of space-time.

**Magick**—The actions of many consciousnesses voluntarily working together within an aware and interconnected universe to bring about one or more desired results.

**Magickal pages**—An alert from the universe, often in the form of an urge or impulse to do something unexpected, which indicates that consciousness has pulled together the people, places, and times necessary to carry out a magickal request.

**Mechanistic view of the universe**—A model of the universe popularized by Sir Isaac Newton in the 1600s, which portrays the universe as a giant machine, operating according to fixed laws of motion and gravitation, and which views matter as distinct, billiard-ball-like particles, and space as empty vacuum.

**Multidimensionality**—The proposed existence of multiple levels or layers of reality and consciousness, many of which may lie outside of space-time as we typically perceive it.

**Mysticism**—The direct personal contact with one's concept of God, the Divine, or the Ground of Being.

**Paganism or Neo-Paganism**—A modern religious movement that encompasses traditions which are generally earth-centered; magickal; indigenous; stress a connection to and respect for the natural world; recognize both male and female deities; encourage diversity in spiritual beliefs, practices, and lifestyles; do not operate under a centralized hierarchy; have no official or standardized dogma that extends beyond the particular tradition; and stresses personal responsibility in matters of belief, ethics, and spiritual practice.

**Pentacle**—A five-pointed star, the points of which represent earth, air, fire, water, and spirit. Pentacles are frequently set within a circle, which can represent the wheel of life, the encircling of the divine, or the union of the material and spiritual realms. Despite Hollywood's insistence otherwise, the pentacle is not a symbol of Satan or evil.

**Principles of Paganism**—(1) We are in control of what we believe, (2) we are responsible for our own actions and spiritual development, (3) we are responsible for deciding who or what God is for us, and forming a relationship with that God, (4) everything contains the spark of intelligence, (5) everything is sacred, (6) each part of the universe can communicate with each other part, and these parts often cooperate for specific ends, and (7) consciousness survives death.

**Rites of passage**—The personal seasons of life, which typically include pregnancy and birth, baby welcomings, coming of age, handfasting and marriage, handparting, croning, saging, death, dedication to a course of study, initiation, and ordination. Although Pagans do not have sacraments per se, the rites of passage resemble some sacramental rites and serve the same purposes.

**Rituals**—A Pagan church service that can be held privately or with a group. Elements of a ritual typically include the preparation of the space and the people; creation of sacred space, often through the casting of a circle, calling of Quarters, Deities, or other energies; a magickal or energetic working; and dismissals. Pagan rituals generally do not include sermons, are frequently performed by clergy, and may involve dancing, drumming, singing, or other activities by the participants.

**Satanism**—Encompasses three distinct groups: (1) Renegade Christians who worship Satan as the principle of evil, and would generally not consider themselves to be Pagan, (2) members of the Church of Satan, who recognize Satan as an archetype and perhaps a being, but do not worship him or any other Deity, and whose guiding principles are autonomy and self-determinism, and (3) members of the Temple of Set, who do not give any attention to Satan at all, actually, but study the deity Set, who represents the principle of independent or "isolate" intelligence.

**Solitaries**—Pagans who prefer to practice alone. Although they may attend public Pagan functions and enjoy group interaction on occasion, they are not interested in joining a Pagan circle or coven on a permanent basis.

**Traditions**—The various spiritual paths within Paganism, roughly equivalent to denominations in Christianity.

**Wheel of the Year**—The Pagan sacred or liturgical year, which begins at Yule (December 21) and proceeds through the eight Pagan holidays of Imbolg (Feb. 1), Spring Equinox

(March 21), Beltane (May 1), Summer Solstice (June 21), Lammas (Aug. 1), Fall Equinox (Sept. 21), Samhain (Nov. 1), and then begins again at Yule.

**Wicca**—The single largest tradition within Paganism, which is earth-centered, celebrates the eight Pagan holidays, envisions Deity as both male and female (which it calls the God and the Goddess), practices magick, and believes in an afterlife known as the Summerland.

**Wiccan ethical system**—Stated in the Rede and the Rule of Threes. The Rede contains the ethical instruction to "harm none and do what you will." The Rule of Threes states that whatever you send out from yourself will come back threefold.

# BIBLIOGRAPHY

Adler, Margot. *Drawing Down the Moon*. Boston: Beacon Press, 1986.

Aquinas, St. Thomas. *The Summa Theologica*. Vol. 2. Translated by the Fathers of the English Dominican Province. New York: Benzinger Brothers, Inc. 1947.

Ashley, Nancy. *Create Your Own Reality: A Seth Workbook*. New York: Prentice Hall, 1981.

Augustine, St. *Tractates on the Gospel of John 112–124: Tractates on the First Epistle of John*. Translated by John W. Rettig. Reprint, Washington, D.C.: The Catholic University of America Press, 1995.

Bonewits, Isaac. "Defining Paganism: Paleo-, Meso-, and Neo- 2.5," 1979. http://www.neopagan.net/PaganDefs.HTML

Blakney, R. B., trans. *The Way of Life: Lao Tzu*. New York: New American Library, 1955.

Brownstein, R. "The Taming of a New Age Prophet." *Christianity Today* (16 June 1989): 28.

Campbell, Joseph. *The Hero With a Thousand Faces*. Princeton: Princeton University Press, 1973.

Clark, Peter. *Zoroastrianism: An Introduction to an Ancient Faith*. Brighton, England: Sussex Academic Press, 1998.

Crowley, Aleister. *Magick in Theory and Practice*. Oxfordshire, England: I-H-O Books, 1999.

Crowley, Vivianne. *Principles of Paganism*. San Francisco: Thorsons, 1996.

Dawson, L. L. "Anti-modernism, Modernism, and Postmodernism: Struggling with the Cultural Significance of New Religious Movements." *Sociology of Religion* 59, no. 2 (1998): 131–56. Quoted in Danny L. Jorgenson and Scott E. Russell, "American Neo-Paganism: The Participants' Social Identities," *Journal for the Scientific Study of Religion* 38 (September 1999): 335.

Dunn, Judy. *The Beginnings of Social Understanding.* Oxford: Blackwell, 1988.

Eibl-Eibesfeldt, Irenaus. *Human Ethology.* New York: De Gruyter, 1989.

Farrar, Janet and Stewart, and Gavin Bone. *The Pagan Path.* Custer, Wash.: Phoenix Publishing, 1995.

Friedman, Norman. *Bridging Science and Spirit: Common Elements in David Bohm's Physics, The Perennial Philosophy and Seth.* St. Louis, Mo.: Living Lake Books, 1994.

———. *The Hidden Domain.* Eugene, Oreg.: The Woodbridge Group, 1997.

Gibbons, Jenny. "Recent Developments in the Study of the Great European Witch Hunt." *The Pomegranate* 5 (August 1998): 2–16.

Greene, Brian. *The Elegant Universe.* New York: Random House, 1999.

Grof, Stanislav. *The Holotropic Mind: The Three Levels of Human Consciousness and How They Shape Our Lives.* New York: HarperCollins, 1993.

Guiley, Rosemary Ellen. *The Encyclopedia of Witches and Witchcraft.* New York: Facts on File, Inc., 1989.

Hart, Mother Columba, O.S.B., trans. *Hadewijch: The Complete Works.* New York: Paulist Press, 1980.

Harvey, Andrew. *The Essential Mystics.* New York: HarperCollins, 1997.

Hume, Robert Ernest, trans. *The Thirteen Principal Upanishads.* London: Oxford University Press, 1951.

Huxley, Aldous. *The Perennial Philosophy.* New York: Harper & Row, 1972.

Irenaeus de Lyon. *Contre Les Heresies: Denonciation et refutation de la gnose au nom menteur.* Translated by Adelin Rousseau. 2d ed. Paris: Les Editions du Cerf: 1985.

Jordan, Michael. *Encyclopedia of Gods.* New York: Facts on File, Inc., 1993.

Jorgenson, Danny L., and Scott E. Russell. "American NeoPaganism: The Participants' Social Identities." *Journal for the Scientific Study of Religion* 38 (September 1999): 325–338.

Kagan, Jerome. *The Second Year: The Emergence of Self-Awareness.* Cambridge, Mass.: Harvard University Press, 1981.

Kagan, Jerome, and Sharon Lamb, eds. *The Emergence of Morality in Young Children.* Chicago: University of Chicago Press, 1987.

Kelly, Aidan. "An Update on Neo-Pagan Witchcraft in America." In *Perspectives on the New Age,* edited by James R. Lewis and J. Gordon Melton, 140–41. New York: State University of New York, 1992.

Kramer, Heinrich, and James Sprenger. *The Malleus Maleficarum.* 1486. Reprint, New York: Dover Publications, Inc., 1971.

Levenson, Jon D. *Creation and the Persistence of Evil: The Jewish Drama of Divine Omnipotence.* San Francisco: Harper & Row, 1988.

Lewis, Hunter. *A Question of Values: Six Ways We Make the Personal Choices that Shape Our Lives.* San Francisco: Harper & Row, 1990.

Lewis, James R., and J. Gordon Melton, eds. *Perspectives on the New Age.* New York: State University of New York, 1992.

Murdock, George P., and D. R. White. "Standard Cross-cultural Sample." *Ethnology* 8 (October 1969): 329–69.

Myss, Caroline. *Anatomy of the Spirit.* New York: Three Rivers Press, 1996.

National Telecommunications and Information Administration. "A Nation Online: How Americans Are Expanding Their Use of the Internet," posted February 5, 2002. http://www.ntia.doc.gov/opadhome/digitalnation/index.html#Previous

Origen. *The Writings of Origen.* Vol. 2 of *Contra Celsus.* Translated by Rev. Frederick Crombie, D.D. Edinburgh, Scotland: Morrison & Gibb Limited for T & T Clark, 1910.

Pagels, Elaine. *The Origins of Satan.* New York: Random House, 1995.

Porter, Burton F. *The Good Life: Alternatives in Ethics.* New York: Ardsley House Publishers, Inc., 1995.

Ranke-Heinemann, Uta. *Eunuchs for the Kingdom of Heaven.* New York: Doubleday, 1990.

RavenWolf, Silver. *To Ride a Silver Broomstick.* St. Paul, Minn.: Llewellyn Publications, 1995.

Roberts, Jane. *The God of Jane.* 1981. Reprint, Portsmouth, N.H.: Moment Point Press, Inc., 2000.

———. *Psychic Politics.* Portsmouth, N.H.: Moment Point Press, Inc., 2000.

Russell, Scott. "The Social Identities of American Neo-Paganism." Master's thesis, University of South Florida, 1999.

Schweder, Richard A., Manamohan Mahaptra, and Joan G. Miller. "Culture and Moral Development." In *The Emergence of Morality in Young Children,* edited by Jerome Kagan and Sharon Lamb. Chicago: University of Chicago Press, 1987.

Starhawk. *Spiral Dance.* New York: HarperCollins, 1989.

Strong, James. *The New Strong's Exhaustive Concordance of the Bible.* Nashville, Tenn.: Thomas Nelson Publishers, 1990.

Talbot, Michael. *The Holographic Universe.* New York: HarperCollins, 1991.

Tertullian. *Traite de la Prescription Contre Les Heretiques.* Translated by P. de Labriolle. Paris: Les Editions du Cerf, 1957.

Thorsson, Edred. *A Book of Troth.* St. Paul, Minn.: Llewellyn Publications, 1989.

Traherne, Thomas. *Poems, Centuries and Three Thanksgivings.* Edited by Anne Ridler. London: Oxford University Press, 1966.

Tresniowski, Alex, and Karen Brailsford. "Making a Joyful Noise." *People* 47, (14 April 1997): 73.

Truzzi, Marcello. "The Occult Revival as Popular Culture: Some Random Observations on the Old and Nouveau Witch." *Sociological Quarterly* 13 (Winter 1972): 16–36.

Valiente, Doreen. *The Rebirth of Witchcraft.* Custer, Wash.: Phoenix Publishing, 1989.

Walsh, Roger. *Essential Spirituality.* New York: John Wiley & Sons, Inc., 1999.

Weber, Renee. "The Physicist and the Mystic—Is a Dialogue Between Them Possible? A Conversation with David Bohm." In *The Holographic Paradigm and Other Paradoxes,* edited by Ken Wilbur, 197. Boulder, Colo.: Shambhala Publications, 1982.

Wilber, Ken, ed. *The Holographic Paradigm and Other Paradoxes.* Boulder, Colo.: Shambhala Publications, 1982.

Wilson, James Q. *The Moral Sense.* New York: The Free Press, 1993.

Wolinsky, Stephen. *Quantum Consciousness.* Las Vegas, Nev.: Bramble Books, 1993.

Wright, L. "The Sensual Christian." *Rolling Stone* issue 617 (14 November 1991): 78.

# RECOMMENDED READING

## Chapter 1

Adler, Margot. *Drawing Down the Moon*. Boston: Beacon Press, 1986.

Ashcroft-Nowicki, Dolores. *First Steps in Ritual*. Wellingborough, Northamptonshire: The Aquarian Press, 1982.

Budapest, Zsuzsanna. *Grandmother of Time: A Women's Book of Celebrations, Spells, and Sacred Objects for Every Month of the Year*. New York: Harper & Row, 1989.

Cabot, Laurie. *Celebrate the Earth: A Year of Holidays in the Pagan Tradition*. New York: Dell Publishing, 1994.

Campanelli, Pauline. *Rites of Passage*. St. Paul, Minn.: Llewellyn Publications, 1994.

———. *Wheel of the Year: Living the Magical Life*. St. Paul, Minn.: Llewellyn Publications, 1989.

Crowley, Vivianne. *Principles of Paganism*. London: Thorsons, 1996.

Eilers, Dana. *The Practical Pagan*. Franklin Lakes, N.J.: New Page Books, 2002.

Farrar, Janet and Stewart. *A Witches Bible Compleat*. New York: Magickal Childe Publishing, Inc., 1991.

Farrar, Janet and Stewart, and Gavin Bone. *The Pagan Path*. Custer, Wash.: Phoenix Publishing, 1995.

Harvey, Graham, and Charlotte Hardman. *Paganism Today*. London: Thorsons, 1995.

Jorgenson, Danny, and Scott Russell. "American NeoPaganism: The Participants' Social Identities." *Journal for the Scientific Study of Religion* 38 (September 1999): 325–338.

Klein, Kenny. *The Flowering Rod*. Oak Park, Ill.: Delphi Press, Inc., 1993.

Lewis, James R., and J. Gordon Melton. *Perspectives on the New Age*. Albany, N.Y.: State University of New York Press, 1992.

RavenWolf, Silver. *To Ride a Silver Broomstick*. St. Paul, Minn.: Llewellyn Publications, 1995.

Starhawk. *The Pagan Book of Living and Dying*. San Francisco: HarperSanFrancisco, 1997.

———. *Spiral Dance*. New York: HarperCollins Publishers, 1989.

Sun Bear, Wabun Wind, and Crysalis Mulligan. *Dancing with the Wheel: The Medicine Wheel Workbook*. New York: Simon & Schuster, 1991.

Telesco, Patricia. *Seasons of the Sun: Celebrations from the World's Spiritual Traditions*. York Beach, Maine: Samuel Weiser, Inc., 1996.

## Chapter 2

Campbell, Joseph. *The Power of Myth*. New York: Doubleday, 1988.

Chopra, Deepak. *Quantum Healing*. New York: Bantam Books, 1990.

———. *The Way of the Wizard: Twenty Spiritual Lessons for Creating the Life You Want*. New York: Harmony Books, 1995.

Hay, Louise L. *Heal Your Body*. Santa Monica, Calif.: Hay House, Inc., 1988.

Roberts, Jane. *The Individual and the Nature of Mass Events*. San Rafael, Calif.: Amber-Allen Publishing, Inc., 1995.

———. *The Nature of Personal Reality*. San Rafael, Calif.: Amber-Allen Publishing, Inc., 1994.

Talbot, Michael. *The Holographic Universe*. New York: HarperCollins, 1991.

## Chapter 3

Campbell, Joseph. *Myths to Live By*. New York: Bantam Books, 1972.

Conway, D. J. *The Ancient and Shining Ones*. St. Paul, Minn.: Llewellyn Publications, 1994.

Fox, Matthew. *Original Blessing: A Primer in Creation Spirituality*. Santa Fe, N.M.: Bear & Company, 1986.

Jordan, Michael. *Encyclopedia of Gods*. New York: Facts on File, Inc., 1993.

Jung, Carl. *The Collected Works of C. G. Jung*. New York: Pantheon Books, 1959.

Peterson, Roland. *Everyone Is Right*. Marina del Rey, Calif.: DeVorss and Company, 1992.

RavenWolf, Silver. *Angels: Companions in Magick*. St. Paul, Minn.: Llewellyn Publications, 1996.

Roberts, Jane. *The God of Jane*. 1981. Reprint, Portsmouth, N.H.: Moment Point Press, Inc., 2000.

Sheldrake, Rupert. *A New Science of Life*. Rochester, N.Y.: Inner Traditions International Ltd., 1995.

———. *The Presence of the Past*. New York: Times Books, 1988.

Sjoo, Monica, and Barbara Mor. *The Great Cosmic Mother: Rediscovering the Religion of the Earth*. San Francisco: HarperSanFrancisco, 1991.

Stone, Merlin. *When God Was a Woman*. San Diego, Calif.: Harcourt Brace Jovanovich, 1976.

Talbot, Michael. *Mysticism and the New Physics*. London: Penguin Group, 1993.

Telesco, Patricia. *Goddess in My Pocket*. San Francisco: HarperSanFrancisco, 1998.

## Chapter 4

Guiley, Rosemary. *The Encyclopedia of Witches and Witchcraft*. New York: Facts on File, 1989.

Kramer, Heinrich, and James Sprenger. *The Malleus Maleficarum*. New York: Dover Publications, Inc., 1971.

LaVey, Anton. *The Satanic Bible*. New York: Avon Books, 1969.

Pagels, Elaine. *The Origin of Satan*. New York: Random House, 1995.

Purkiss, Diane. *The Witch in History*. London: Routledge, 1996.

Ranke-Heinemann, Uta. *Eunuchs for the Kingdom of Heaven*. New York: Doubleday, 1990.

## Chapter 5

Bohm, David. *Wholeness and the Implicate Order*. London: Routledge and Kegan Paul, 1980.

Friedman, Norman. *Bridging Science and Spirit: Common Elements in David Bohm's Physics, The Perennial Philosophy and Seth*. St. Louis, Mo.: Living Lake Books, 1994.

———. *The Hidden Domain*. Eugene, Oreg.: The Woodbridge Group, 1997.

Grof, Stanislav. *The Holotropic Mind: The Three Levels of Human Consciousness and How They Shape Our Lives*. New York: HarperCollins, 1993.

Huxley, Aldous. *The Perennial Philosophy*. New York: Harper & Row, 1972.

Talbot, Michael. *The Holographic Universe*. New York: HarperCollins, 1991.

———. *Mysticism and the New Physics*. London: Penguin Group, 1993.


# Chapter 6

Farrar, Janet and Stewart. *Spells and How They Work*. Custer, Wash.: Phoenix Publishing, Inc., 1990.

Gawain, Shakti. *Creative Visualization*. Novato, Calif.: New World Library, 1995.

Harper, Josephine M., and R. Michael Miller. *The Psychic Energy Workbook: An Illustrated Course in Practical Psychic Skills*. New York: Sterling Publishing Company, Inc., 1986.

Hoffman, Enid. *Develop Your Psychic Skills*. West Chester, Pa.: Whitford Press, 1981.

Kraig, Donald Michael. *Modern Magick: Eleven Lessons in the High Magickal Arts*. St. Paul, Minn.: Llewellyn Publications, 1998.

———. *Modern Sex Magick: Secrets of Erotic Spirituality*. St. Paul, Minn.: Llewellyn Publications, 1998.

Peat, F. David. *Synchronicity: The Bridge Between Matter and Mind*. New York: Bantam Books, 1988.

Plummer, George Winslow. *Consciously Creating Circumstances*. New York: Society of Rosicrucians, Inc., 1992.

RavenWolf, Silver. *To Stir a Magick Cauldron*. St. Paul, Minn.: Llewellyn Publications, 1997.

Roberts, Jane. *The Magical Approach: Seth Speaks About the Art of Creative Living*. San Rafael, Calif.: Amber-Allen Publishing, 1995.

Vaughan, Frances E. *Awakening Intuition*. New York: Anchor Books, 1979.


# Chapter 7

Crowley, Vivianne. *Principles of Paganism*. London: Thorsons, 1996, pages 20–32.

Cunningham, Scott. *Wicca: A Guide for the Solitary Practitioner*. St. Paul, Minn.: Llewellyn Publications, 1997, chapter 1.

Farrar, Janet and Stewart. *Spells and How They Work*. Custer, Wash.: Phoenix Publishing, Inc., 1990, chapter 3.

————. *A Witches Bible Compleat*. New York: Magickal Childe Publishing, Inc., 1991, vol. 2, pages 135–44.

Lewis, Hunter. *A Question of Values: Six Ways We Make the Personal Choices that Shape Our Lives*. San Francisco: Harper & Row, 1990.

Porter, Burton F. *The Good Life: Alternatives in Ethics*. New York: Ardsley House Publishers, Inc., 1995.

Starhawk. *Spiral Dance*. San Francisco: Harper SanFrancisco, 1989, chapter 1.

Thorsson, Edred. *A Book of Troth*. St. Paul, Minn.: Llewellyn Publications, 1989, pages 114–19.

Wilson, James Q. *The Moral Sense*. New York: The Free Press, 1993.

# INDEX